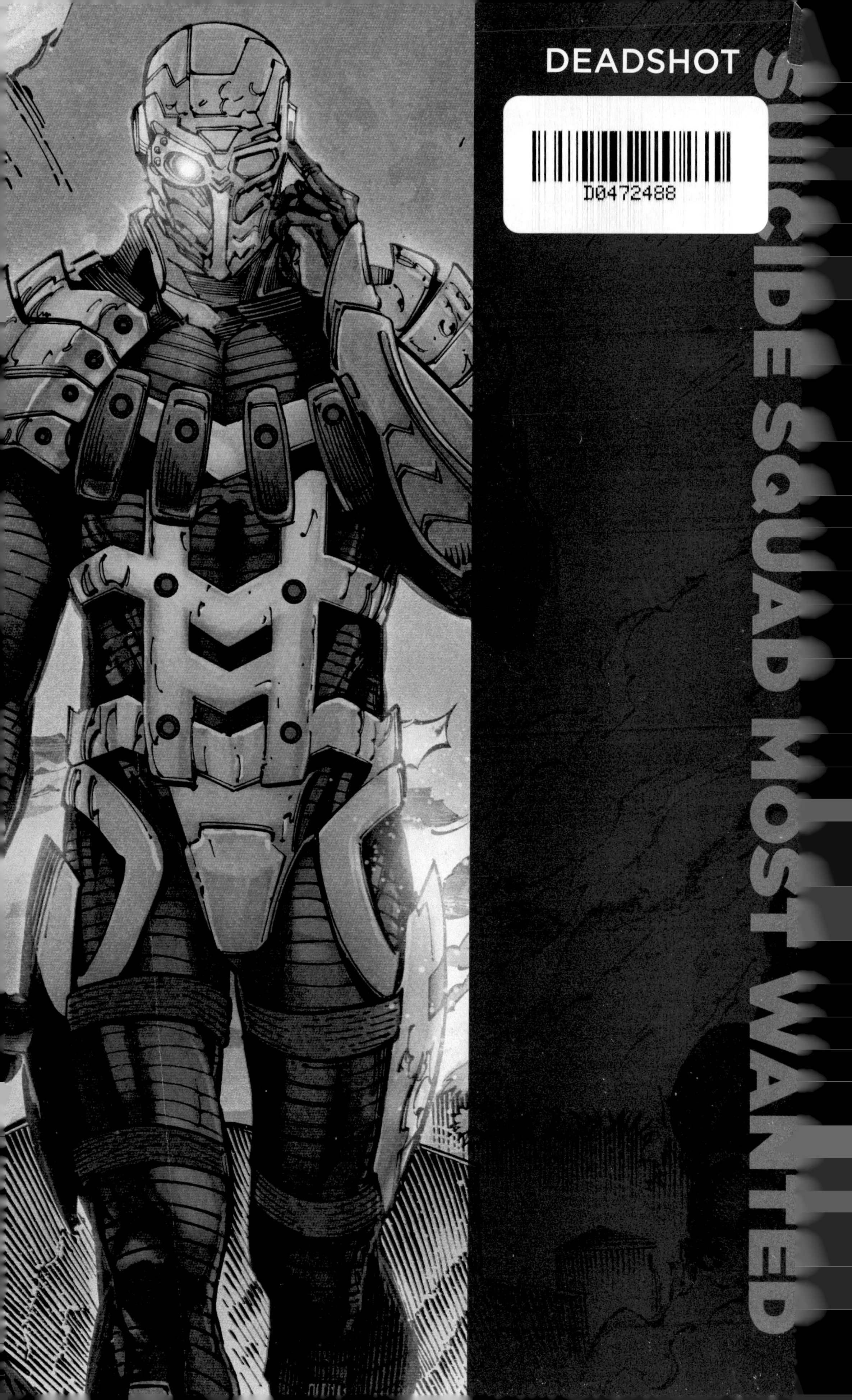

DEADSHOT

SUICIDE SQUAD MOST WANTED

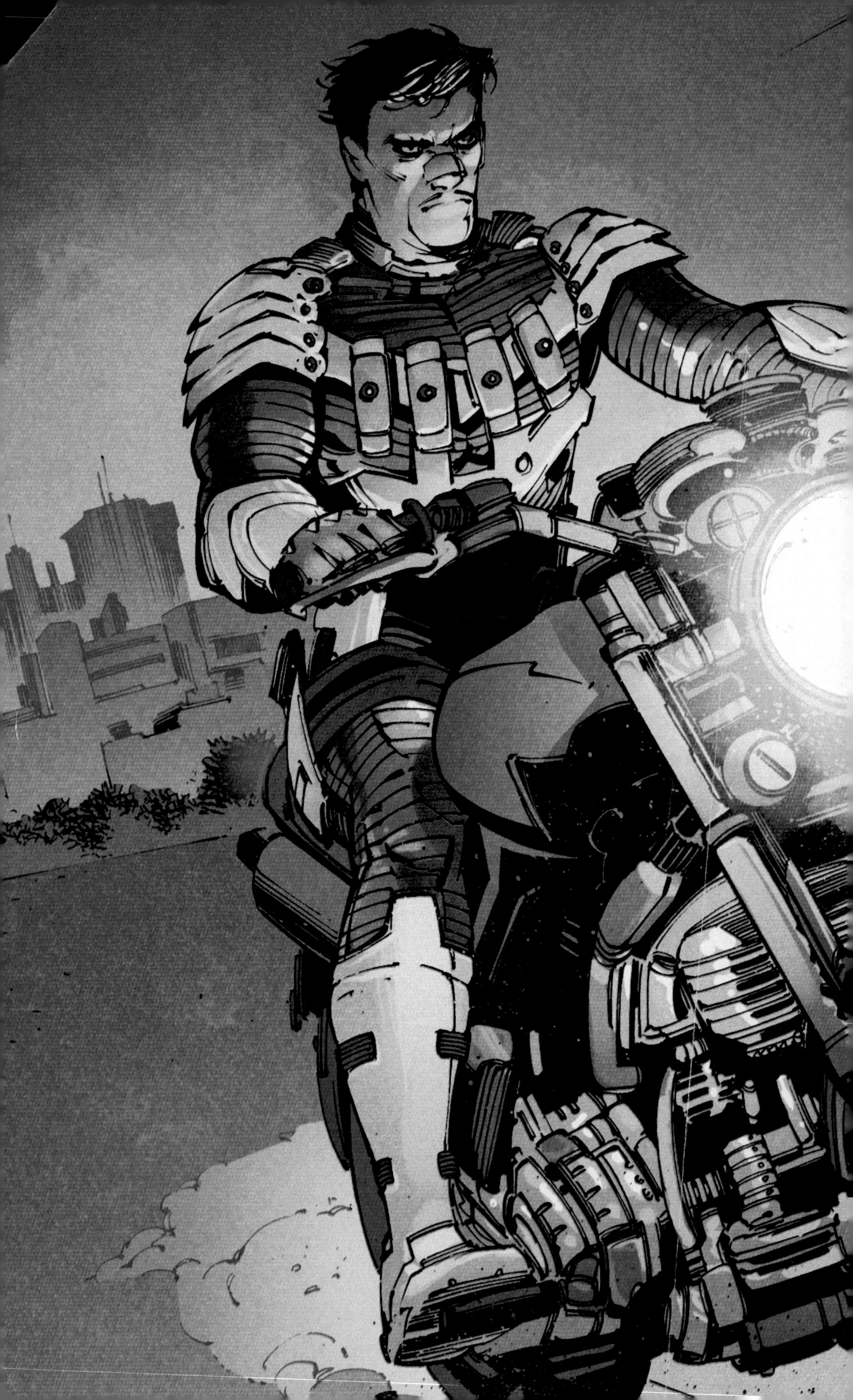

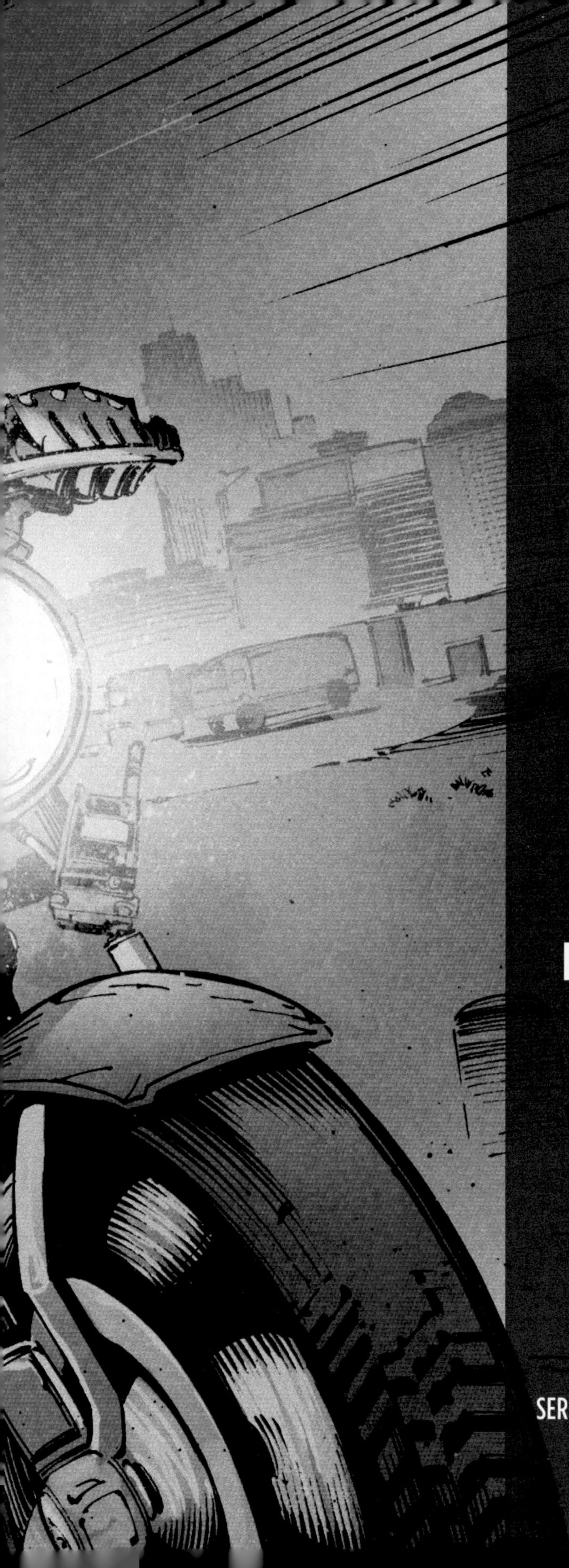

SUICIDE SQUAD MOST WANTED

DEADSHOT

WRITTEN BY
BRIAN BUCCELLATO

PENCILS BY
VIKTOR BOGDANOVIC

INKS BY
RICHARD FRIEND

COLOR BY
MICHAEL SPICER

LETTERS BY
CLEM ROBINS

SERIES & COLLECTION COVER ART BY
CARY NORD

DEADSHOT CO-CREATED BY
LEW SAYRE SCHWARTZ

ALEX ANTONE Editor - Original Series
BRITTANY HOLZHERR Assistant Editor - Original Series
JEB WOODARD Group Editor - Collected Editions
PAUL SANTOS Editor - Collected Edition
STEVE COOK Design Director - Books
DAMIAN RYLAND Publication Design

BOB HARRAS Senior VP - Editor-in-Chief, DC Comics

DIANE NELSON President
DAN DIDIO and JIM LEE Co-Publishers
GEOFF JOHNS Chief Creative Officer
AMIT DESAI Senior VP - Marketing & Global Franchise Management
NAIRI GARDINER Senior VP - Finance
SAM ADES VP - Digital Marketing
BOBBIE CHASEVP - Talent Development
MARK CHIARELLO Senior VP - Art, Design & Collected Editions
JOHN CUNNINGHAM VP - Content Strategy
ANNE DEPIES VP - Strategy Planning & Reporting
DON FALLETTI VP - Manufacturing Operations
LAWRENCE GANEM VP - Editorial Administration & Talent Relations
ALISON GILL Senior VP - Manufacturing & Operations
HANK KANALZ Senior VP - Editorial Strategy & Administration
JAY KOGAN VP - Legal Affairs
DEREK MADDALENA Senior VP - Sales & Business Development
JACK MAHAN VP - Business Affairs
DAN MIRON VP - Sales Planning & Trade Development
NICK NAPOLITANO VP - Manufacturing Administration
CAROL ROEDER VP - Marketing
EDDIE SCANNELL VP - Mass Account & Digital Sales
COURTNEY SIMMONS Senior VP - Publicity & Communications
JIM (SKI) SOKOLOWSKI VP - Comic Book Specialty & Newsstand Sales
SANDY YI Senior VP - Global Franchise Management

SUICIDE SQUAD MOST WANTED: DEADSHOT

DC Comics, 2900 West Alameda Ave., Burbank, CA 91505
Printed by RR Donnelley, Owensville, MO, USA. 7/1/16 First Printing.
ISBN: 978-1-4012-6380-5

Library of Congress Cataloging-in-Publication Data

Names: Buccellato, Brian, author. | Bogdanovic, Viktor (Artist), illustrator. | Friend, Richard (Illustrator), illustrator. | Spicer, Michael (Colorist), illustrator. | Robins, Clem, 1955- illustrator. | Nord, Cary, illustrator.
Title: Suicide Squad Most Wanted : Deadshot / Brian Buccellato, writer ; Viktor Bogdanovic, pencils ; Richard Friend, inks ; Michael Spicer, color ; Clem Robins, letters ; Cary Nord, cover.
Description: Burbank, CA : DC Comics, [2016].
Identifiers: LCCN 2016024661 | ISBN 9781401263805 (paperback)
Subjects: LCSH: Comic books, strips, etc. | BISAC: COMICS & GRAPHIC NOVELS / Superheroes.
Classification: LCC PN6728.S825 B83 2016 | DDC 741.5/973—dc23
LC record available at https://lccn.loc.gov/2016024661

PEFC Certified
Printed on paper from sustainably managed forests and controlled sources
PEFC
PEFC/29-31-75
www.pefc.org

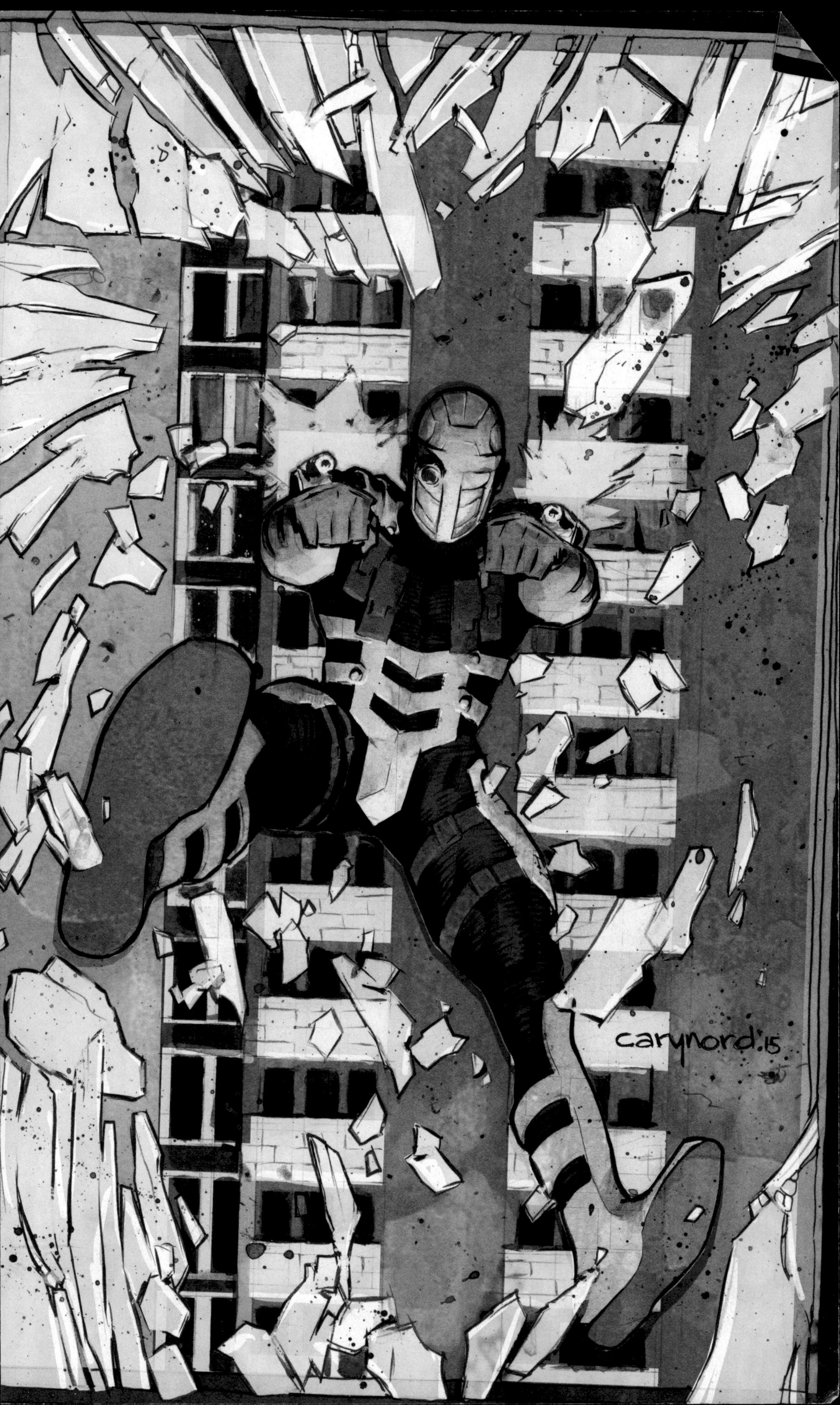
carynord'15

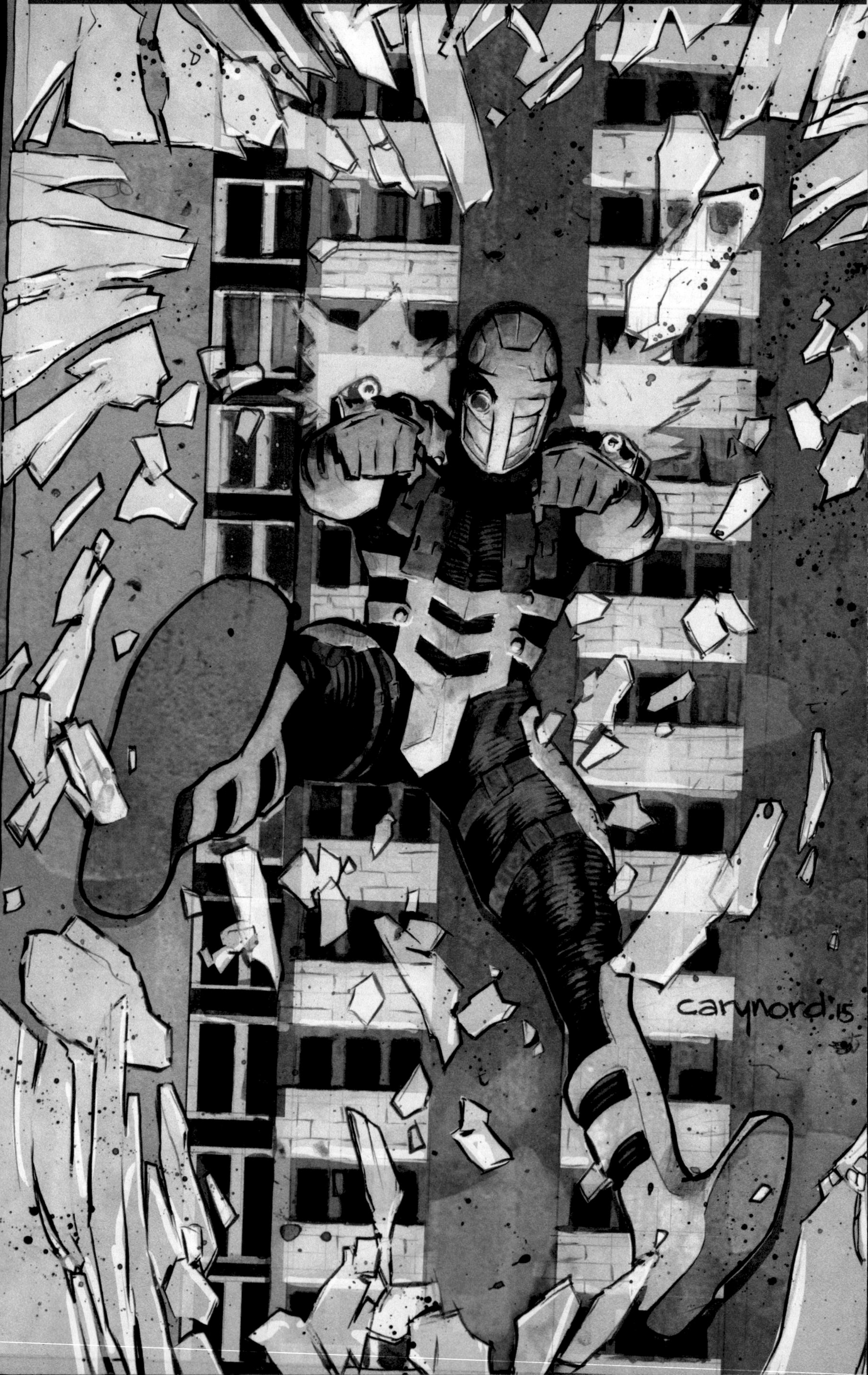
carynord.15

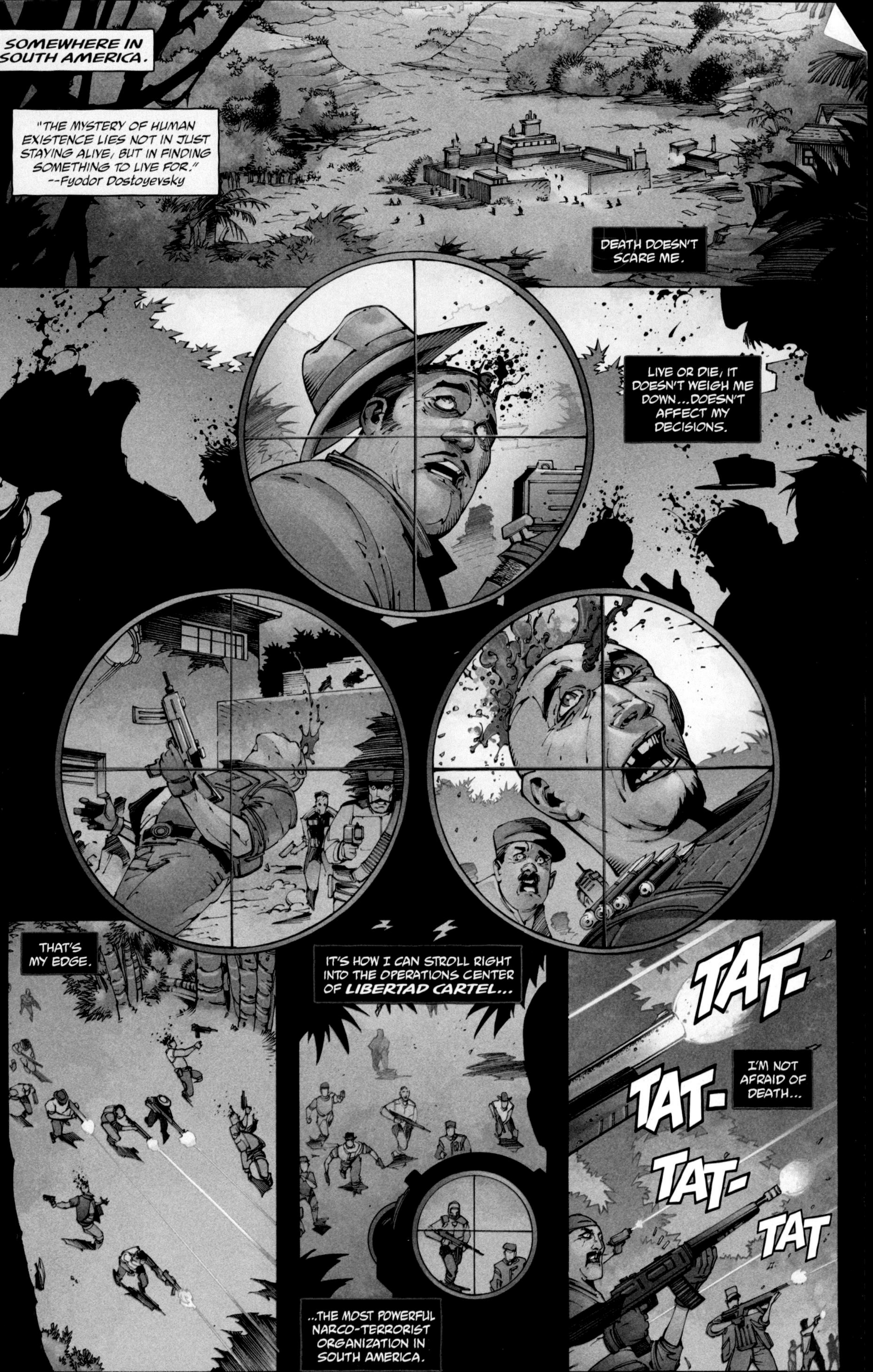
SOMEWHERE IN SOUTH AMERICA.
"THE MYSTERY OF HUMAN EXISTENCE LIES NOT IN JUST STAYING ALIVE, BUT IN FINDING SOMETHING TO LIVE FOR." --Fyodor Dostoyevsky
DEATH DOESN'T SCARE ME.
LIVE OR DIE, IT DOESN'T WEIGH ME DOWN...DOESN'T AFFECT MY DECISIONS.
THAT'S MY EDGE.
IT'S HOW I CAN STROLL RIGHT INTO THE OPERATIONS CENTER OF LIBERTAD CARTEL...
...THE MOST POWERFUL NARCO-TERRORIST ORGANIZATION IN SOUTH AMERICA.
TAT-
TAT-
TAT-
TAT
I'M NOT AFRAID OF DEATH...

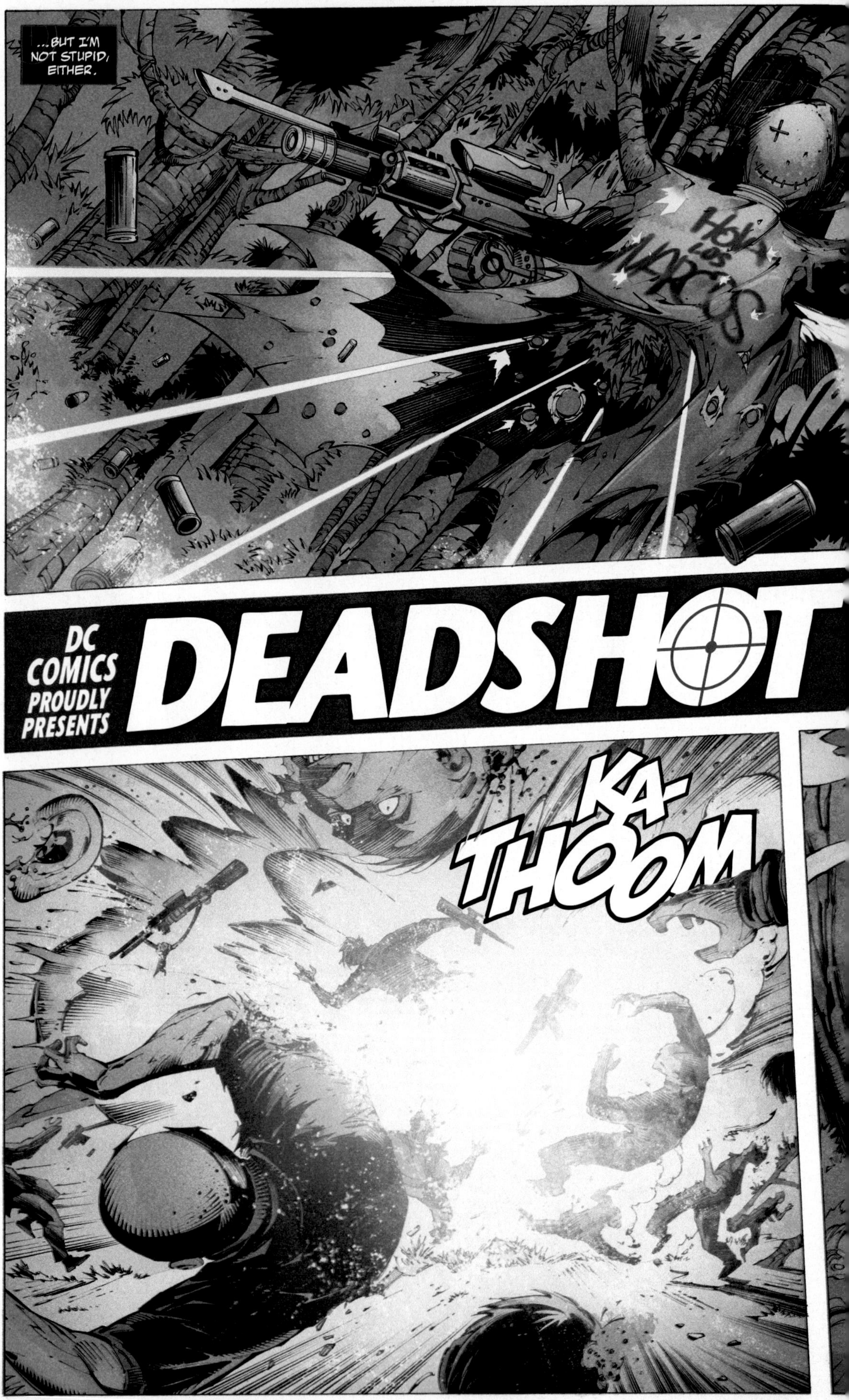
...BUT I'M NOT STUPID, EITHER.
DC COMICS PROUDLY PRESENTS
DEADSHOT
KA-THOOM

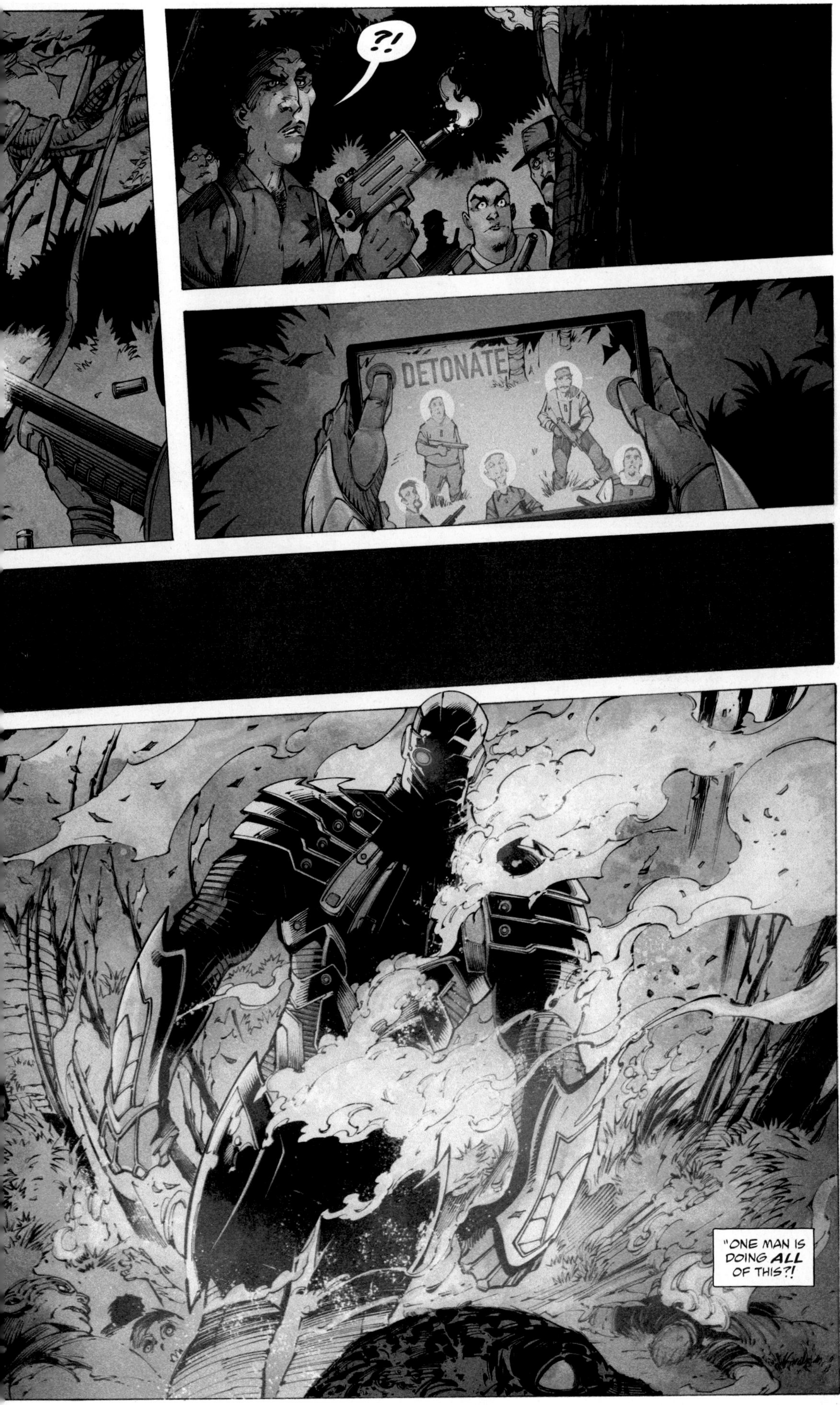
?!
DETONATE
"ONE MAN IS DOING ALL OF THIS?!

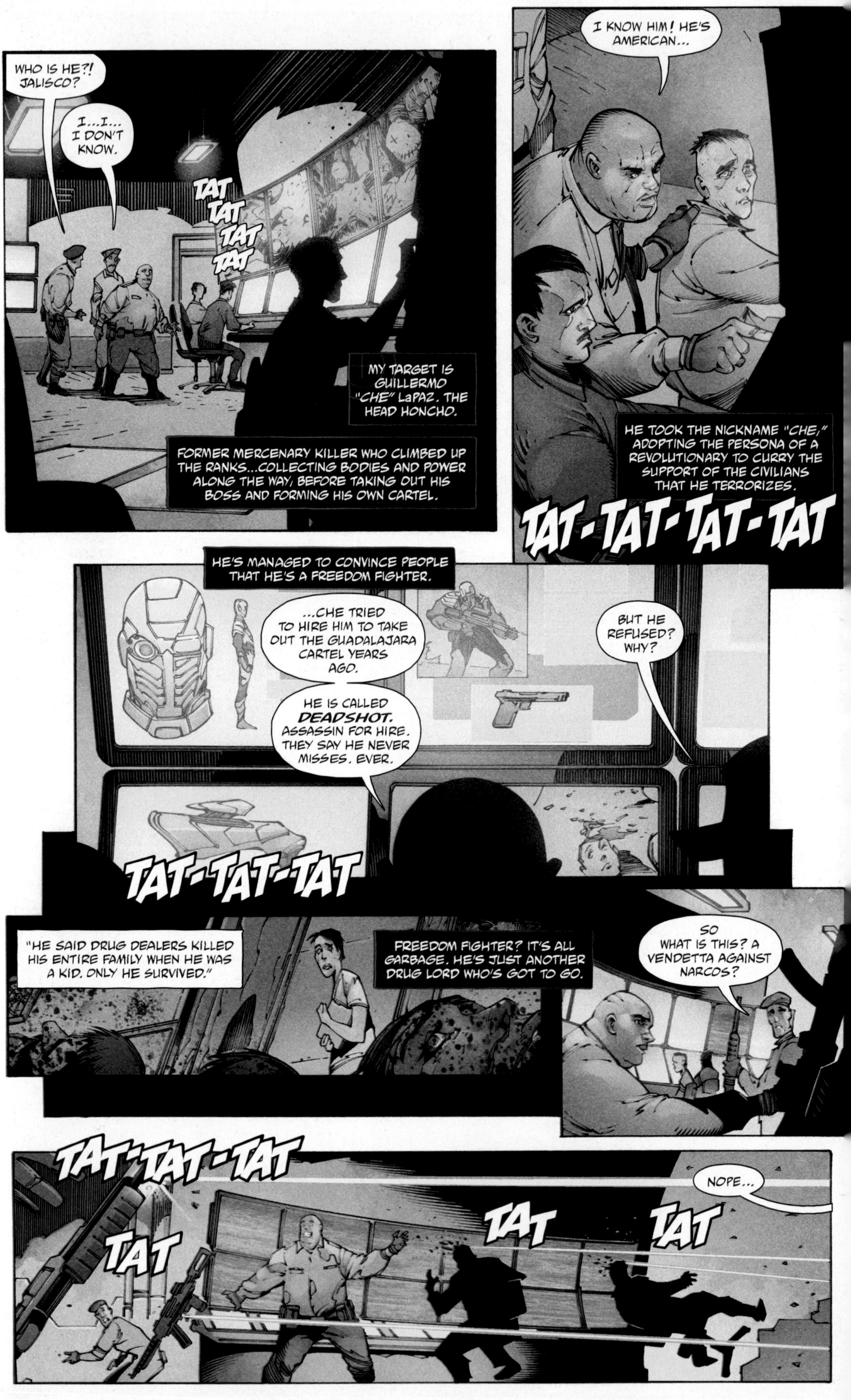

WHO IS HE?! JALISCO?
I...I... I DON'T KNOW.
TAT TAT TAT TAT
MY TARGET IS GUILLERMO "CHE" LaPAZ. THE HEAD HONCHO.
FORMER MERCENARY KILLER WHO CLIMBED UP THE RANKS...COLLECTING BODIES AND POWER ALONG THE WAY, BEFORE TAKING OUT HIS BOSS AND FORMING HIS OWN CARTEL.
I KNOW HIM! HE'S AMERICAN...
HE TOOK THE NICKNAME "CHE," ADOPTING THE PERSONA OF A REVOLUTIONARY TO CURRY THE SUPPORT OF THE CIVILIANS THAT HE TERRORIZES.
TAT-TAT-TAT-TAT
HE'S MANAGED TO CONVINCE PEOPLE THAT HE'S A FREEDOM FIGHTER.
...CHE TRIED TO HIRE HIM TO TAKE OUT THE GUADALAJARA CARTEL YEARS AGO.
HE IS CALLED DEADSHOT. ASSASSIN FOR HIRE. THEY SAY HE NEVER MISSES. EVER.
BUT HE REFUSED? WHY?
TAT-TAT-TAT
"HE SAID DRUG DEALERS KILLED HIS ENTIRE FAMILY WHEN HE WAS A KID. ONLY HE SURVIVED."
FREEDOM FIGHTER? IT'S ALL GARBAGE. HE'S JUST ANOTHER DRUG LORD WHO'S GOT TO GO.
SO WHAT IS THIS? A VENDETTA AGAINST NARCOS?
TAT-TAT-TAT
NOPE...
TAT
TAT
TAT

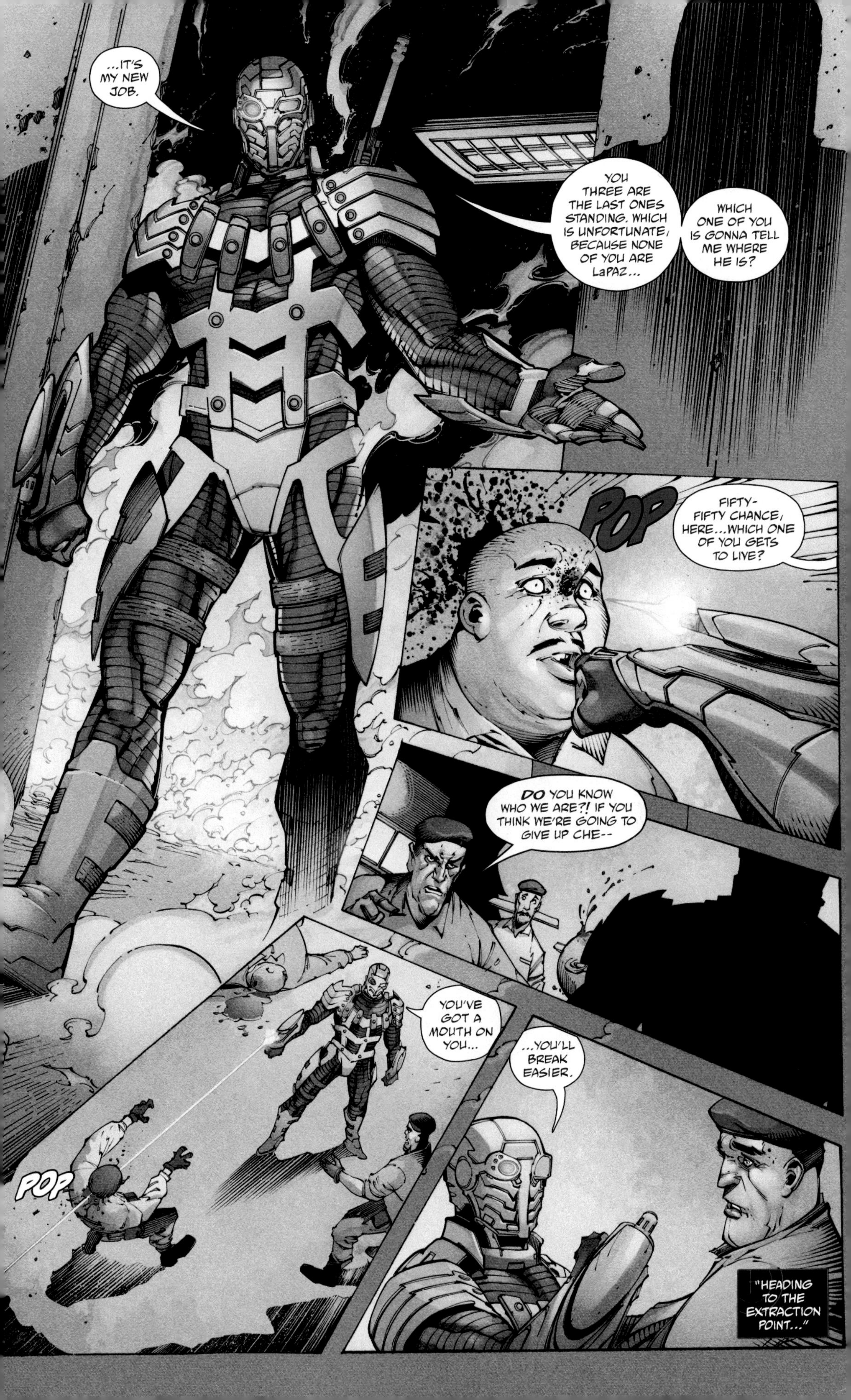
...IT'S MY NEW JOB.
YOU THREE ARE THE LAST ONES STANDING. WHICH IS UNFORTUNATE, BECAUSE NONE OF YOU ARE LaPAZ...
WHICH ONE OF YOU IS GONNA TELL ME WHERE HE IS?
POP
FIFTY-FIFTY CHANCE, HERE...WHICH ONE OF YOU GETS TO LIVE?
DO YOU KNOW WHO WE ARE?! IF YOU THINK WE'RE GOING TO GIVE UP CHE--
YOU'VE GOT A MOUTH ON YOU...
POP
...YOU'LL BREAK EASIER.
"HEADING TO THE EXTRACTION POINT..."

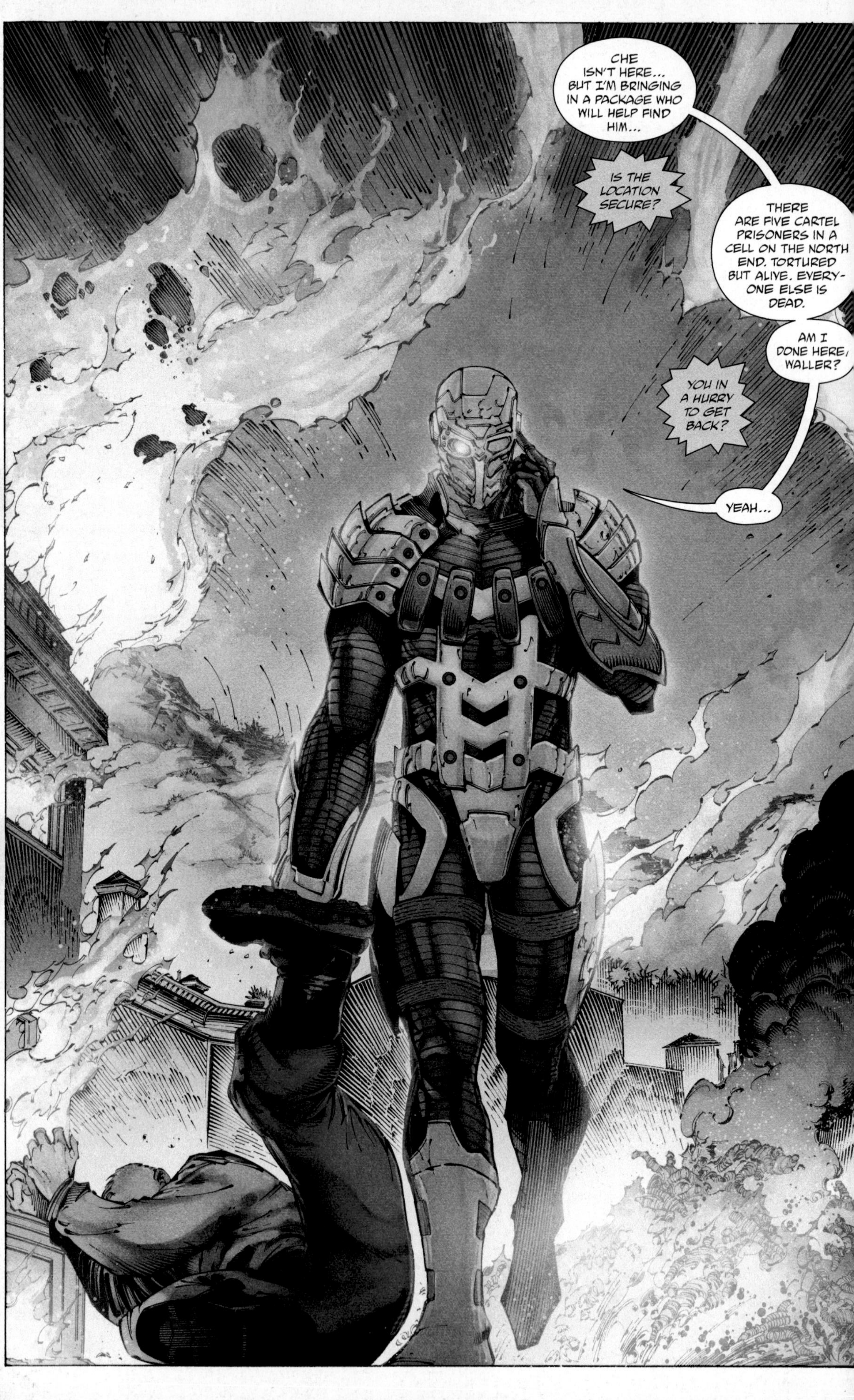
CHE ISN'T HERE... BUT I'M BRINGING IN A PACKAGE WHO WILL HELP FIND HIM...
IS THE LOCATION SECURE?
THERE ARE FIVE CARTEL PRISONERS IN A CELL ON THE NORTH END. TORTURED BUT ALIVE. EVERY-ONE ELSE IS DEAD.
AM I DONE HERE, WALLER?
YOU IN A HURRY TO GET BACK?
YEAH...

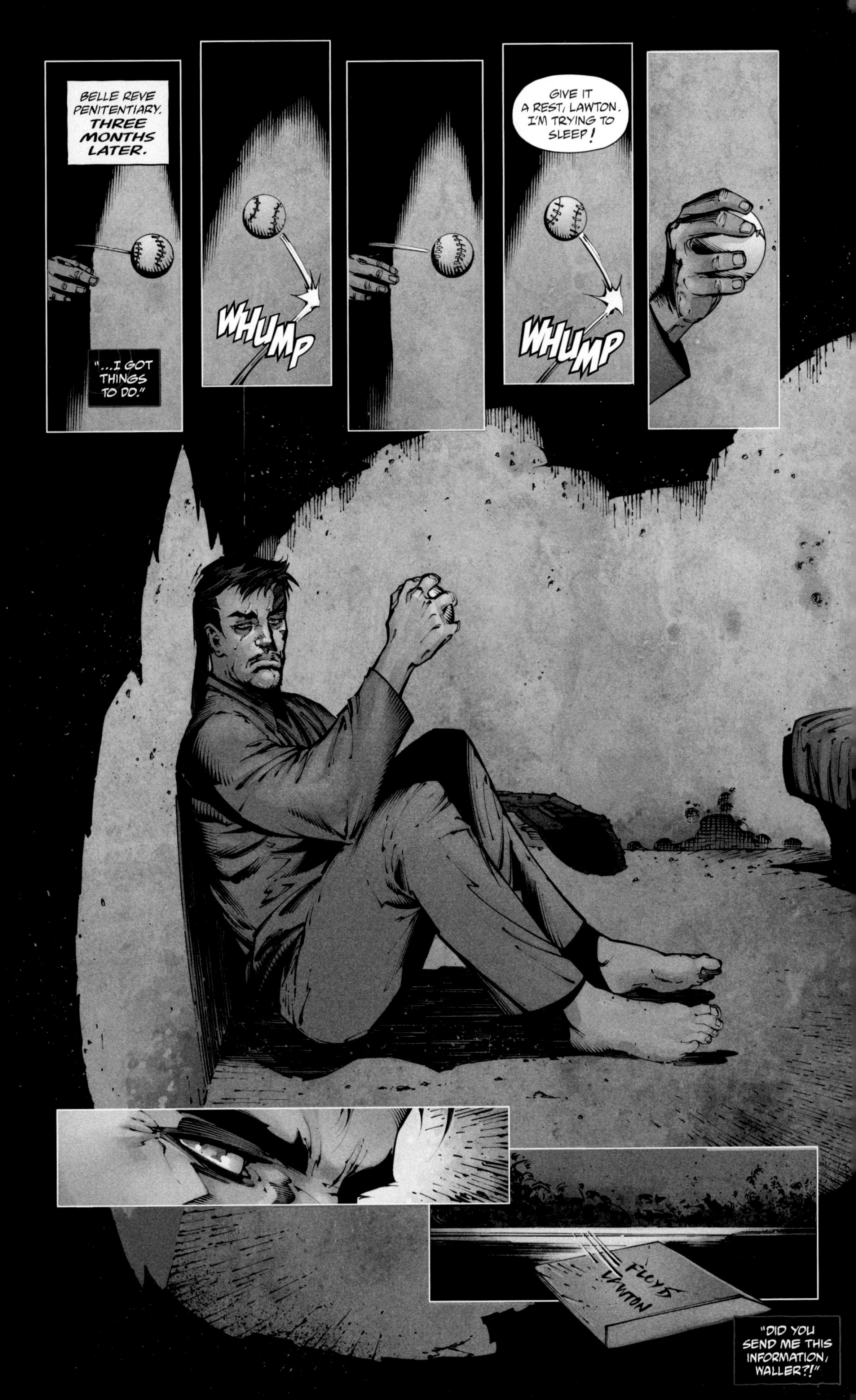
BELLE REVE PENITENTIARY. THREE MONTHS LATER.
"...I GOT THINGS TO DO."
WHUMP
GIVE IT A REST, LAWTON. I'M TRYING TO SLEEP!
WHUMP
FLOYD LAWTON
"DID YOU SEND ME THIS INFORMATION, WALLER?!"

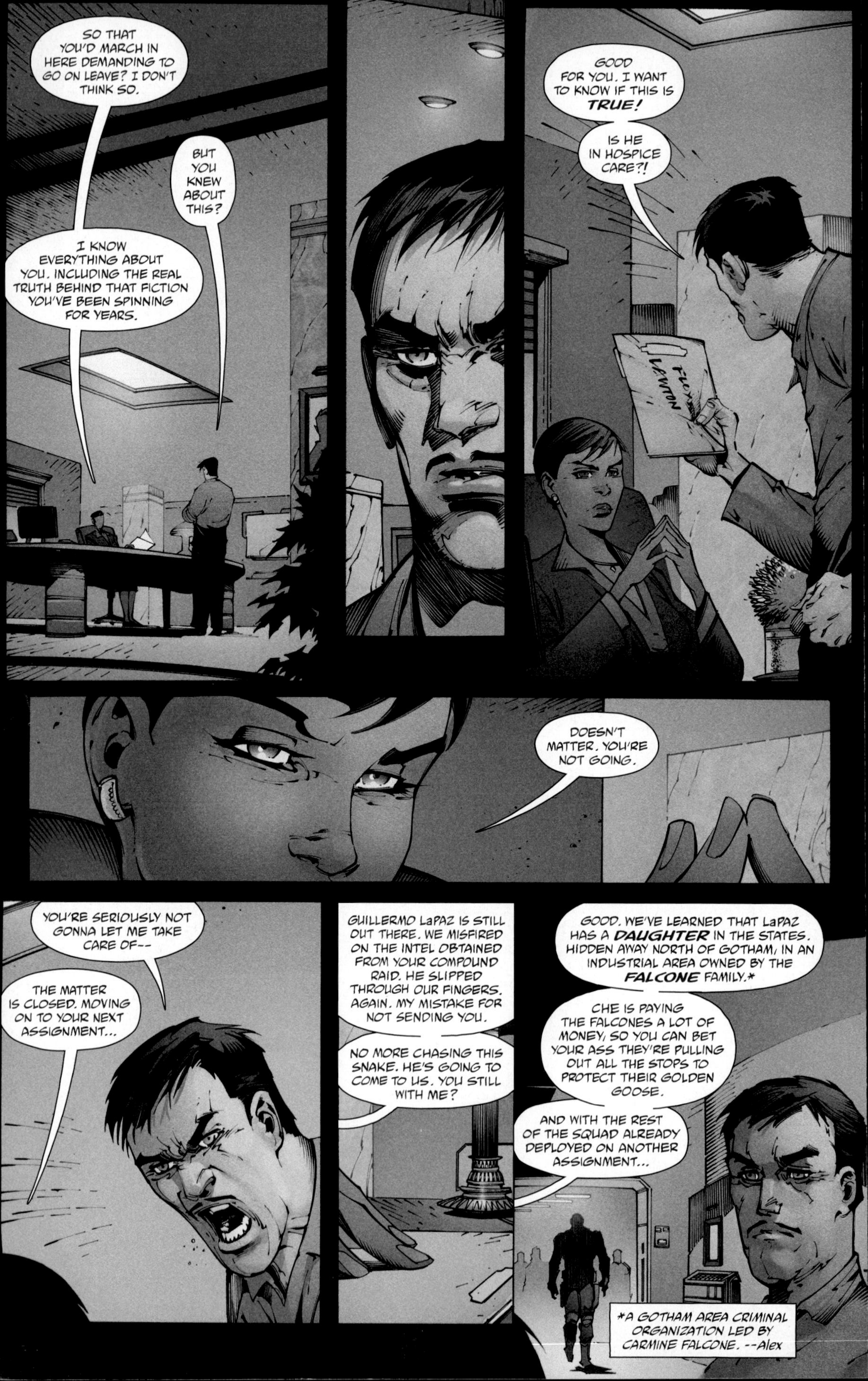
SO THAT YOU'D MARCH IN HERE DEMANDING TO GO ON LEAVE? I DON'T THINK SO.
BUT YOU KNEW ABOUT THIS?
I KNOW EVERYTHING ABOUT YOU. INCLUDING THE REAL TRUTH BEHIND THAT FICTION YOU'VE BEEN SPINNING FOR YEARS.
GOOD FOR YOU. I WANT TO KNOW IF THIS IS TRUE!
IS HE IN HOSPICE CARE?!
FLOYD LAWTON
DOESN'T MATTER. YOU'RE NOT GOING.
YOU'RE SERIOUSLY NOT GONNA LET ME TAKE CARE OF--
THE MATTER IS CLOSED. MOVING ON TO YOUR NEXT ASSIGNMENT...
GUILLERMO LaPAZ IS STILL OUT THERE. WE MISFIRED ON THE INTEL OBTAINED FROM YOUR COMPOUND RAID. HE SLIPPED THROUGH OUR FINGERS. AGAIN. MY MISTAKE FOR NOT SENDING YOU.
NO MORE CHASING THIS SNAKE. HE'S GOING TO COME TO US. YOU STILL WITH ME?
GOOD. WE'VE LEARNED THAT LaPAZ HAS A DAUGHTER IN THE STATES. HIDDEN AWAY NORTH OF GOTHAM, IN AN INDUSTRIAL AREA OWNED BY THE FALCONE FAMILY.*
CHE IS PAYING THE FALCONES A LOT OF MONEY, SO YOU CAN BET YOUR ASS THEY'RE PULLING OUT ALL THE STOPS TO PROTECT THEIR GOLDEN GOOSE.
AND WITH THE REST OF THE SQUAD ALREADY DEPLOYED ON ANOTHER ASSIGNMENT...
*A GOTHAM AREA CRIMINAL ORGANIZATION LED BY CARMINE FALCONE. --Alex

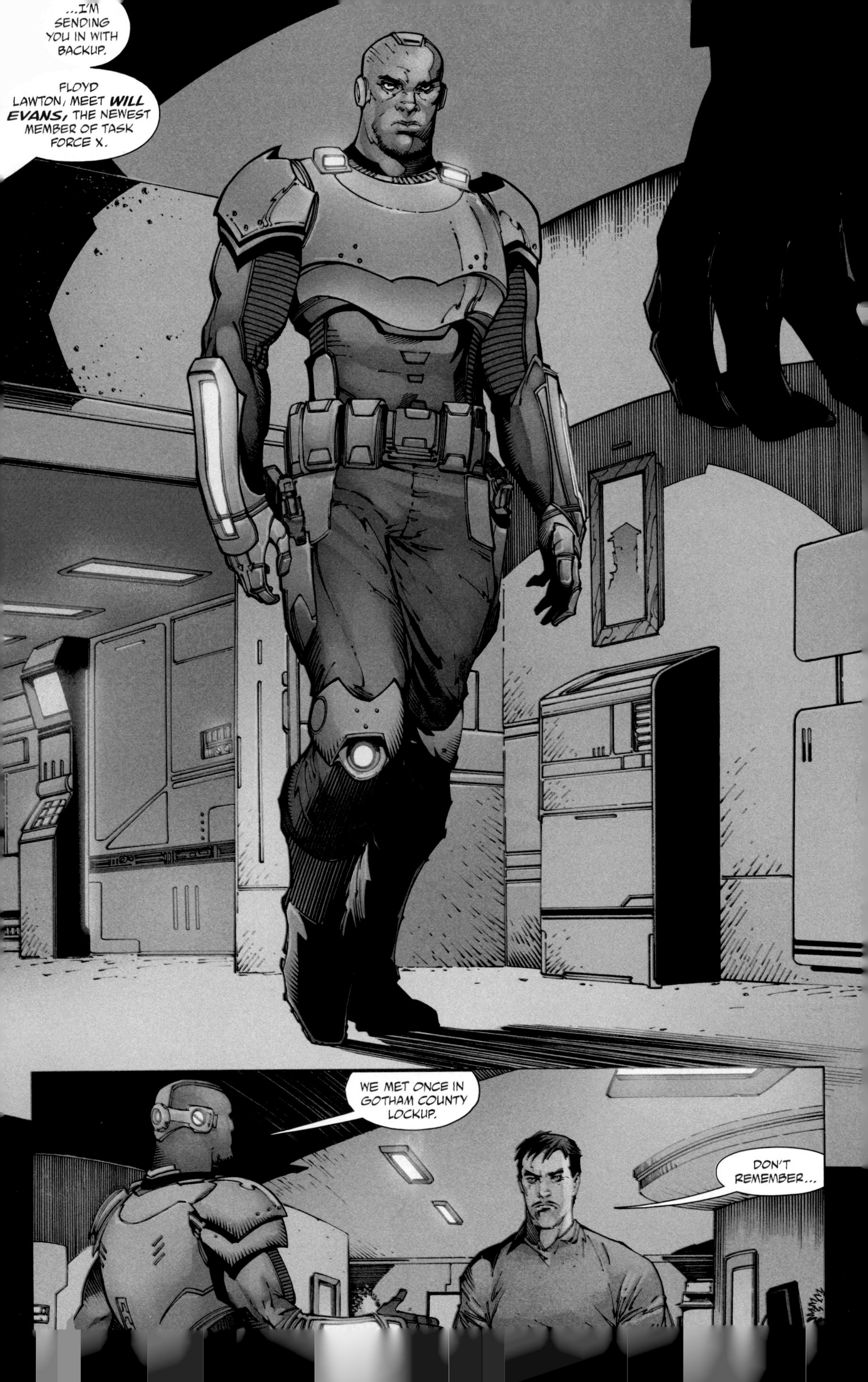
...I'M SENDING YOU IN WITH BACKUP.
FLOYD LAWTON, MEET WILL EVANS, THE NEWEST MEMBER OF TASK FORCE X.
WE MET ONCE IN GOTHAM COUNTY LOCKUP.
DON'T REMEMBER...

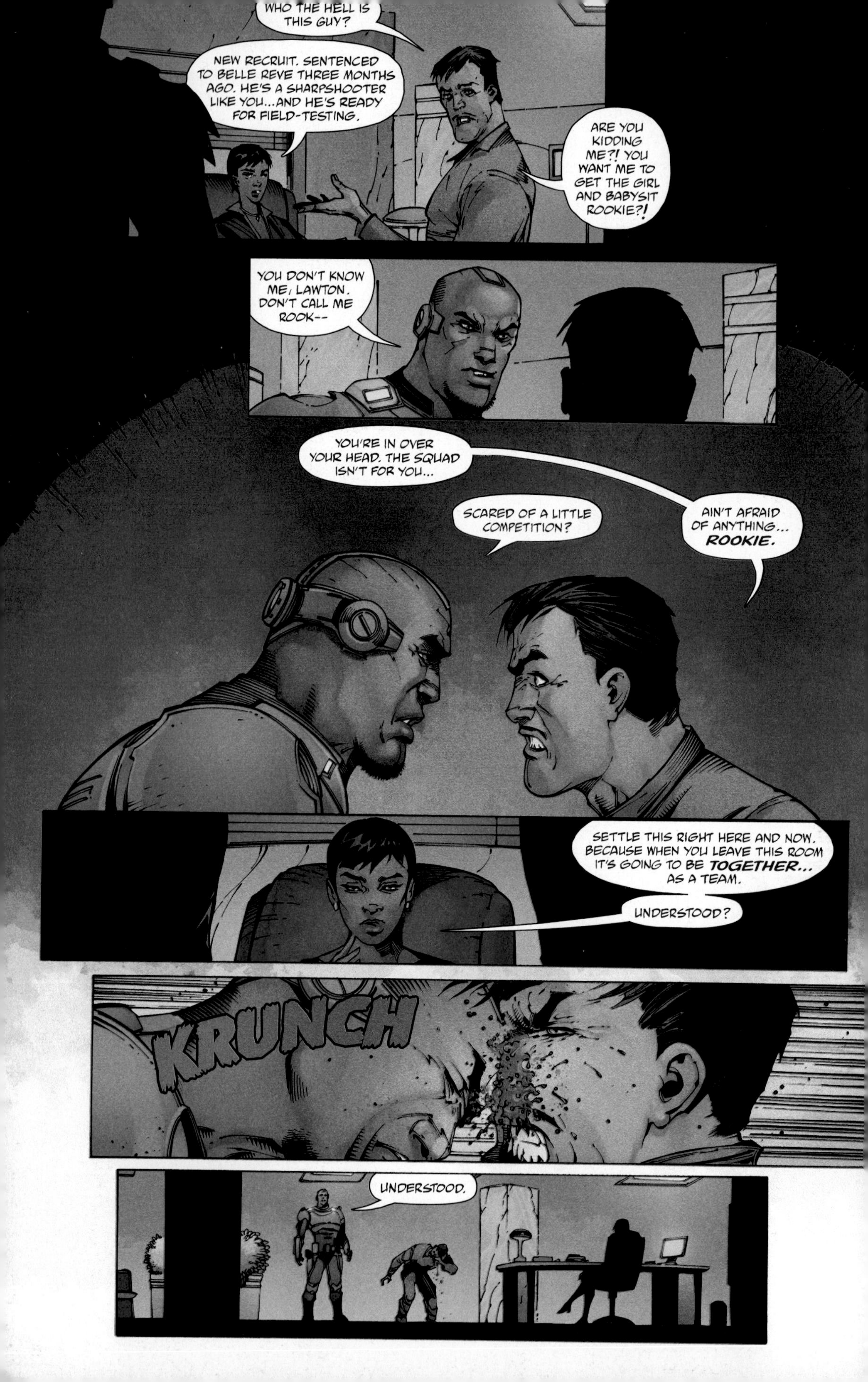
WHO THE HELL IS THIS GUY?
NEW RECRUIT. SENTENCED TO BELLE REVE THREE MONTHS AGO. HE'S A SHARPSHOOTER LIKE YOU...AND HE'S READY FOR FIELD-TESTING.
ARE YOU KIDDING ME?! YOU WANT ME TO GET THE GIRL AND BABYSIT ROOKIE?!
YOU DON'T KNOW ME, LAWTON. DON'T CALL ME ROOK--
YOU'RE IN OVER YOUR HEAD. THE SQUAD ISN'T FOR YOU...
SCARED OF A LITTLE COMPETITION?
AIN'T AFRAID OF ANYTHING... ROOKIE.
SETTLE THIS RIGHT HERE AND NOW. BECAUSE WHEN YOU LEAVE THIS ROOM IT'S GOING TO BE TOGETHER... AS A TEAM.
UNDERSTOOD?
KRUNCH
UNDERSTOOD.

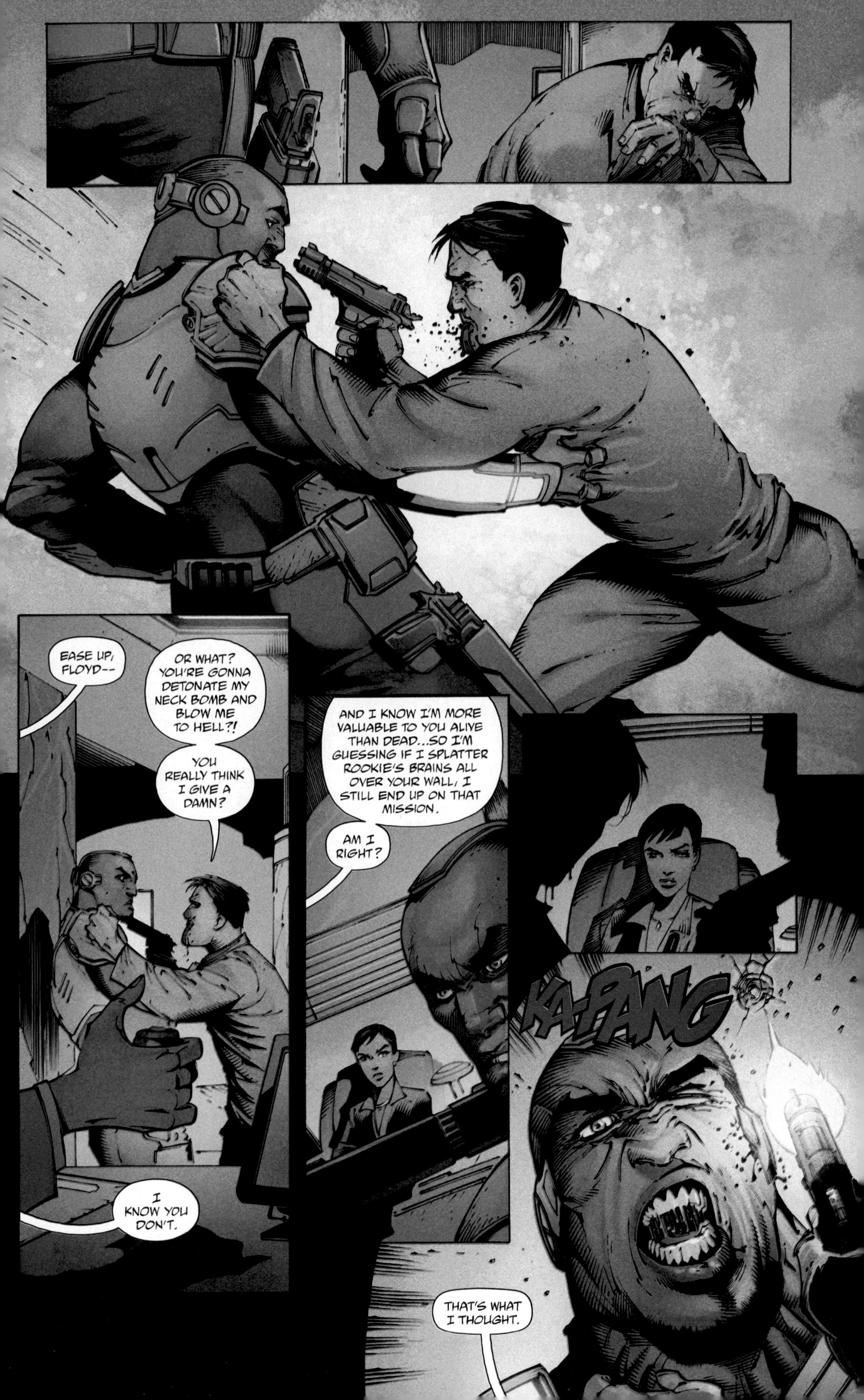
EASE UP, FLOYD--
OR WHAT? YOU'RE GONNA DETONATE MY NECK BOMB AND BLOW ME TO HELL?!
YOU REALLY THINK I GIVE A DAMN?
I KNOW YOU DON'T.
AND I KNOW I'M MORE VALUABLE TO YOU ALIVE THAN DEAD...SO I'M GUESSING IF I SPLATTER ROOKIE'S BRAINS ALL OVER YOUR WALL, I STILL END UP ON THAT MISSION.
AM I RIGHT?
KA-PANG
THAT'S WHAT I THOUGHT.

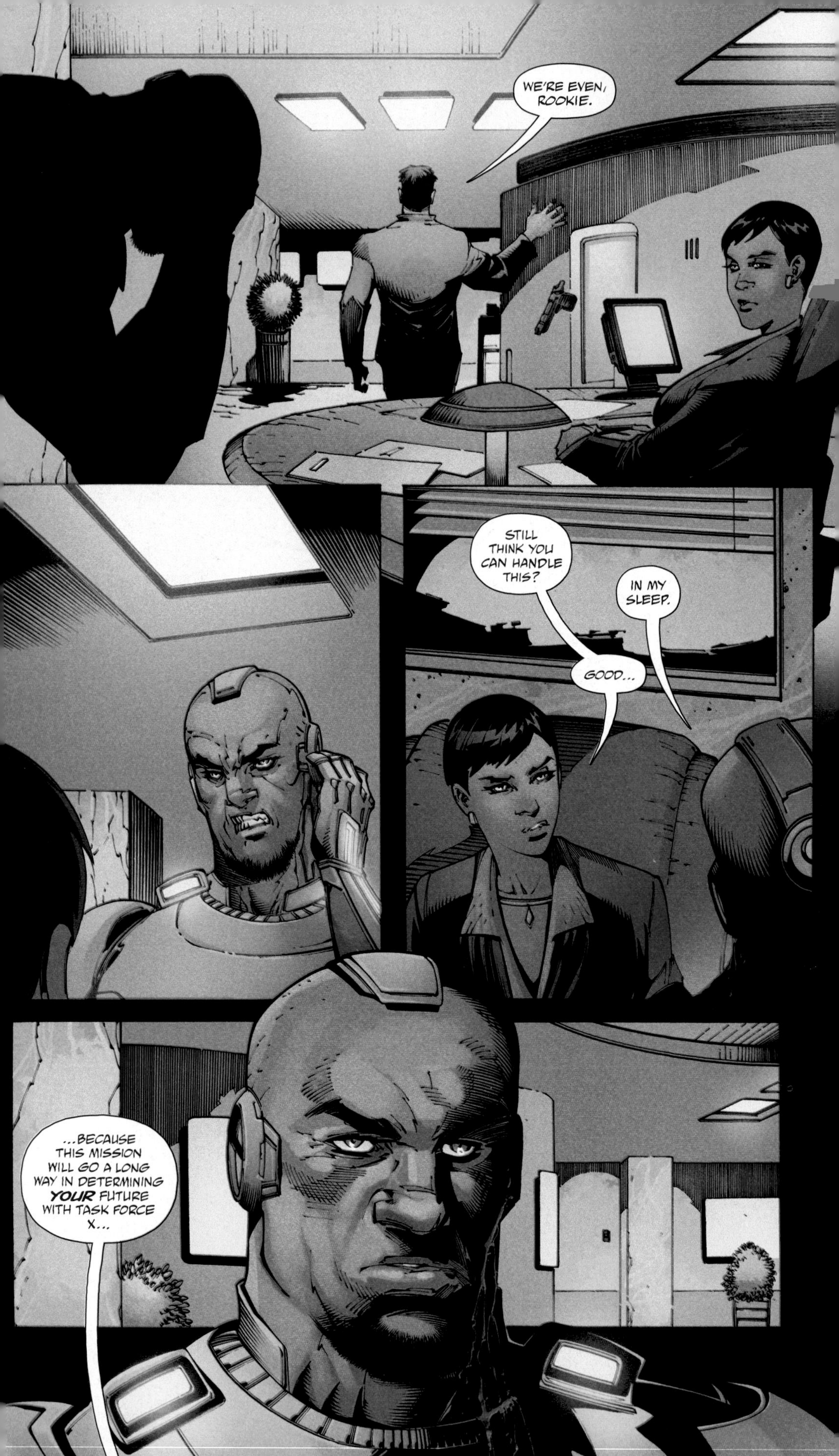
WE'RE EVEN, ROOKIE.
STILL THINK YOU CAN HANDLE THIS?
IN MY SLEEP.
GOOD...
...BECAUSE THIS MISSION WILL GO A LONG WAY IN DETERMINING *YOUR* FUTURE WITH TASK FORCE X...

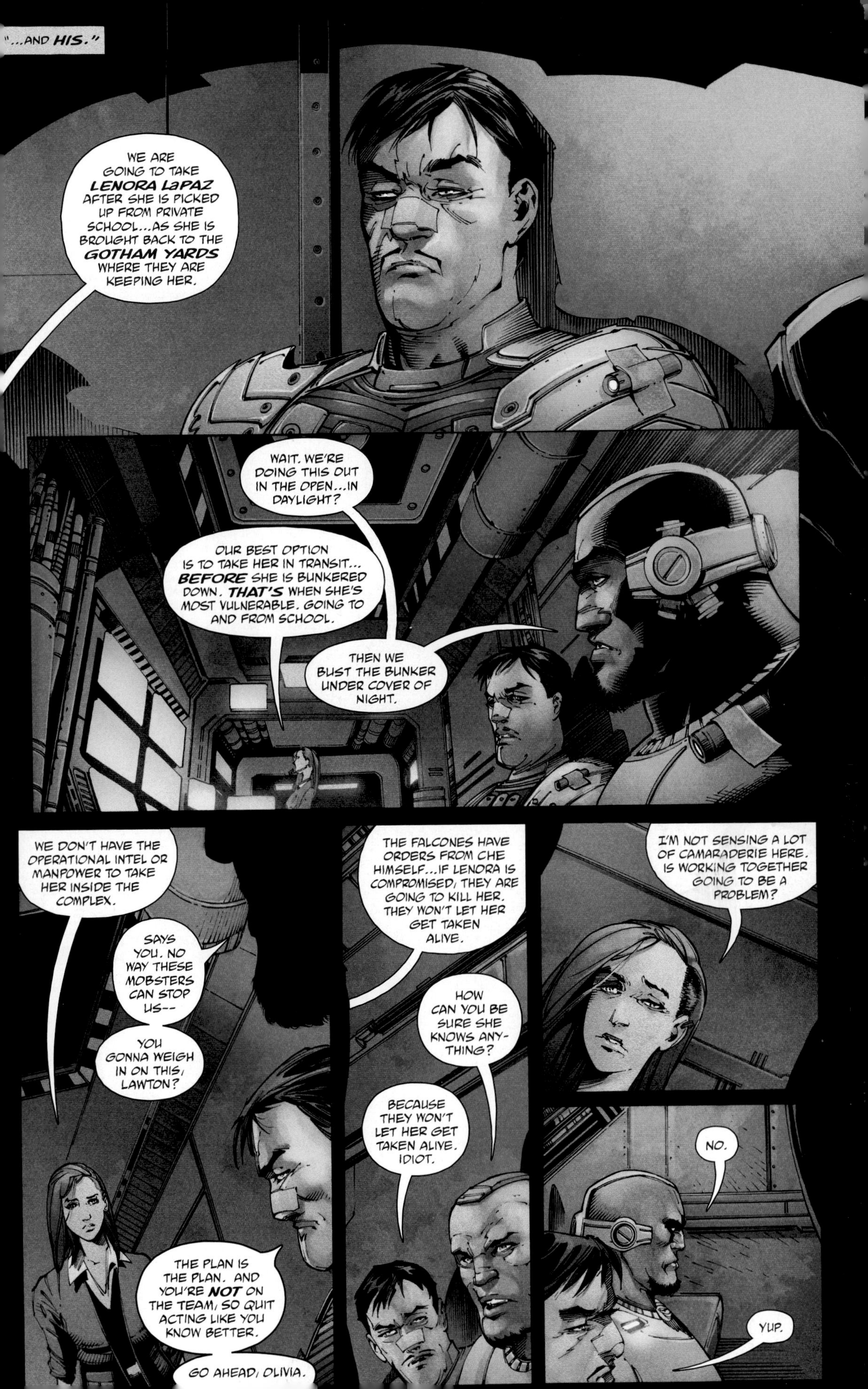
"...AND HIS."
WE ARE GOING TO TAKE LENORA LaPAZ AFTER SHE IS PICKED UP FROM PRIVATE SCHOOL...AS SHE IS BROUGHT BACK TO THE GOTHAM YARDS WHERE THEY ARE KEEPING HER.
WAIT. WE'RE DOING THIS OUT IN THE OPEN...IN DAYLIGHT?
OUR BEST OPTION IS TO TAKE HER IN TRANSIT... BEFORE SHE IS BUNKERED DOWN. THAT'S WHEN SHE'S MOST VULNERABLE. GOING TO AND FROM SCHOOL.
THEN WE BUST THE BUNKER UNDER COVER OF NIGHT.
WE DON'T HAVE THE OPERATIONAL INTEL OR MANPOWER TO TAKE HER INSIDE THE COMPLEX.
SAYS YOU. NO WAY THESE MOBSTERS CAN STOP US--
YOU GONNA WEIGH IN ON THIS, LAWTON?
THE PLAN IS THE PLAN. AND YOU'RE NOT ON THE TEAM, SO QUIT ACTING LIKE YOU KNOW BETTER.
GO AHEAD, OLIVIA.
THE FALCONES HAVE ORDERS FROM CHE HIMSELF...IF LENORA IS COMPROMISED, THEY ARE GOING TO KILL HER. THEY WON'T LET HER GET TAKEN ALIVE.
HOW CAN YOU BE SURE SHE KNOWS ANY-THING?
BECAUSE THEY WON'T LET HER GET TAKEN ALIVE. IDIOT.
I'M NOT SENSING A LOT OF CAMARADERIE HERE. IS WORKING TOGETHER GOING TO BE A PROBLEM?
NO.
YUP.

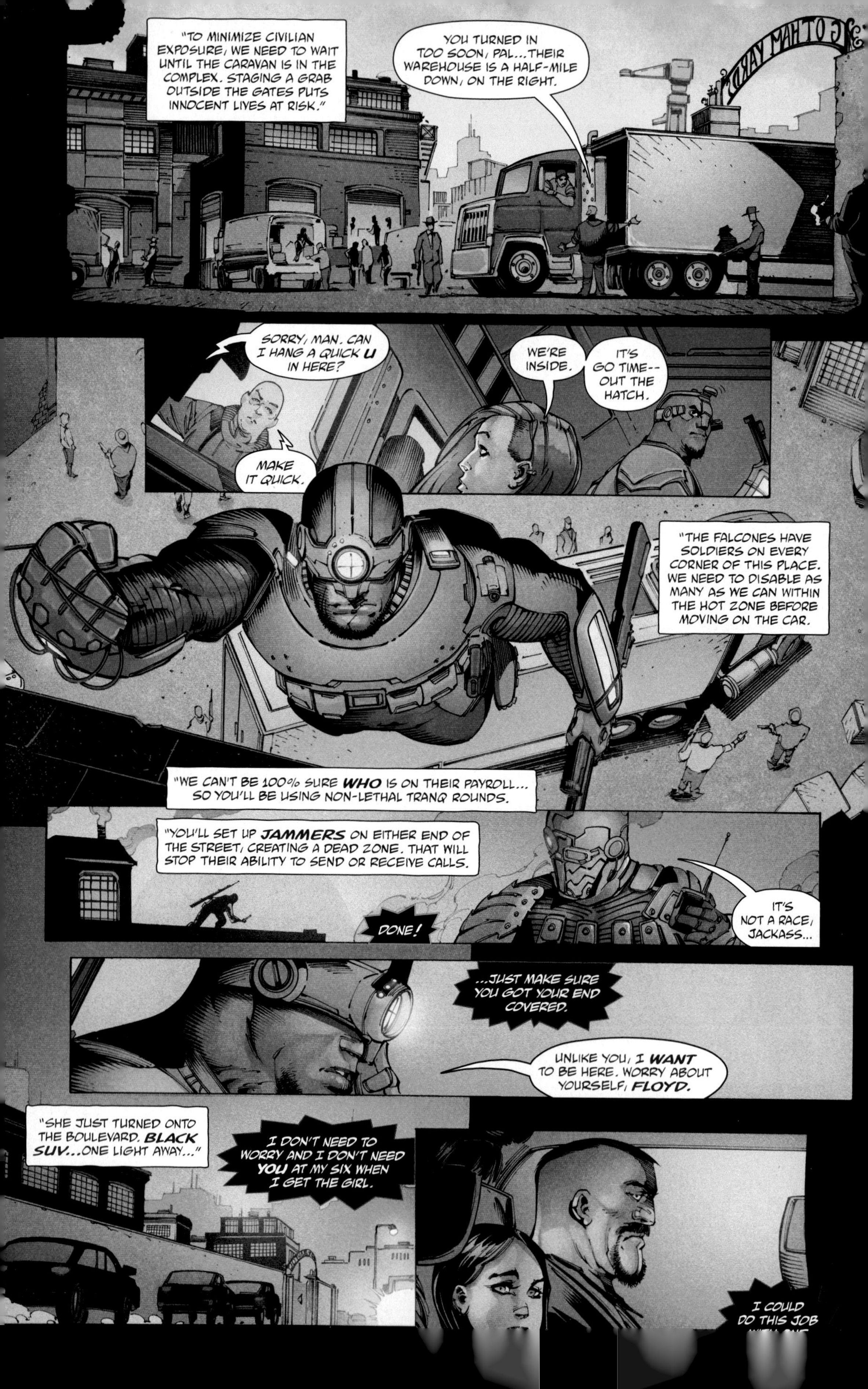
"TO MINIMIZE CIVILIAN EXPOSURE, WE NEED TO WAIT UNTIL THE CARAVAN IS IN THE COMPLEX. STAGING A GRAB OUTSIDE THE GATES PUTS INNOCENT LIVES AT RISK."
YOU TURNED IN TOO SOON, PAL... THEIR WAREHOUSE IS A HALF-MILE DOWN, ON THE RIGHT.
SORRY, MAN. CAN I HANG A QUICK U IN HERE?
MAKE IT QUICK.
WE'RE INSIDE.
IT'S GO TIME-- OUT THE HATCH.
"THE FALCONES HAVE SOLDIERS ON EVERY CORNER OF THIS PLACE. WE NEED TO DISABLE AS MANY AS WE CAN WITHIN THE HOT ZONE BEFORE MOVING ON THE CAR.
"WE CAN'T BE 100% SURE WHO IS ON THEIR PAYROLL... SO YOU'LL BE USING NON-LETHAL TRANQ ROUNDS.
"YOU'LL SET UP JAMMERS ON EITHER END OF THE STREET, CREATING A DEAD ZONE. THAT WILL STOP THEIR ABILITY TO SEND OR RECEIVE CALLS.
DONE!
IT'S NOT A RACE, JACKASS...
...JUST MAKE SURE YOU GOT YOUR END COVERED.
UNLIKE YOU, I WANT TO BE HERE. WORRY ABOUT YOURSELF, FLOYD.
"SHE JUST TURNED ONTO THE BOULEVARD. BLACK SUV...ONE LIGHT AWAY..."
I DON'T NEED TO WORRY AND I DON'T NEED YOU AT MY SIX WHEN I GET THE GIRL.
I COULD DO THIS JOB

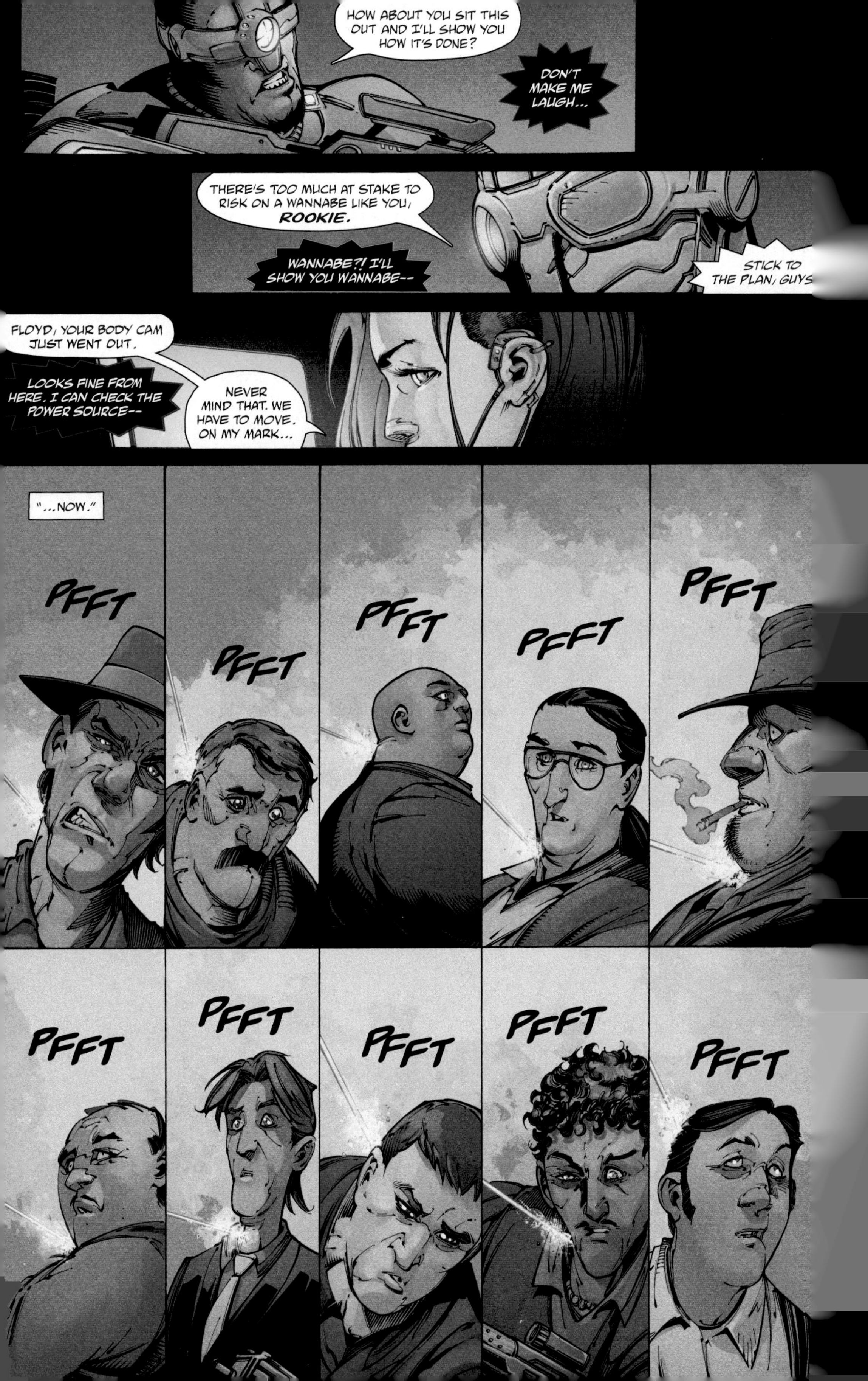
HOW ABOUT YOU SIT THIS OUT AND I'LL SHOW YOU HOW IT'S DONE?
DON'T MAKE ME LAUGH...
THERE'S TOO MUCH AT STAKE TO RISK ON A WANNABE LIKE YOU, ROOKIE.
WANNABE?! I'LL SHOW YOU WANNABE--
STICK TO THE PLAN, GUYS
FLOYD, YOUR BODY CAM JUST WENT OUT.
LOOKS FINE FROM HERE. I CAN CHECK THE POWER SOURCE--
NEVER MIND THAT. WE HAVE TO MOVE. ON MY MARK...
"...NOW."
PFFT
PFFT
PFFT
PFFT
PFFT
PFFT
PFFT
PFFT
PFFT
PFFT

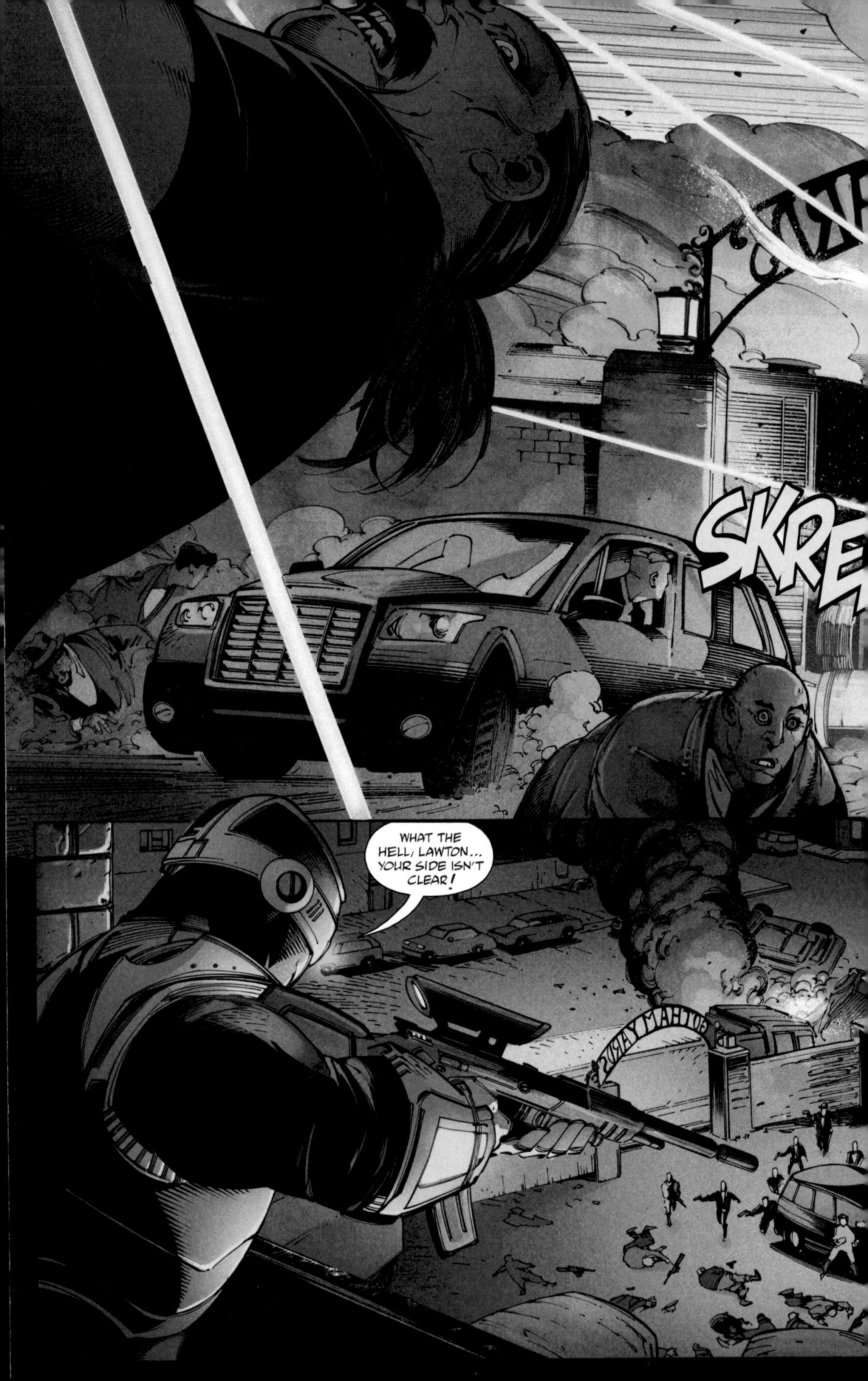
SKRE
WHAT THE HELL, LAWTON... YOUR SIDE ISN'T CLEAR!

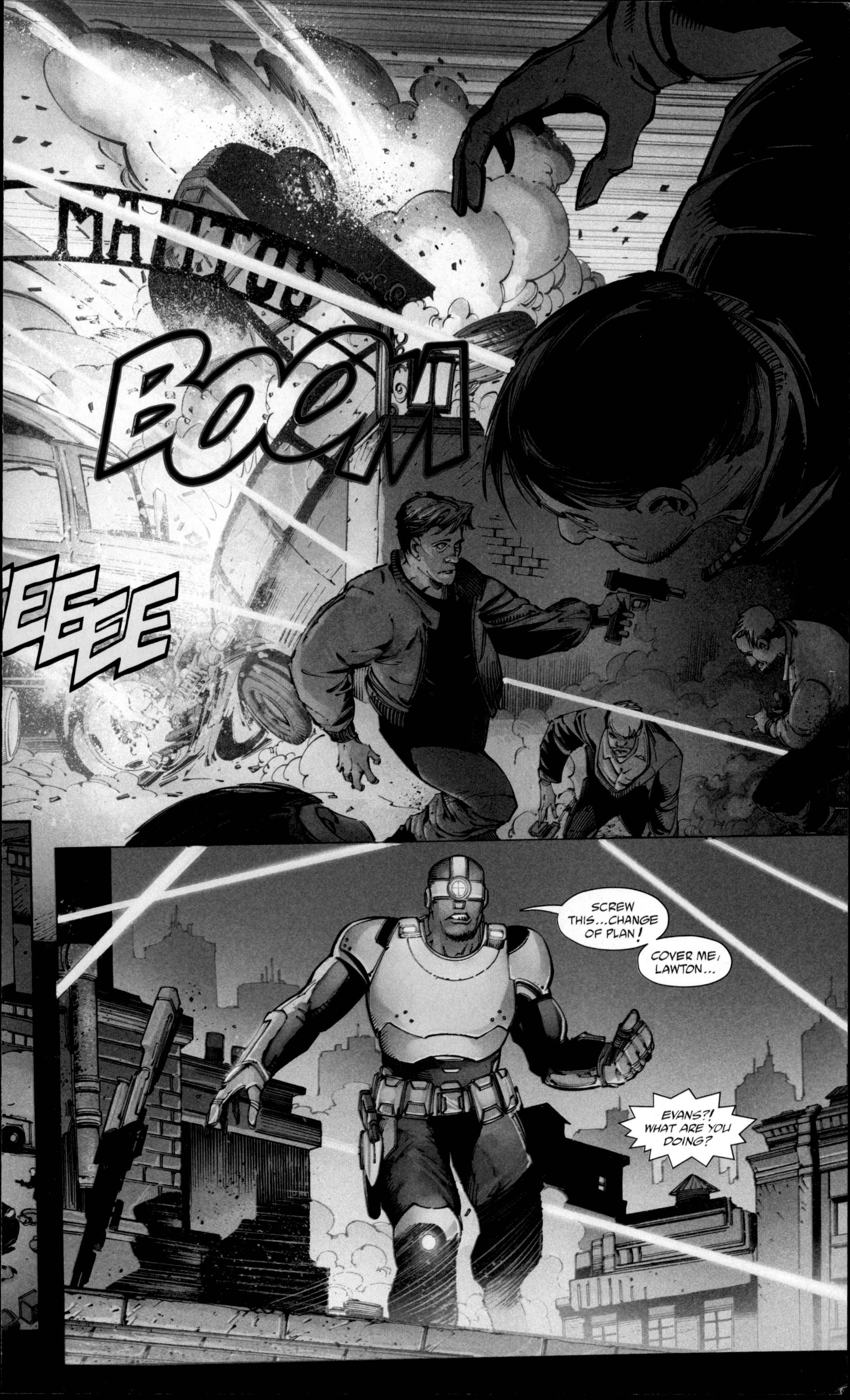
BOOM
SCREW THIS...CHANGE OF PLAN!
COVER ME, LAWTON...
EVANS?! WHAT ARE YOU DOING?

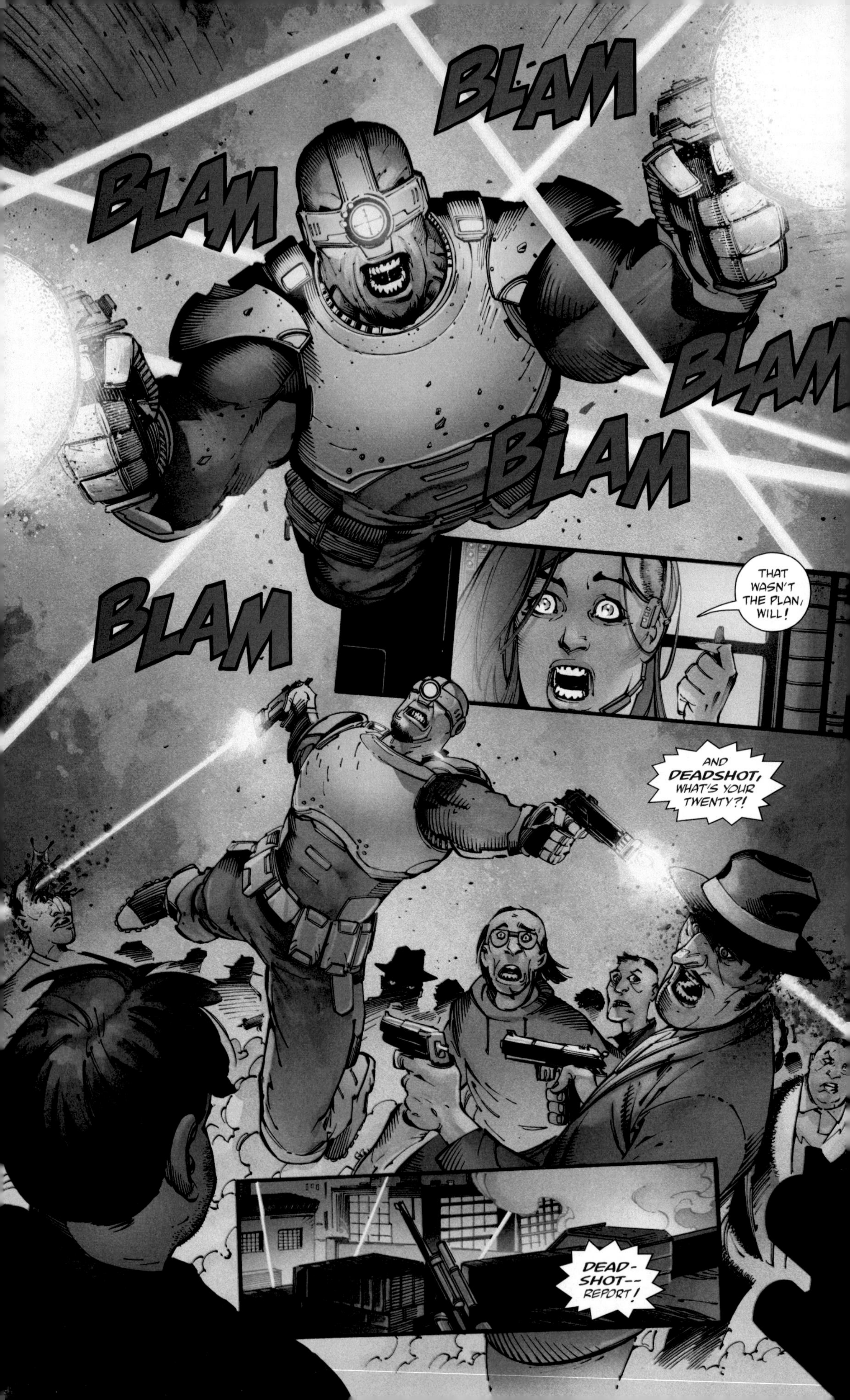
BLAM
BLAM
BLAM
BLAM
BLAM
THAT WASN'T THE PLAN, WILL!
AND DEADSHOT, WHAT'S YOUR TWENTY?!
DEAD-SHOT-- REPORT!

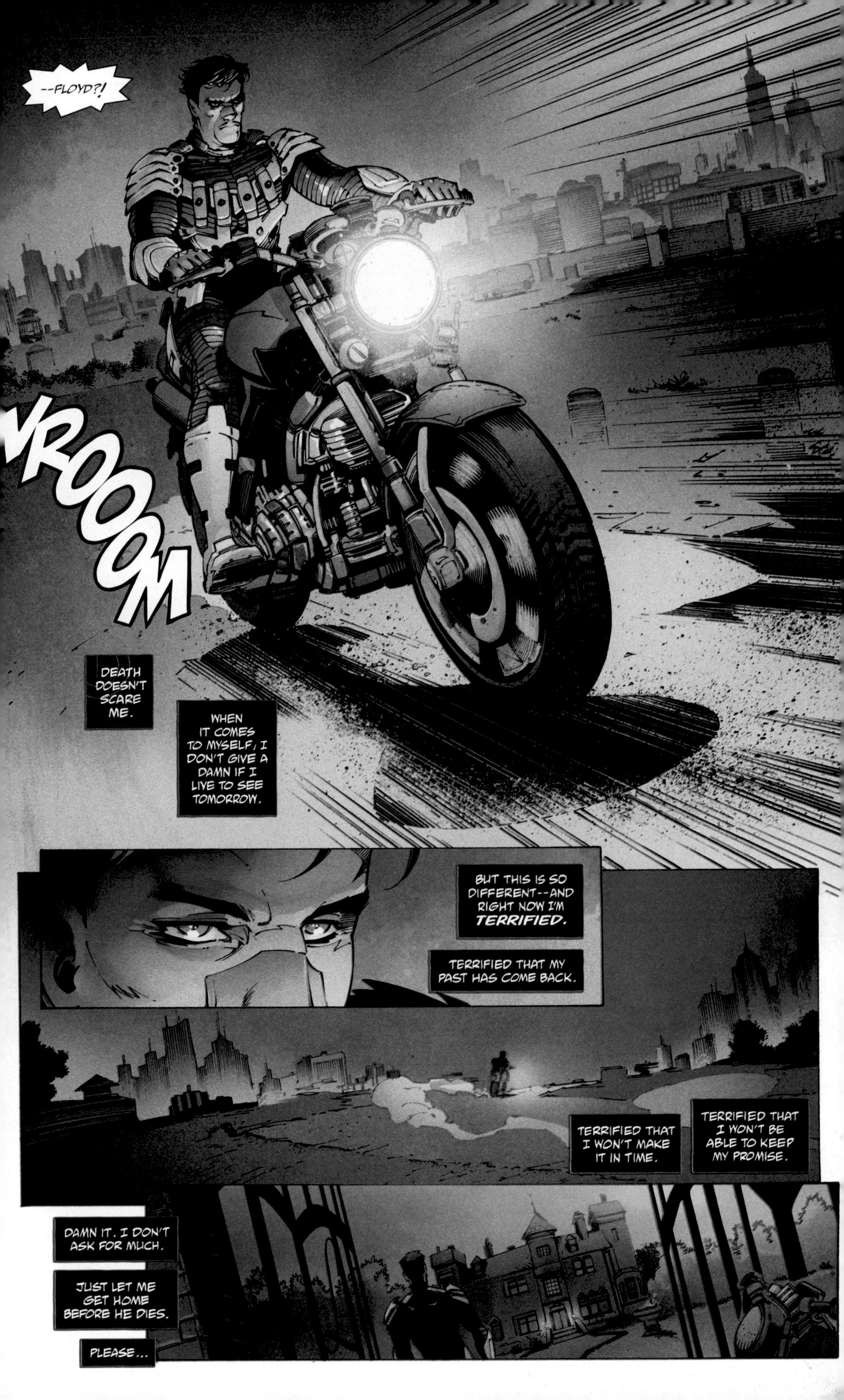
--FLOYD?!
VROOOM
DEATH DOESN'T SCARE ME.
WHEN IT COMES TO MYSELF, I DON'T GIVE A DAMN IF I LIVE TO SEE TOMORROW.
BUT THIS IS SO DIFFERENT--AND RIGHT NOW I'M TERRIFIED.
TERRIFIED THAT MY PAST HAS COME BACK.
TERRIFIED THAT I WON'T MAKE IT IN TIME.
TERRIFIED THAT I WON'T BE ABLE TO KEEP MY PROMISE.
DAMN IT. I DON'T ASK FOR MUCH.
JUST LET ME GET HOME BEFORE HE DIES.
PLEASE...

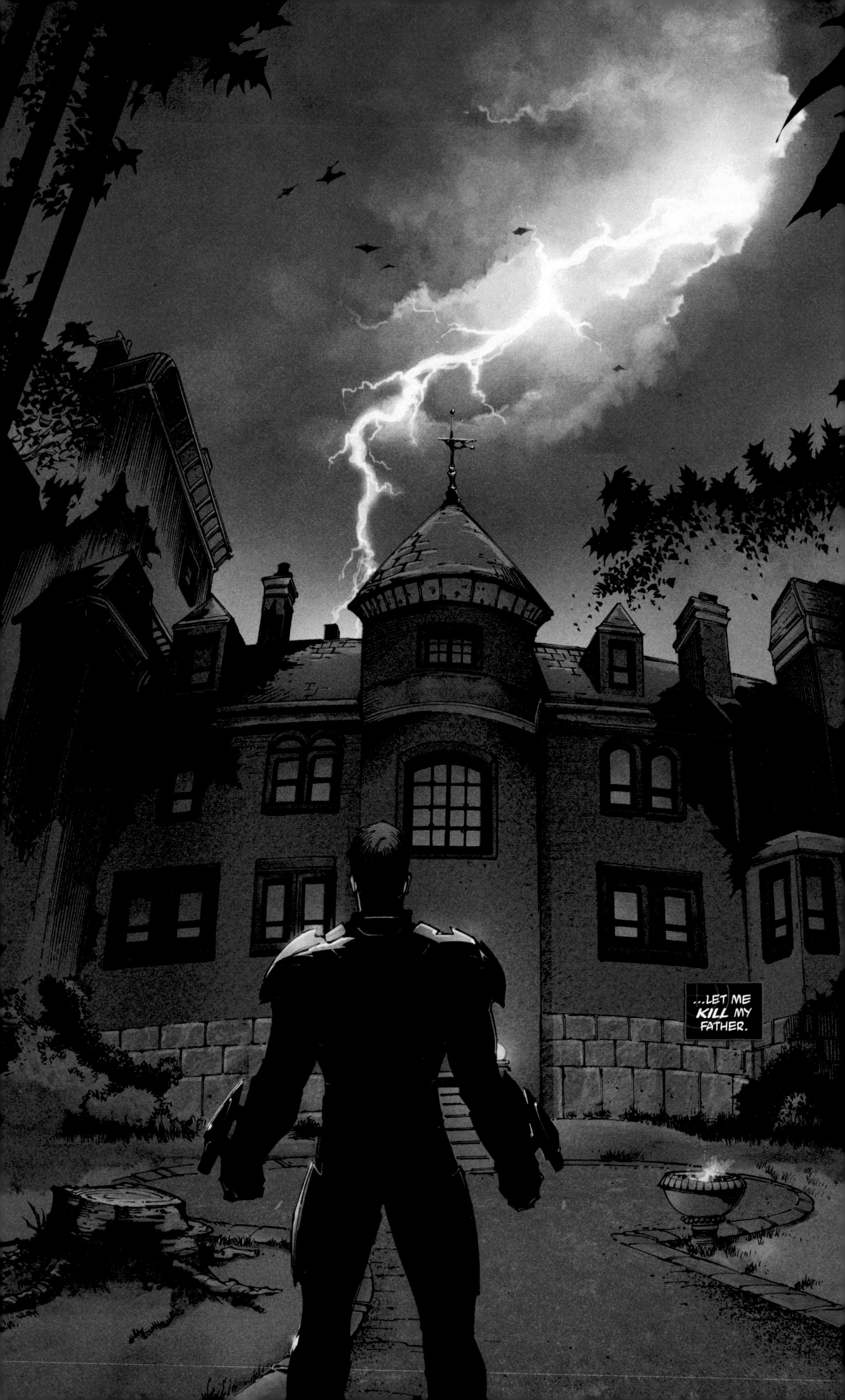
...LET ME KILL MY FATHER.

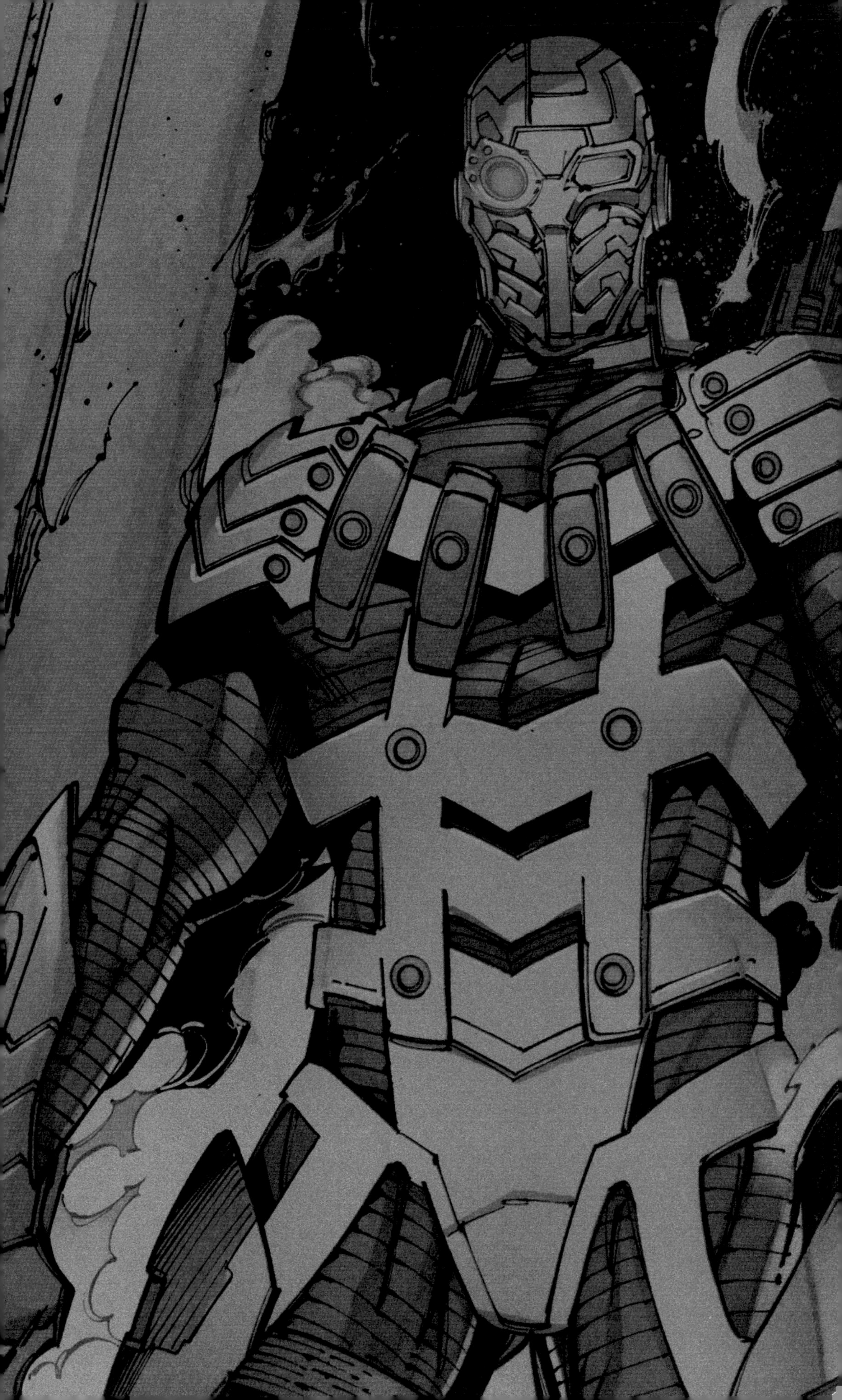

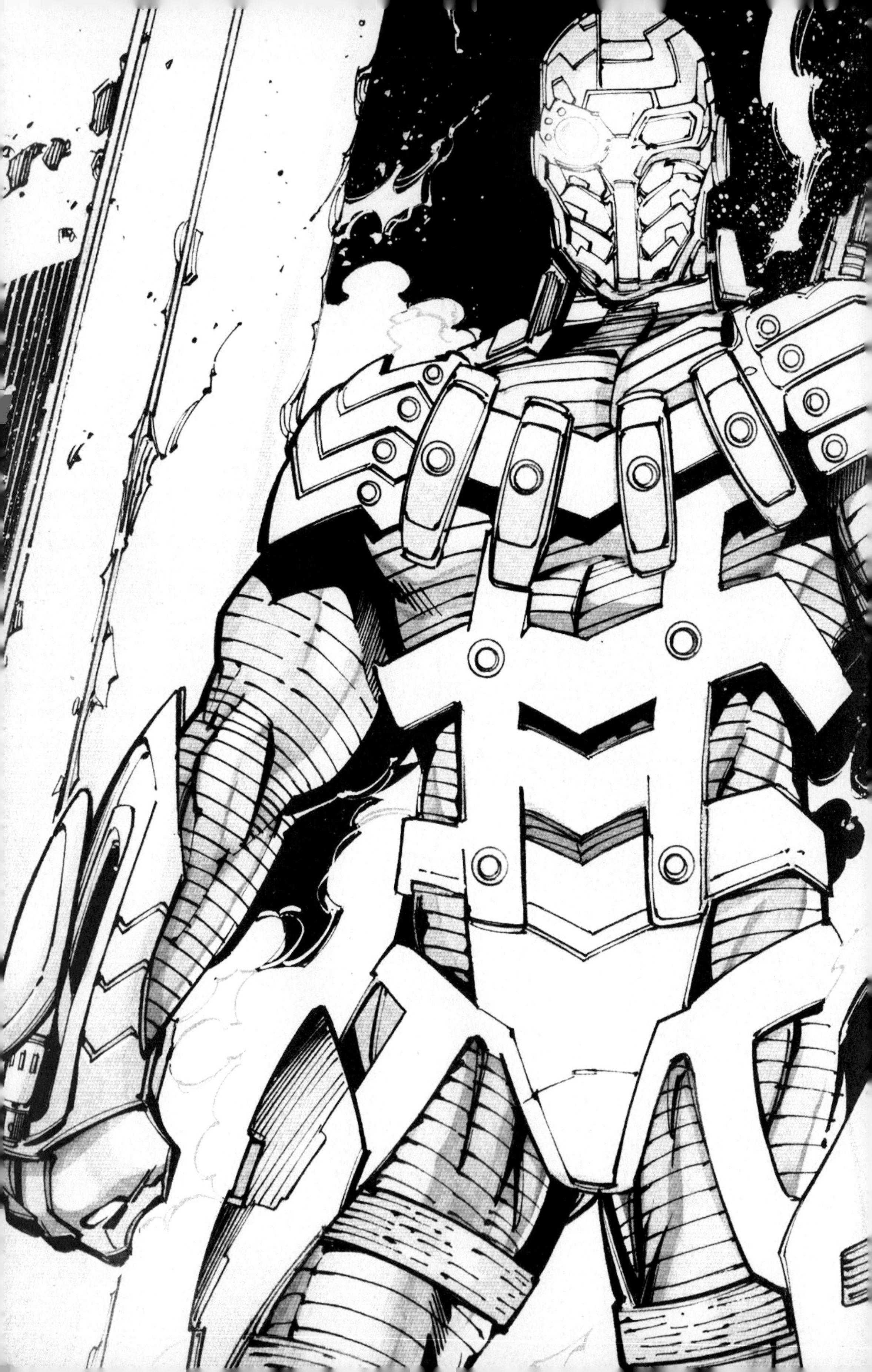

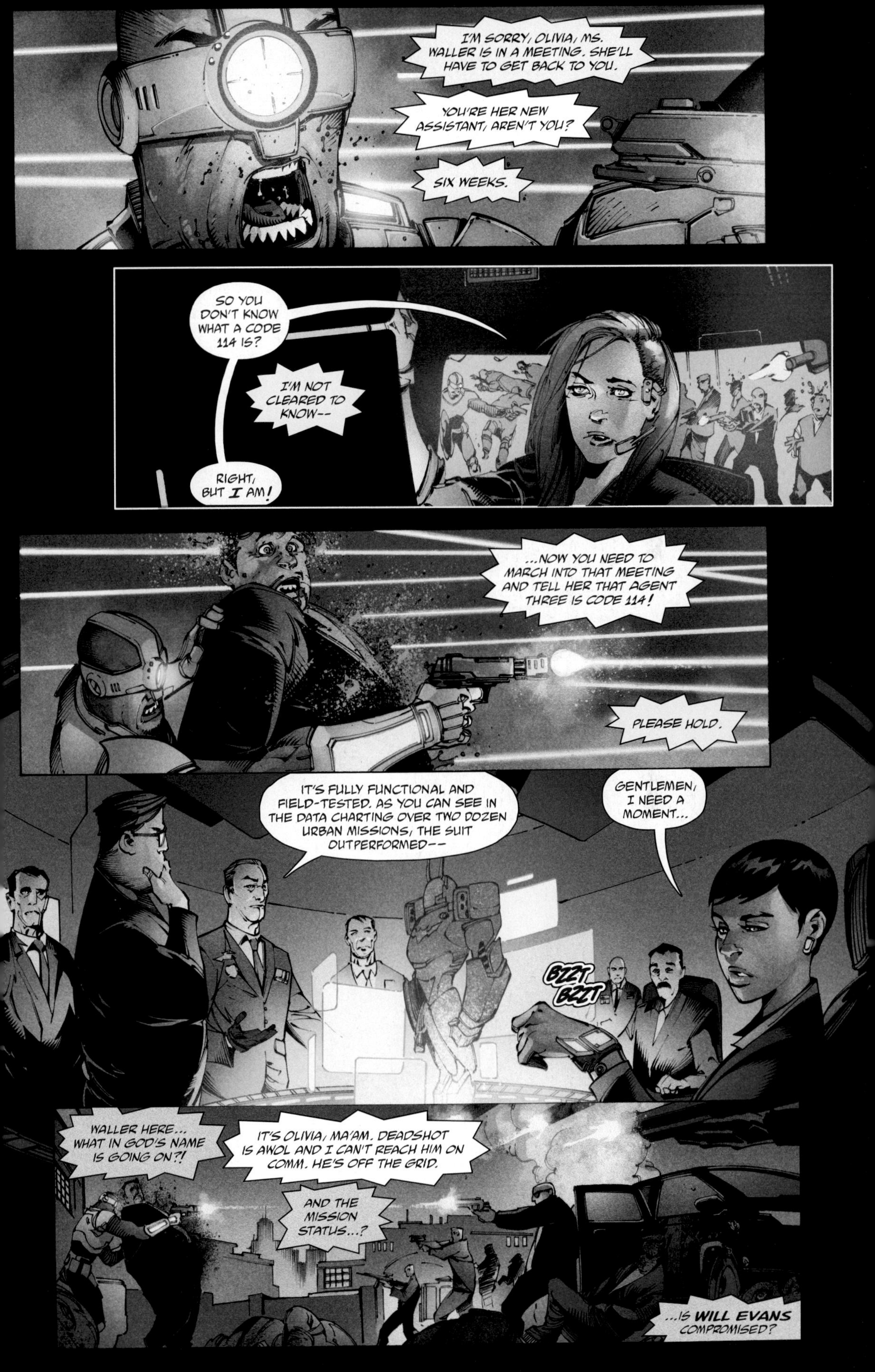
I'M SORRY, OLIVIA, MS. WALLER IS IN A MEETING. SHE'LL HAVE TO GET BACK TO YOU.
YOU'RE HER NEW ASSISTANT, AREN'T YOU?
SIX WEEKS.
SO YOU DON'T KNOW WHAT A CODE 114 IS?
I'M NOT CLEARED TO KNOW--
RIGHT, BUT I AM!
...NOW YOU NEED TO MARCH INTO THAT MEETING AND TELL HER THAT AGENT THREE IS CODE 114!
PLEASE HOLD.
IT'S FULLY FUNCTIONAL AND FIELD-TESTED. AS YOU CAN SEE IN THE DATA CHARTING OVER TWO DOZEN URBAN MISSIONS, THE SUIT OUTPERFORMED--
GENTLEMEN, I NEED A MOMENT...
BZZT BZZT
WALLER HERE... WHAT IN GOD'S NAME IS GOING ON?!
IT'S OLIVIA, MA'AM. DEADSHOT IS AWOL AND I CAN'T REACH HIM ON COMM. HE'S OFF THE GRID.
AND THE MISSION STATUS...?
...IS WILL EVANS COMPROMISED?

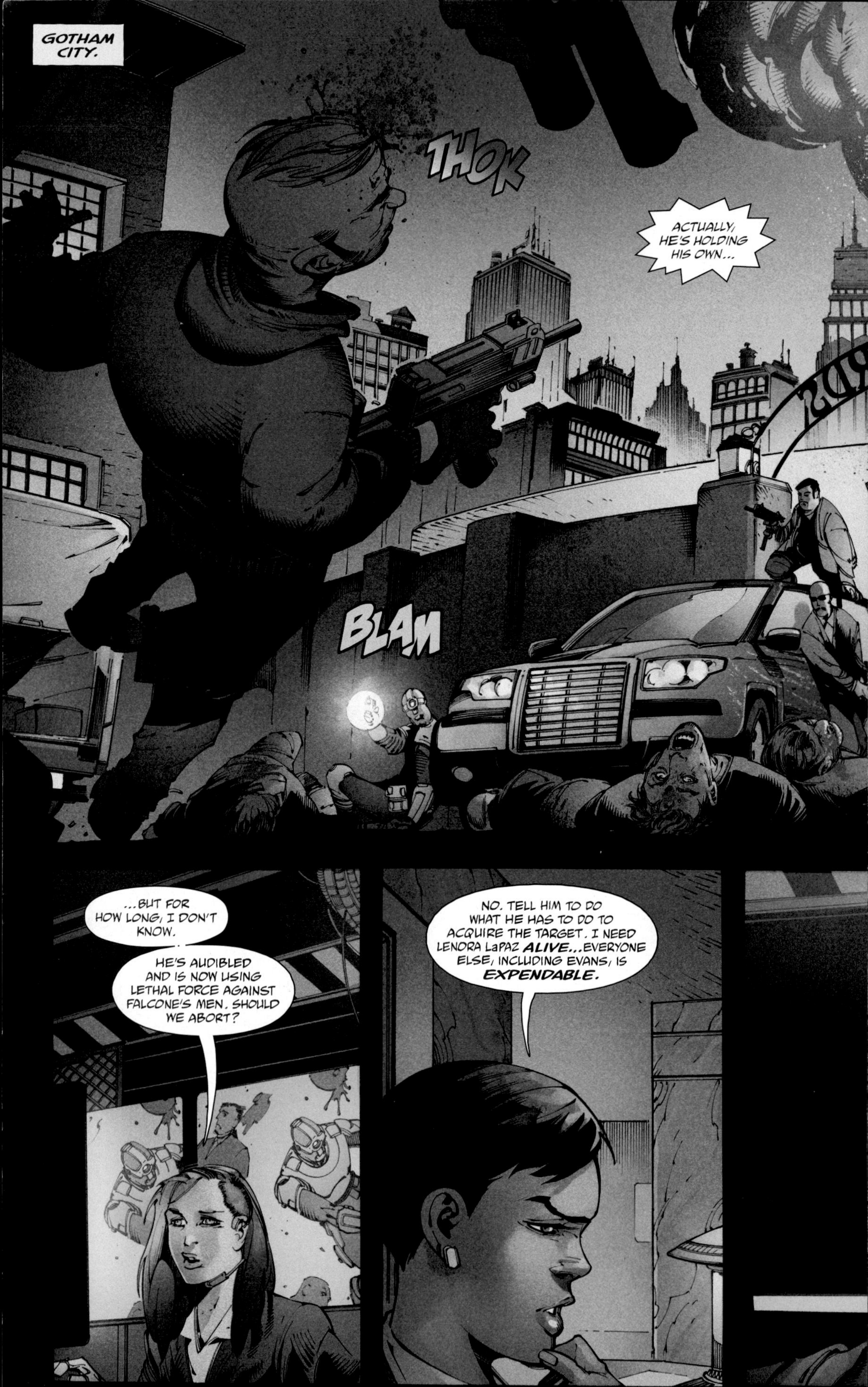
GOTHAM CITY.
THOK
ACTUALLY, HE'S HOLDING HIS OWN...
BLAM
...BUT FOR HOW LONG, I DON'T KNOW.
HE'S AUDIBLED AND IS NOW USING LETHAL FORCE AGAINST FALCONE'S MEN. SHOULD WE ABORT?
NO. TELL HIM TO DO WHAT HE HAS TO DO TO ACQUIRE THE TARGET. I NEED LENORA LaPAZ ALIVE...EVERYONE ELSE, INCLUDING EVANS, IS EXPENDABLE.

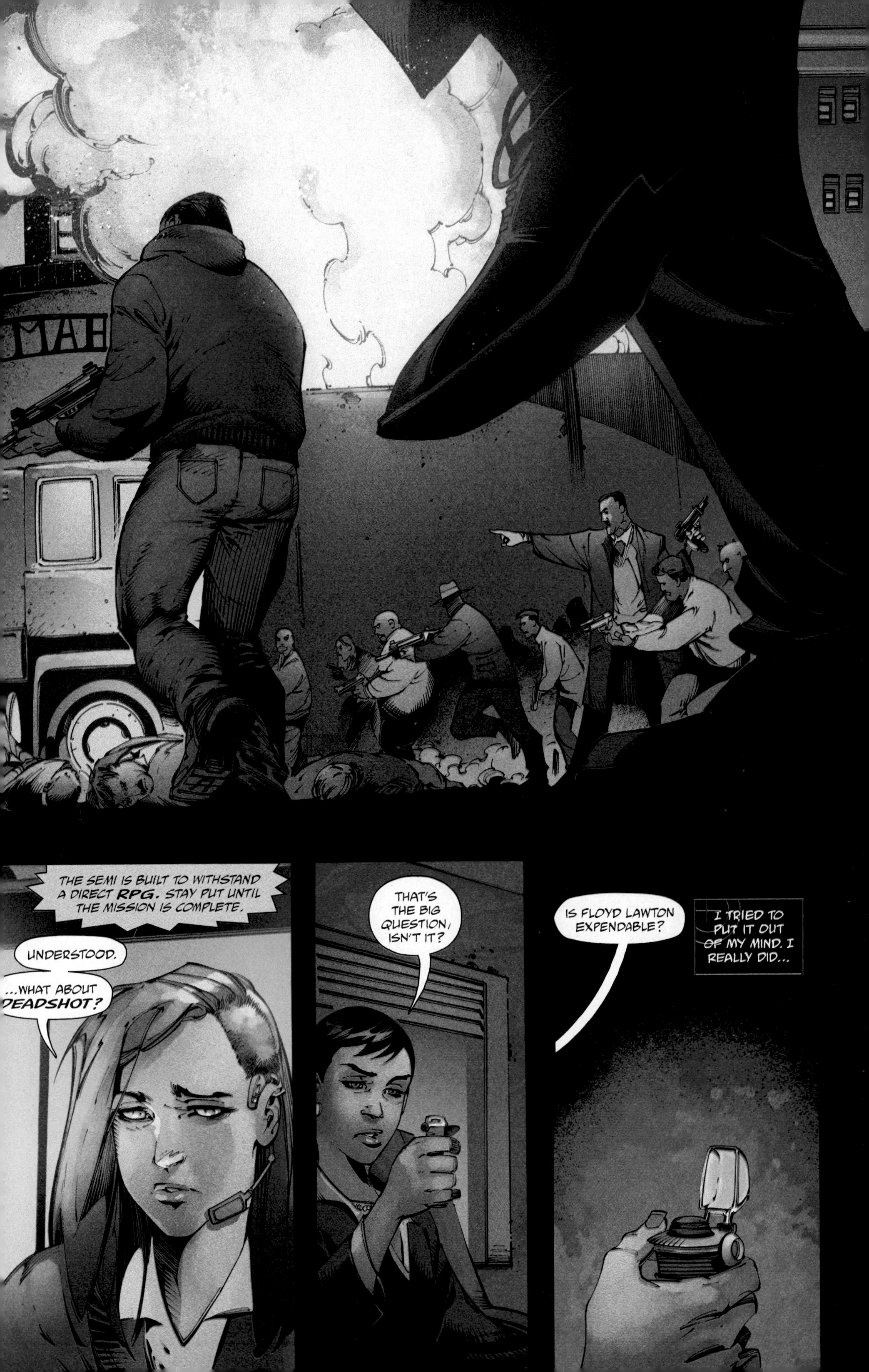

THE SEMI IS BUILT TO WITHSTAND A DIRECT RPG. STAY PUT UNTIL THE MISSION IS COMPLETE.
UNDERSTOOD.
...WHAT ABOUT DEADSHOT?
THAT'S THE BIG QUESTION, ISN'T IT?
IS FLOYD LAWTON EXPENDABLE?
I TRIED TO PUT IT OUT OF MY MIND. I REALLY DID...

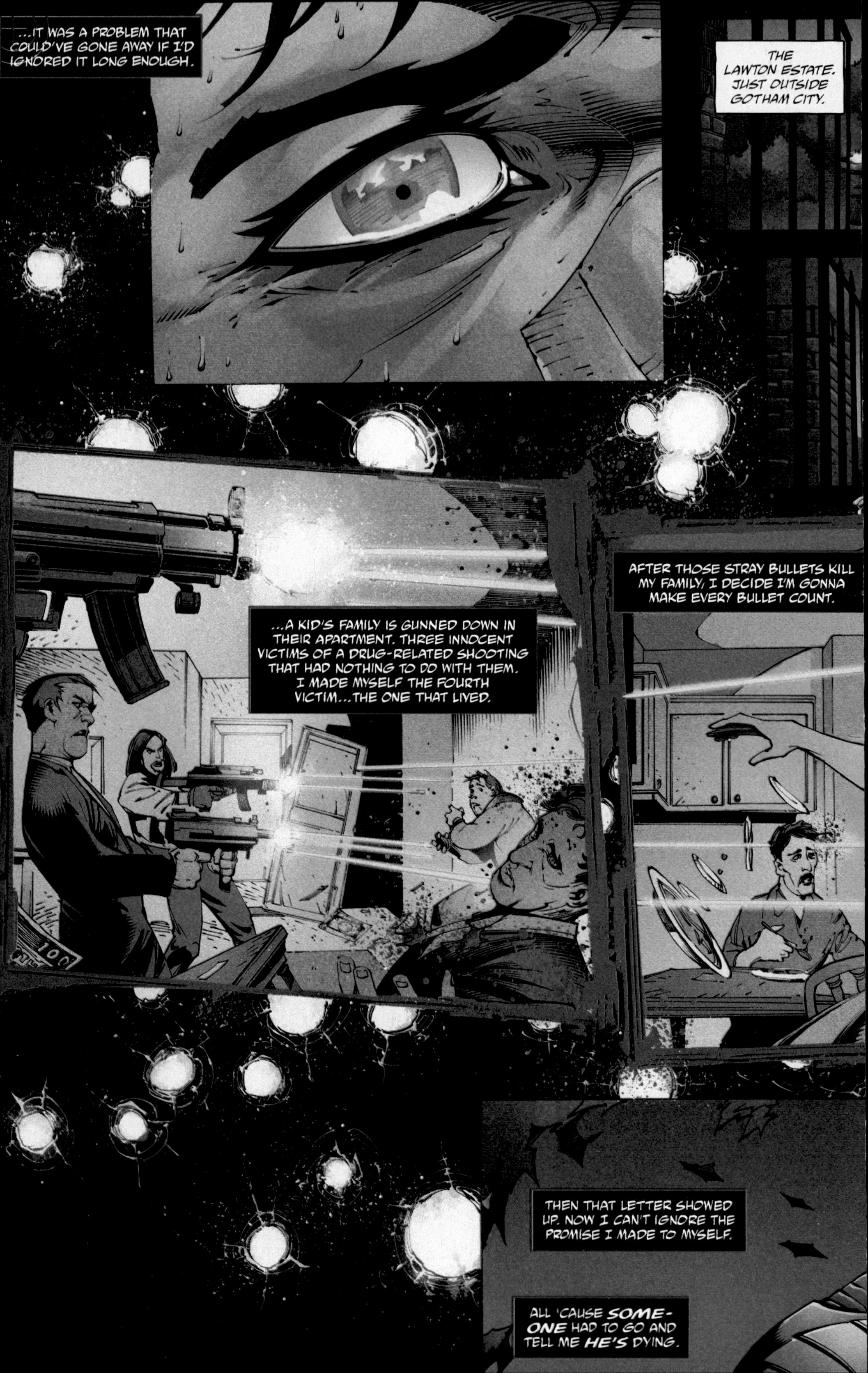
...IT WAS A PROBLEM THAT COULD'VE GONE AWAY IF I'D IGNORED IT LONG ENOUGH.
THE LAWTON ESTATE. JUST OUTSIDE GOTHAM CITY.
...A KID'S FAMILY IS GUNNED DOWN IN THEIR APARTMENT. THREE INNOCENT VICTIMS OF A DRUG-RELATED SHOOTING THAT HAD NOTHING TO DO WITH THEM. I MADE MYSELF THE FOURTH VICTIM...THE ONE THAT LIVED.
AFTER THOSE STRAY BULLETS KILL MY FAMILY, I DECIDE I'M GONNA MAKE EVERY BULLET COUNT.
THEN THAT LETTER SHOWED UP. NOW I CAN'T IGNORE THE PROMISE I MADE TO MYSELF.
ALL 'CAUSE SOME-ONE HAD TO GO AND TELL ME HE'S DYING.

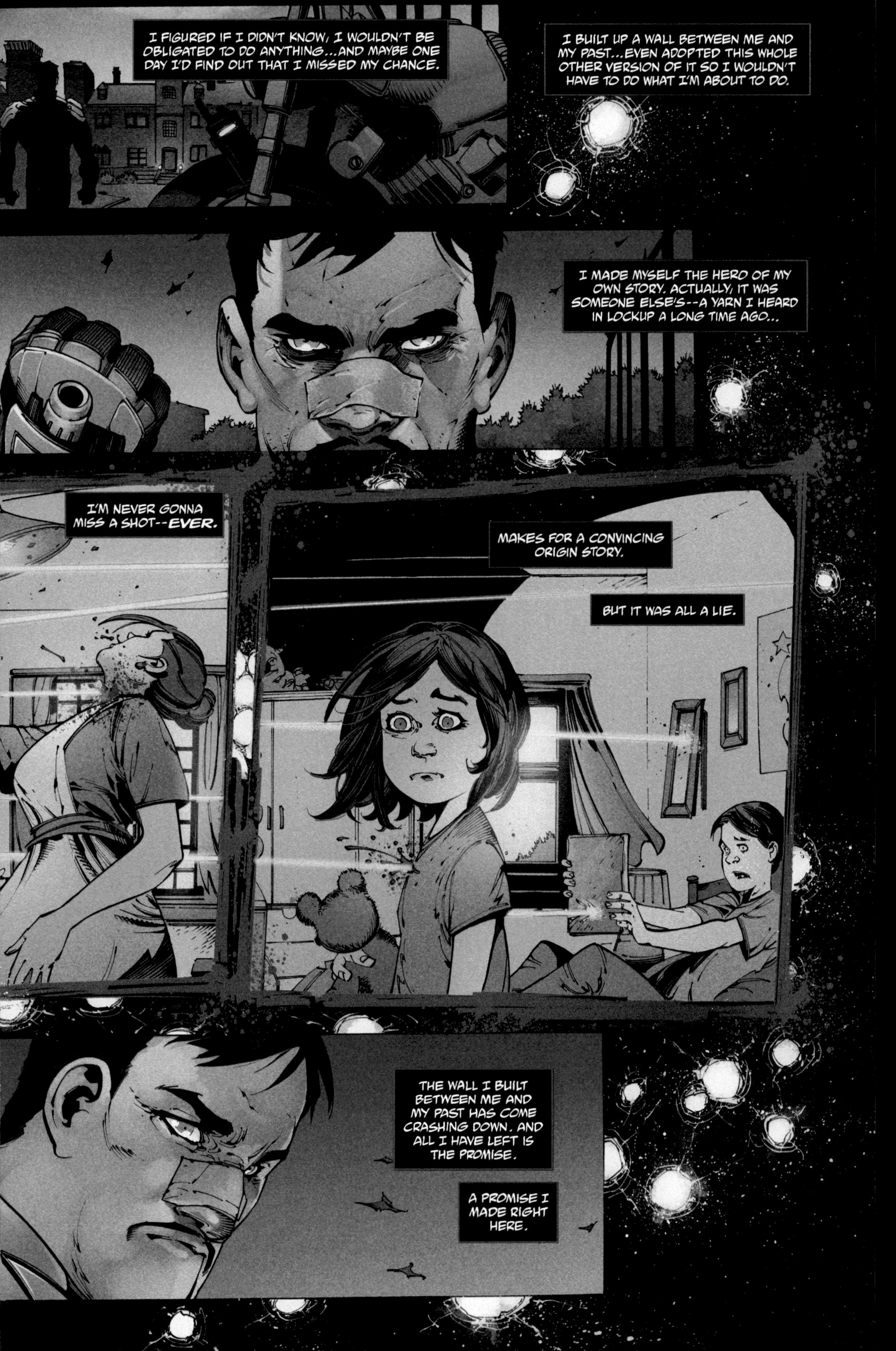
I FIGURED IF I DIDN'T KNOW, I WOULDN'T BE OBLIGATED TO DO ANYTHING...AND MAYBE ONE DAY I'D FIND OUT THAT I MISSED MY CHANCE.
I BUILT UP A WALL BETWEEN ME AND MY PAST...EVEN ADOPTED THIS WHOLE OTHER VERSION OF IT SO I WOULDN'T HAVE TO DO WHAT I'M ABOUT TO DO.
I MADE MYSELF THE HERO OF MY OWN STORY. ACTUALLY, IT WAS SOMEONE ELSE'S--A YARN I HEARD IN LOCKUP A LONG TIME AGO...
I'M NEVER GONNA MISS A SHOT--EVER.
MAKES FOR A CONVINCING ORIGIN STORY.
BUT IT WAS ALL A LIE.
THE WALL I BUILT BETWEEN ME AND MY PAST HAS COME CRASHING DOWN. AND ALL I HAVE LEFT IS THE PROMISE.
A PROMISE I MADE RIGHT HERE.

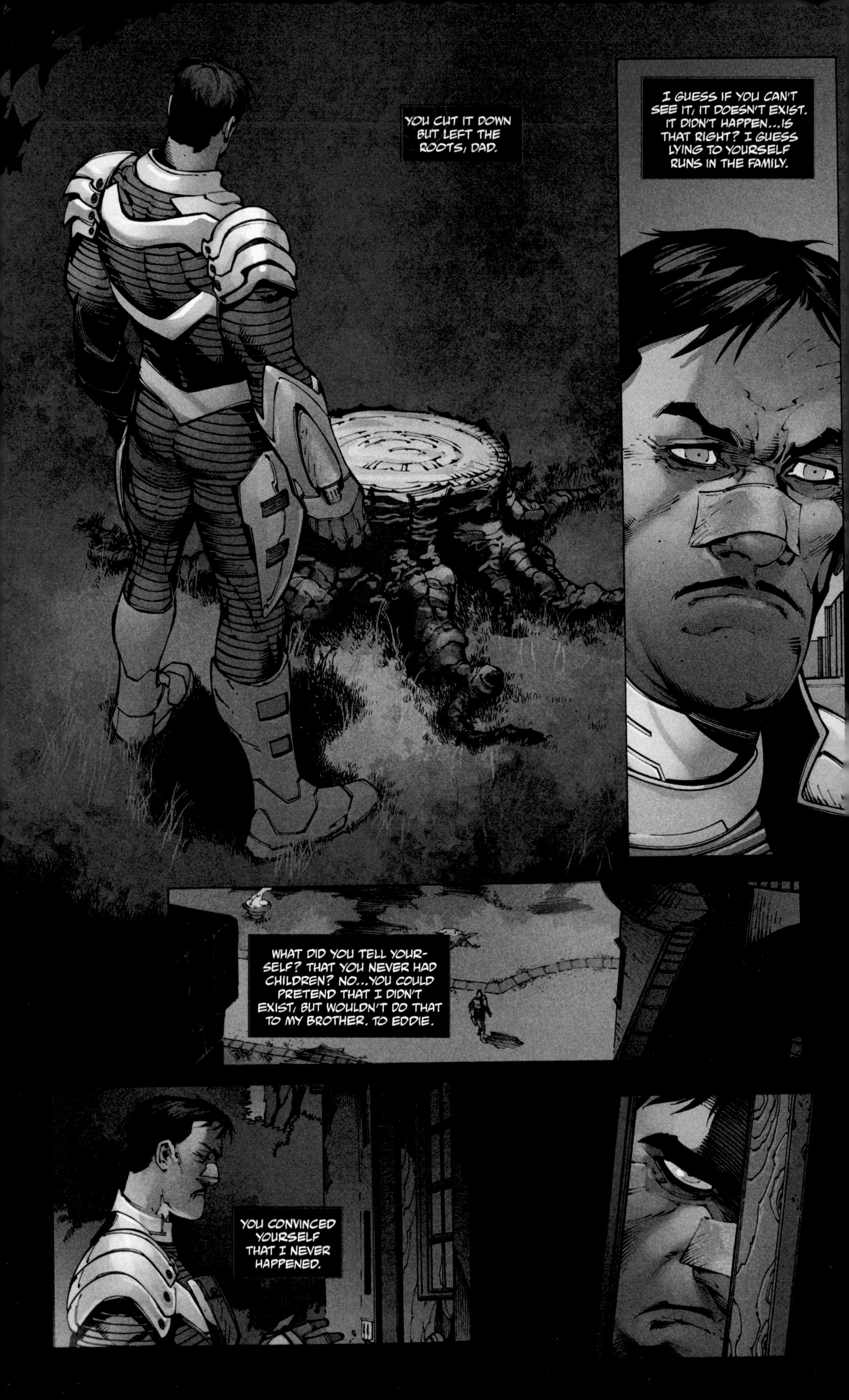
YOU CUT IT DOWN BUT LEFT THE ROOTS, DAD.
I GUESS IF YOU CAN'T SEE IT, IT DOESN'T EXIST. IT DIDN'T HAPPEN...IS THAT RIGHT? I GUESS LYING TO YOURSELF RUNS IN THE FAMILY.
WHAT DID YOU TELL YOUR-SELF? THAT YOU NEVER HAD CHILDREN? NO...YOU COULD PRETEND THAT I DIDN'T EXIST, BUT WOULDN'T DO THAT TO MY BROTHER. TO EDDIE.
YOU CONVINCED YOURSELF THAT I NEVER HAPPENED.

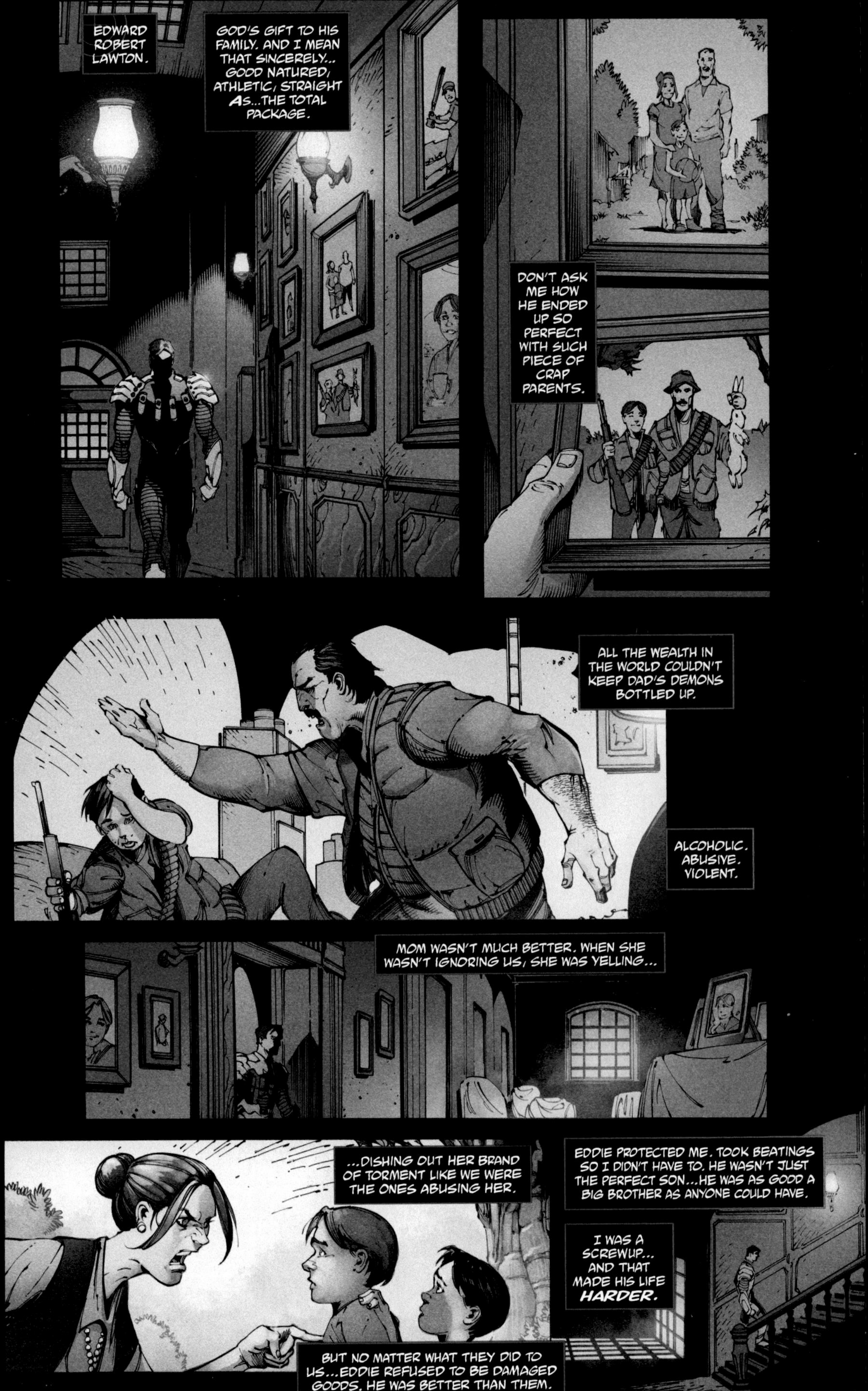
EDWARD ROBERT LAWTON.
GOD'S GIFT TO HIS FAMILY. AND I MEAN THAT SINCERELY... GOOD NATURED, ATHLETIC, STRAIGHT As...THE TOTAL PACKAGE.
DON'T ASK ME HOW HE ENDED UP SO PERFECT WITH SUCH PIECE OF CRAP PARENTS.
ALL THE WEALTH IN THE WORLD COULDN'T KEEP DAD'S DEMONS BOTTLED UP.
ALCOHOLIC. ABUSIVE. VIOLENT.
MOM WASN'T MUCH BETTER. WHEN SHE WASN'T IGNORING US, SHE WAS YELLING...
...DISHING OUT HER BRAND OF TORMENT LIKE WE WERE THE ONES ABUSING HER.
EDDIE PROTECTED ME. TOOK BEATINGS SO I DIDN'T HAVE TO. HE WASN'T JUST THE PERFECT SON...HE WAS AS GOOD A BIG BROTHER AS ANYONE COULD HAVE.
I WAS A SCREWUP... AND THAT MADE HIS LIFE HARDER.
BUT NO MATTER WHAT THEY DID TO US...EDDIE REFUSED TO BE DAMAGED GOODS. HE WAS BETTER THAN THEM.

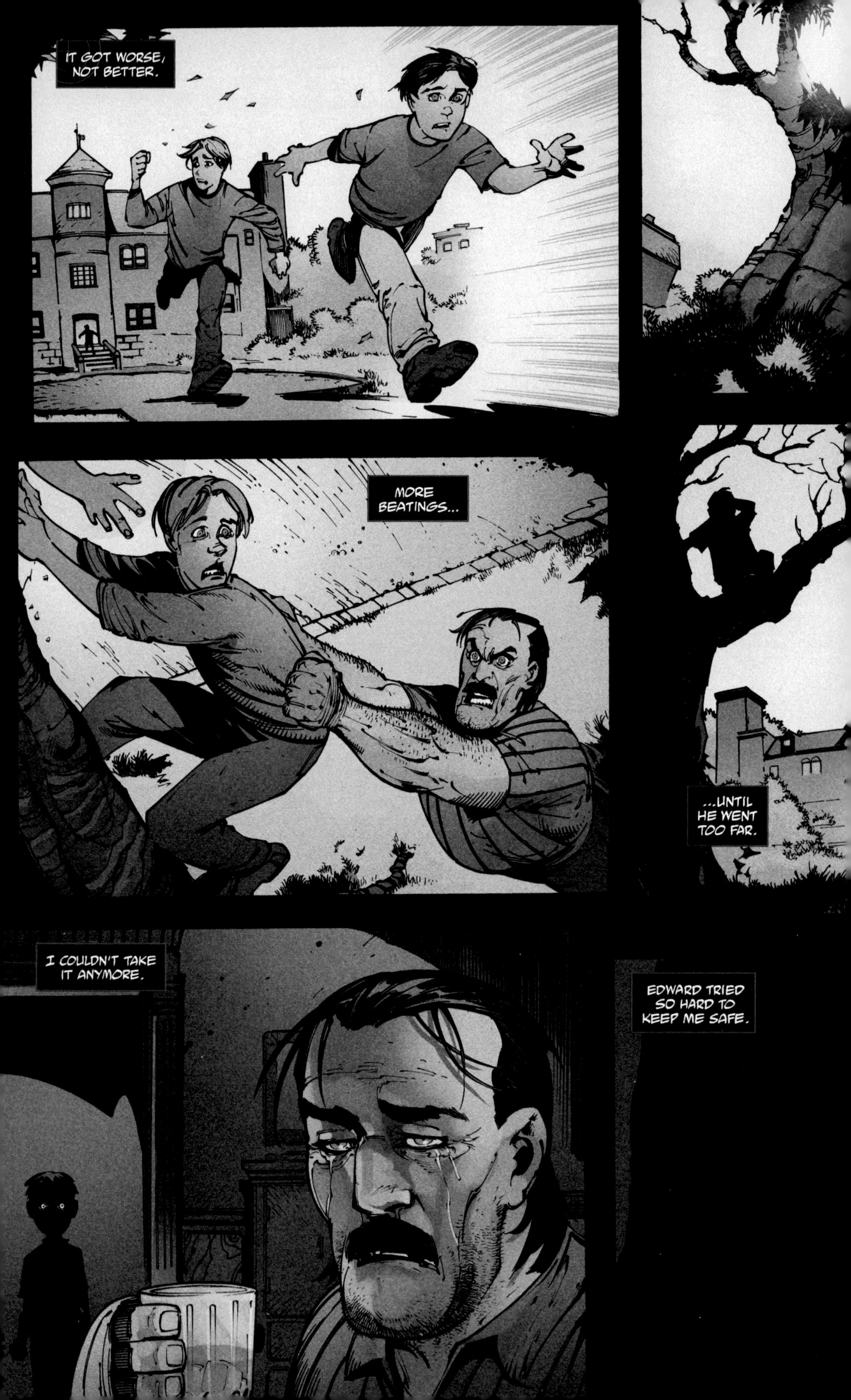
IT GOT WORSE, NOT BETTER.
MORE BEATINGS...
...UNTIL HE WENT TOO FAR.
I COULDN'T TAKE IT ANYMORE.
EDWARD TRIED SO HARD TO KEEP ME SAFE.

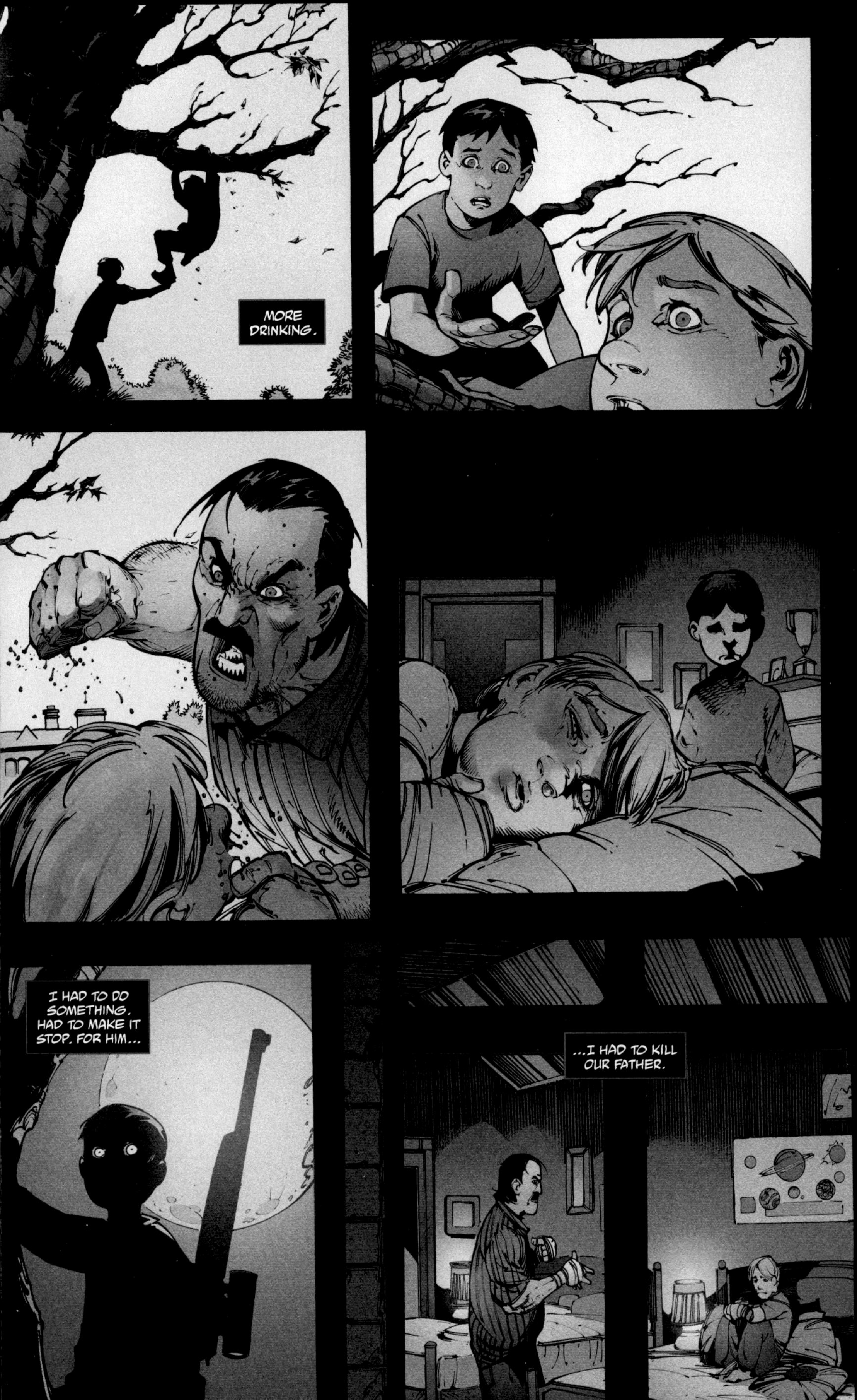

MORE DRINKING.
I HAD TO DO SOMETHING. HAD TO MAKE IT STOP. FOR HIM...
...I HAD TO KILL OUR FATHER.

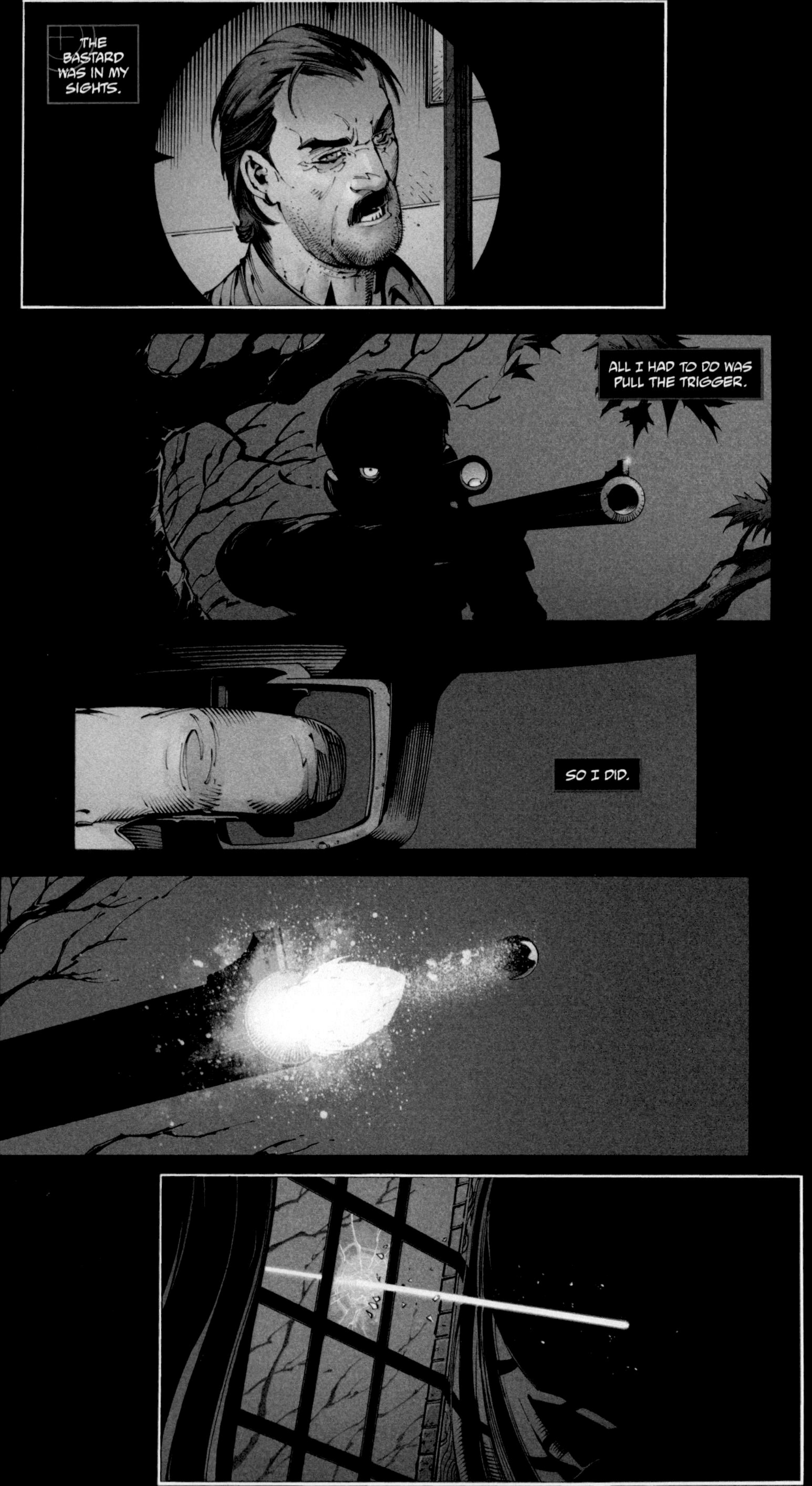
THE BASTARD WAS IN MY SIGHTS.
ALL I HAD TO DO WAS PULL THE TRIGGER.
SO I DID.

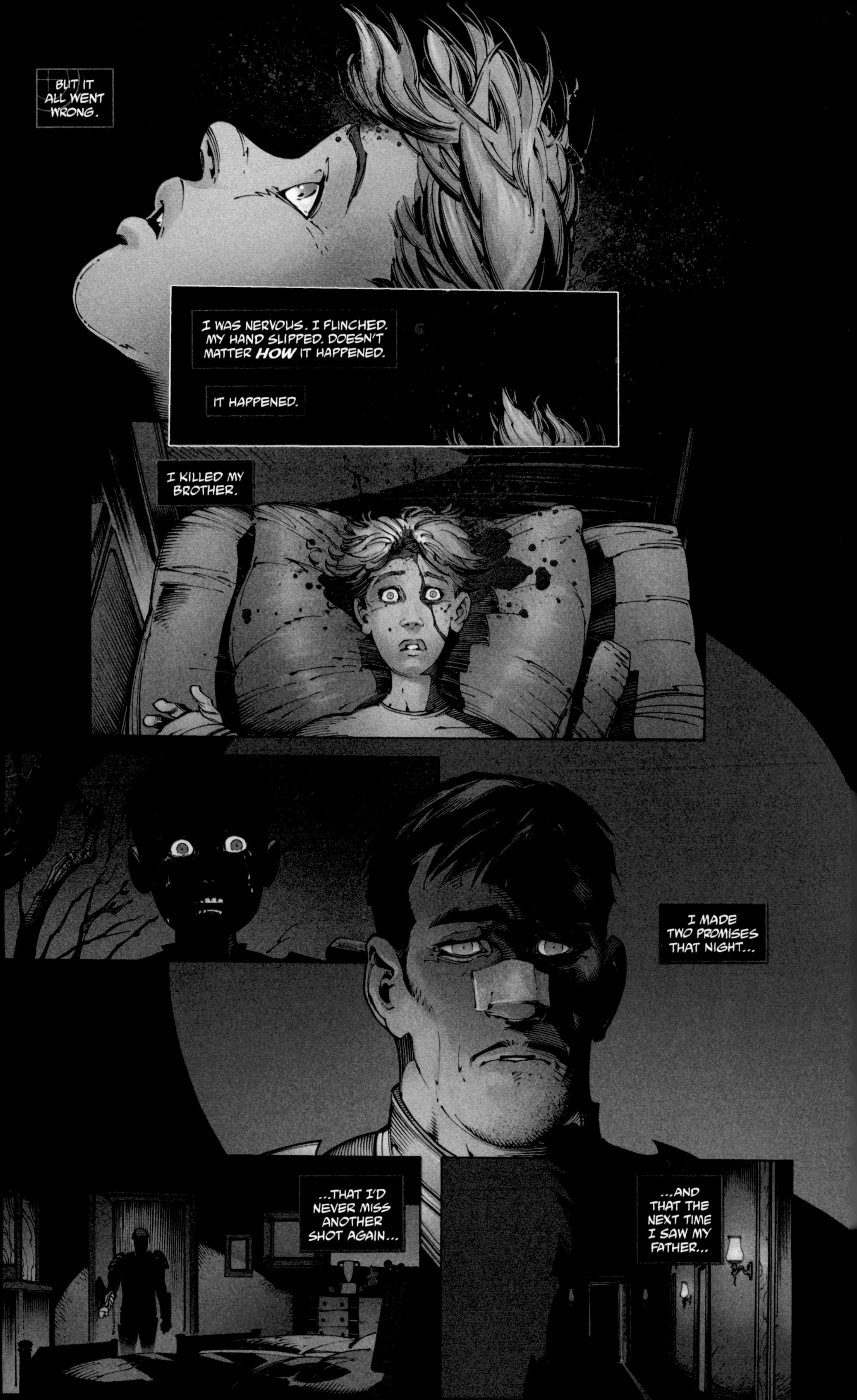
BUT IT ALL WENT WRONG.
I WAS NERVOUS. I FLINCHED. MY HAND SLIPPED. DOESN'T MATTER HOW IT HAPPENED.
IT HAPPENED.
I KILLED MY BROTHER.
I MADE TWO PROMISES THAT NIGHT...
...THAT I'D NEVER MISS ANOTHER SHOT AGAIN...
...AND THAT THE NEXT TIME I SAW MY FATHER...

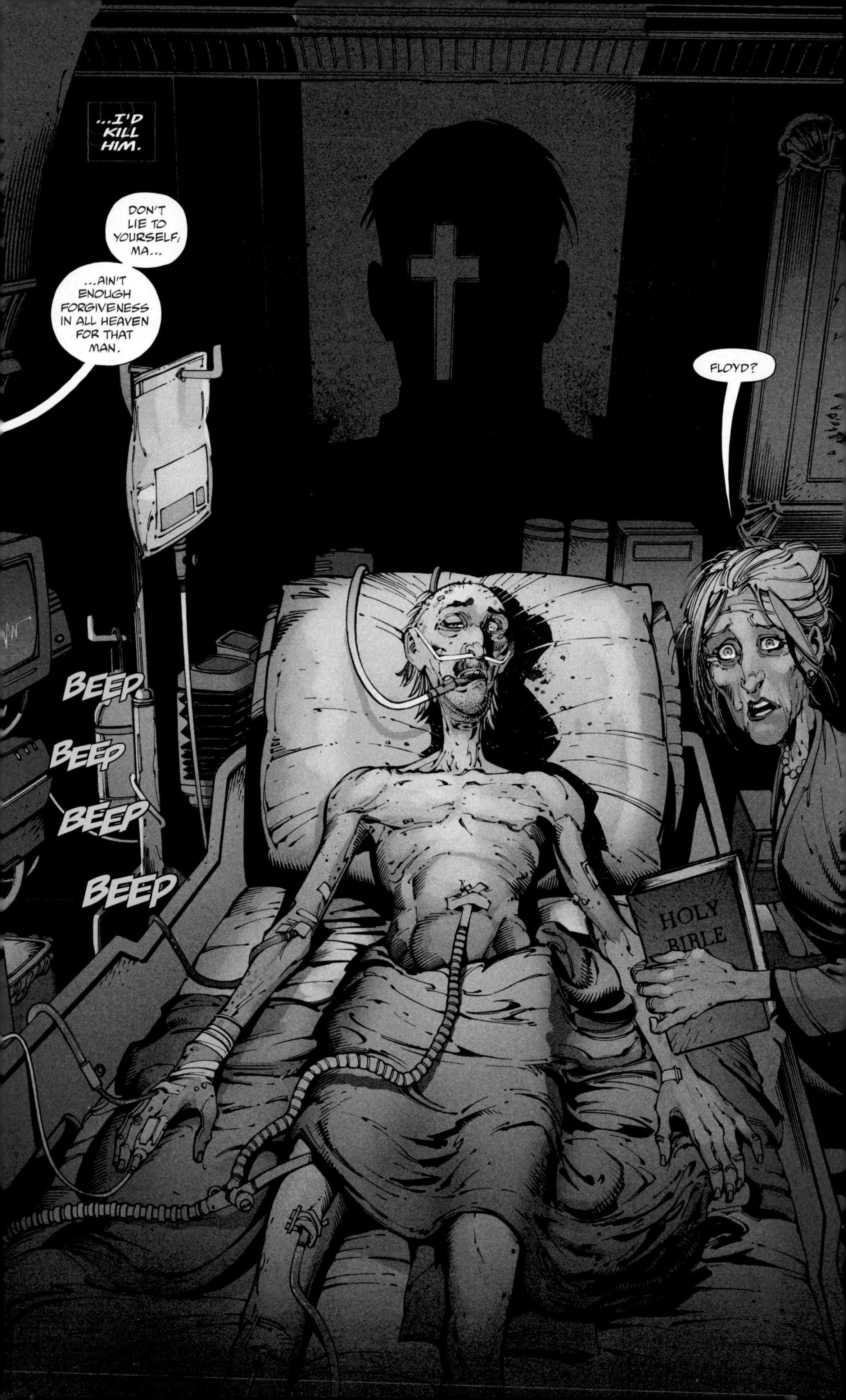
...I'D KILL HIM.
DON'T LIE TO YOURSELF, MA...
...AIN'T ENOUGH FORGIVENESS IN ALL HEAVEN FOR THAT MAN.
FLOYD?
BEEP
BEEP
BEEP
BEEP
HOLY BIBLE

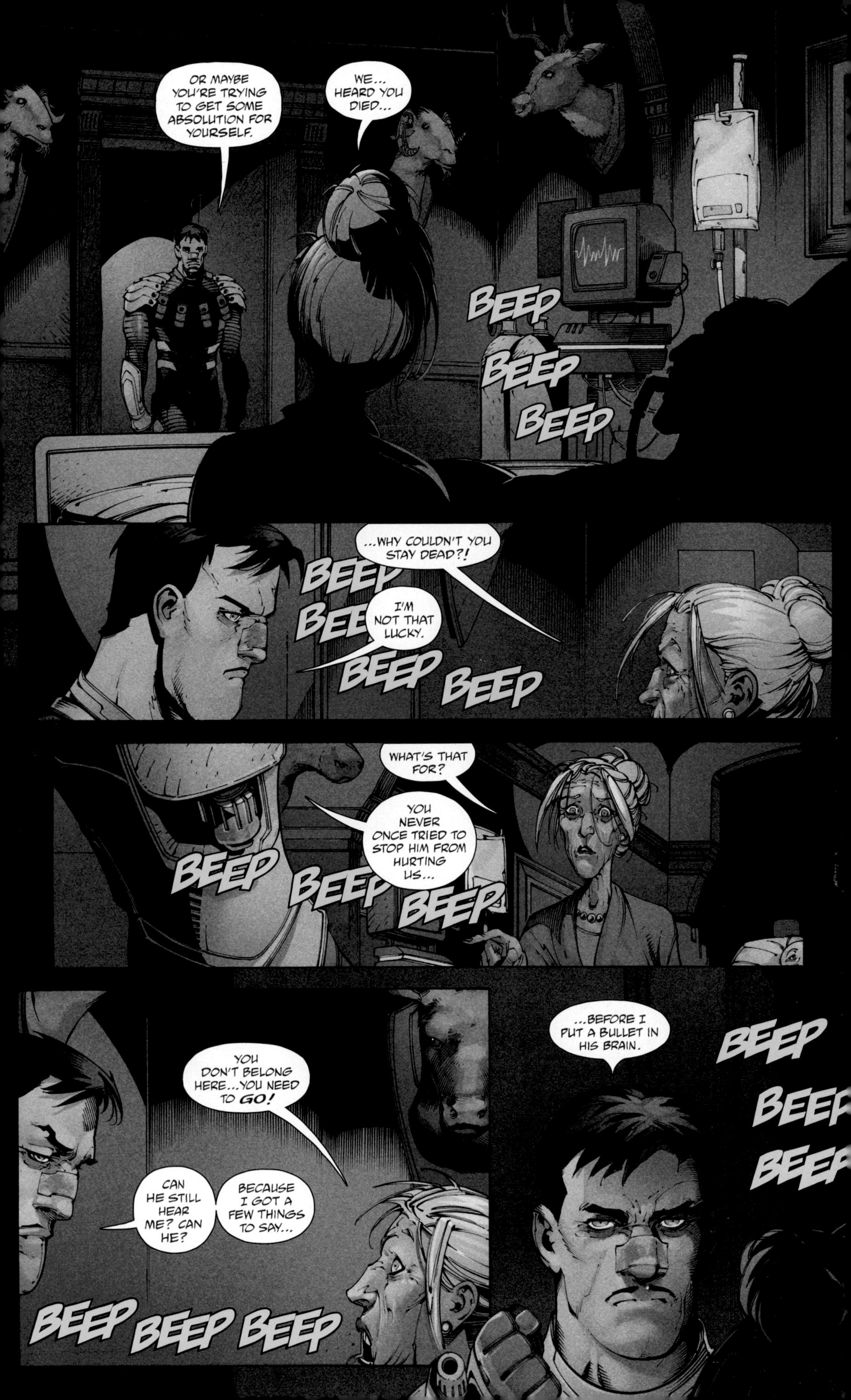
OR MAYBE YOU'RE TRYING TO GET SOME ABSOLUTION FOR YOURSELF.
WE... HEARD YOU DIED...
BEEP
BEEP
BEEP
...WHY COULDN'T YOU STAY DEAD?!
BEEP
BEEP
I'M NOT THAT LUCKY.
BEEP
BEEP
WHAT'S THAT FOR?
YOU NEVER ONCE TRIED TO STOP HIM FROM HURTING US...
BEEP
BEEP
BEEP
YOU DON'T BELONG HERE...YOU NEED TO GO!
CAN HE STILL HEAR ME? CAN HE?
BECAUSE I GOT A FEW THINGS TO SAY...
BEEP
BEEP
BEEP
...BEFORE I PUT A BULLET IN HIS BRAIN.
BEEP
BEEP

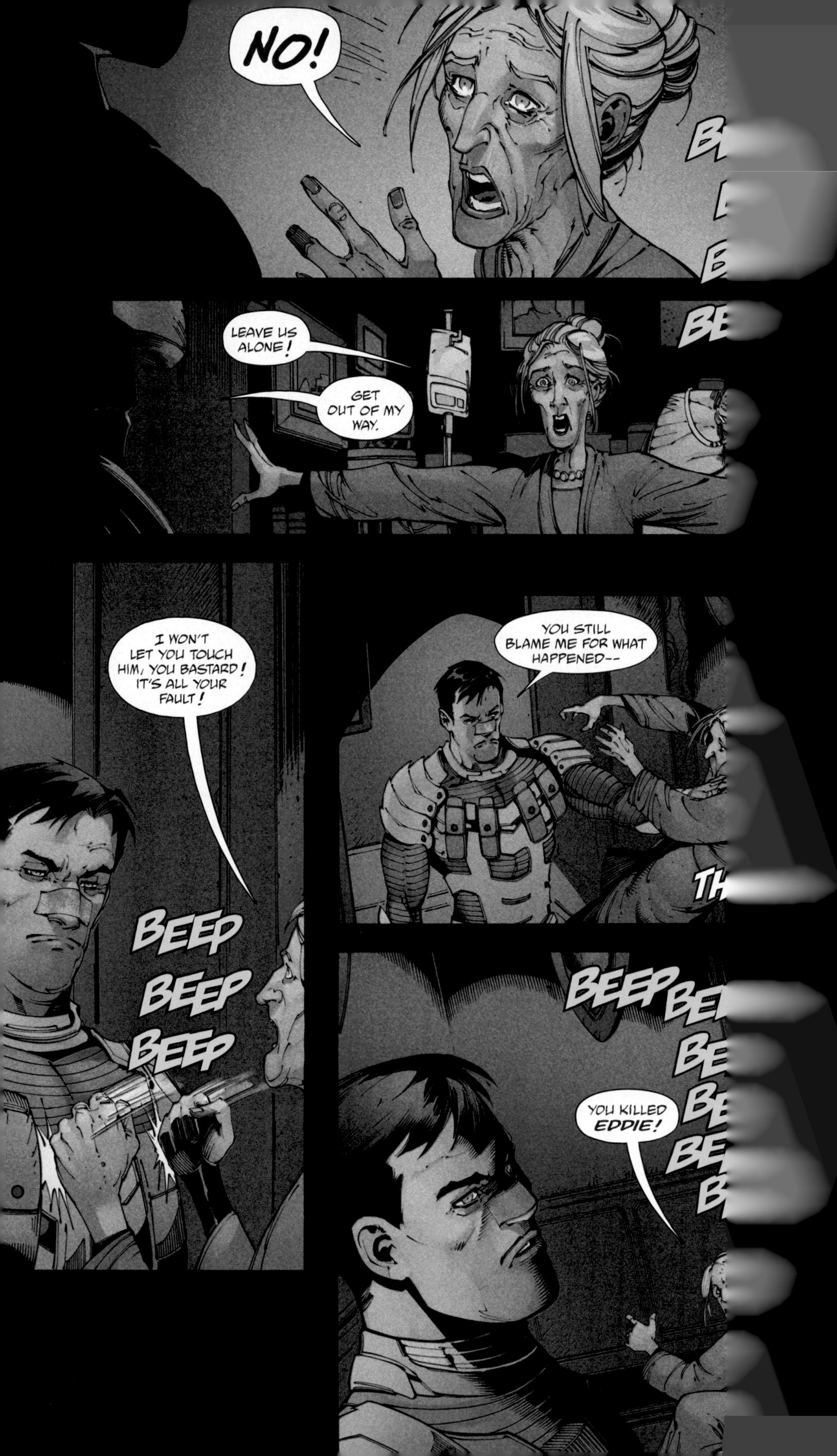
NO!
LEAVE US ALONE!
GET OUT OF MY WAY.
I WON'T LET YOU TOUCH HIM, YOU BASTARD! IT'S ALL YOUR FAULT!
BEEP
BEEP
BEEP
YOU STILL BLAME ME FOR WHAT HAPPENED--
BEEP
YOU KILLED EDDIE!

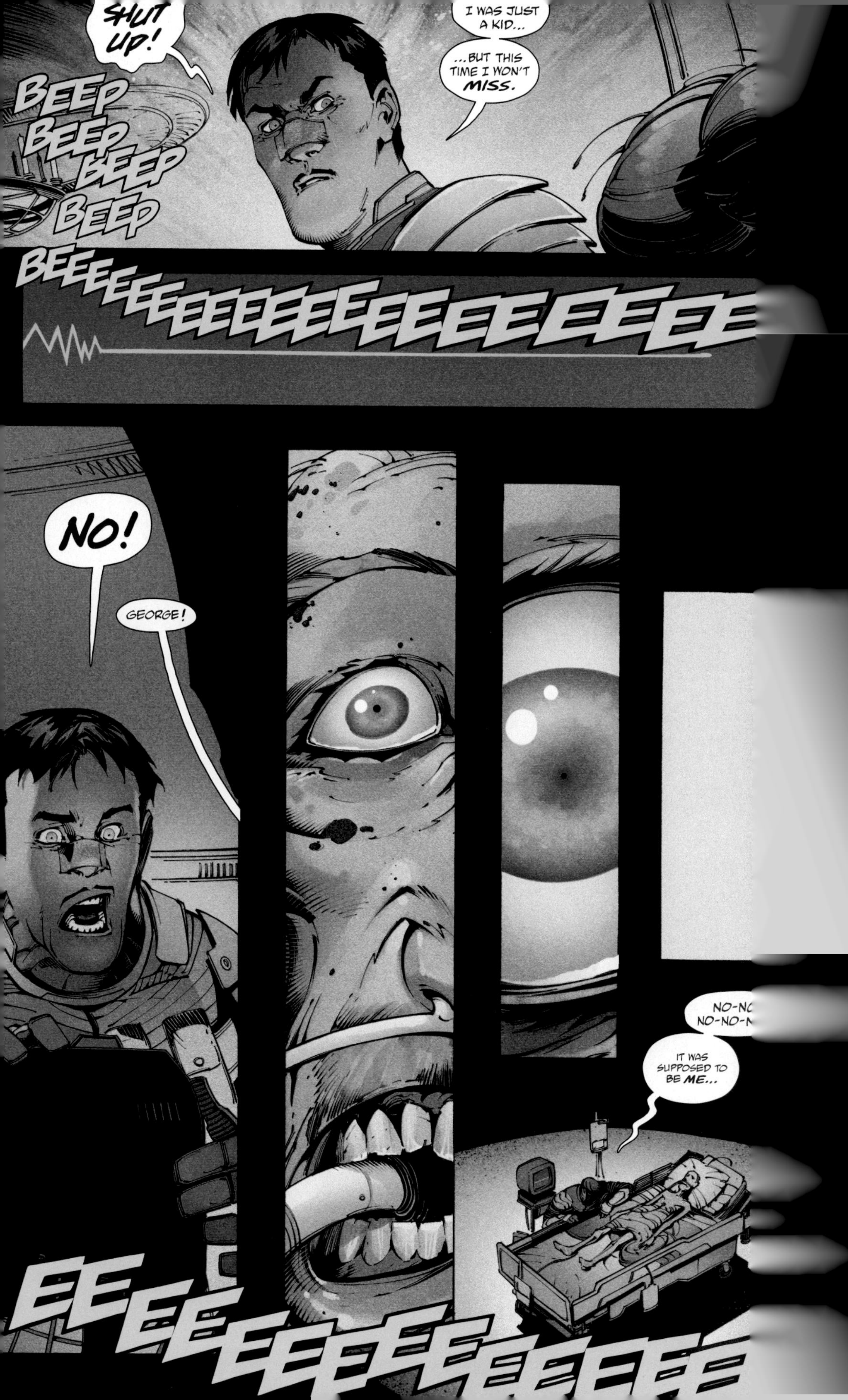
SHUT UP!
I WAS JUST A KID...
...BUT THIS TIME I WON'T MISS.
BEEP
BEEP
BEEP
BEEP
BEEEEEEEEEEEEEEEEEEEE
NO!
GEORGE!
IT WAS SUPPOSED TO BE ME...
EEEEEEEEEEEEE

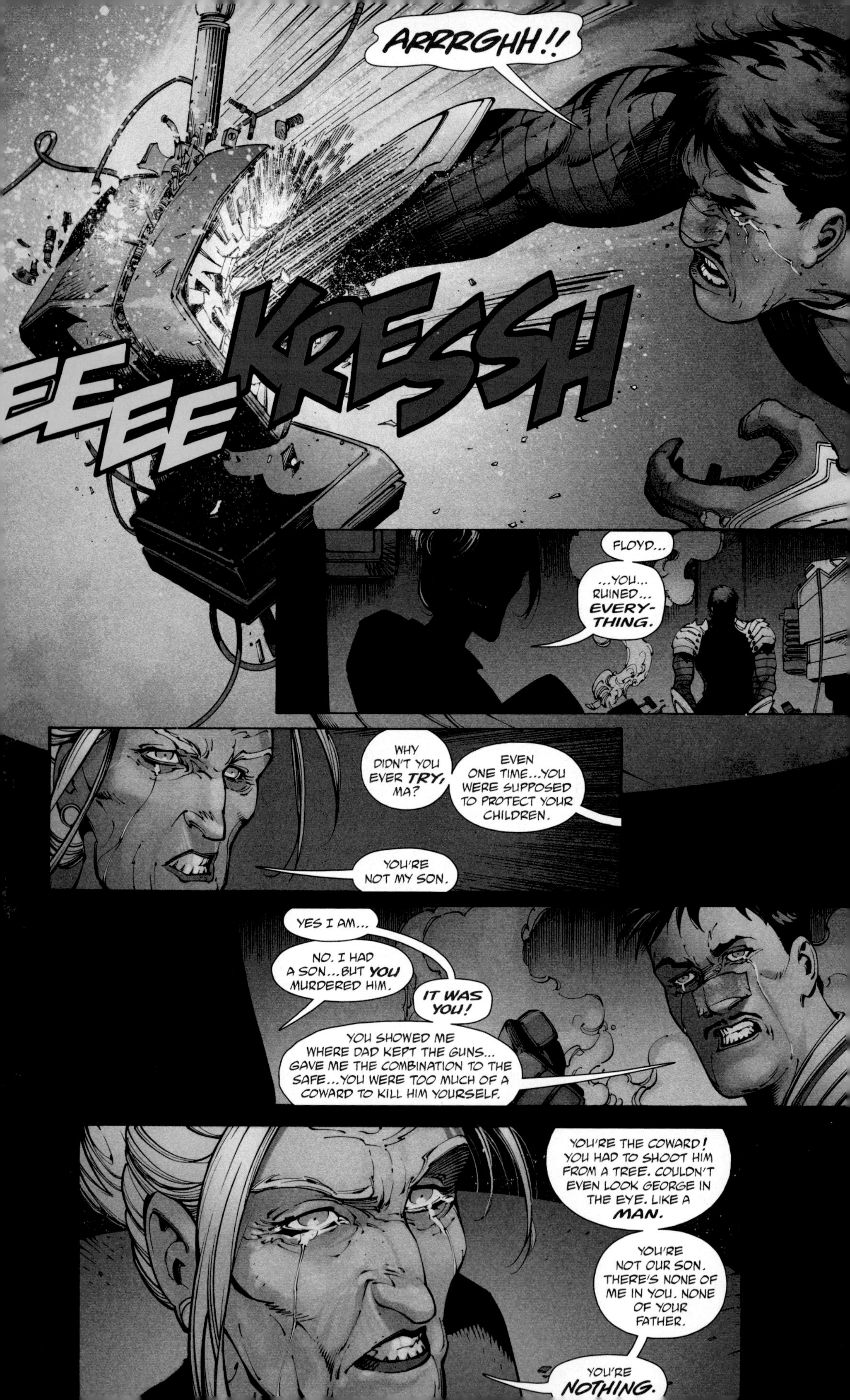
ARRRGHH!!
EEEE
KRESSH
FLOYD...
...YOU... RUINED... EVERY-THING.
WHY DIDN'T YOU EVER TRY, MA?
EVEN ONE TIME...YOU WERE SUPPOSED TO PROTECT YOUR CHILDREN.
YOU'RE NOT MY SON.
YES I AM...
NO. I HAD A SON...BUT YOU MURDERED HIM.
IT WAS YOU!
YOU SHOWED ME WHERE DAD KEPT THE GUNS... GAVE ME THE COMBINATION TO THE SAFE...YOU WERE TOO MUCH OF A COWARD TO KILL HIM YOURSELF.
YOU'RE THE COWARD! YOU HAD TO SHOOT HIM FROM A TREE. COULDN'T EVEN LOOK GEORGE IN THE EYE. LIKE A MAN.
YOU'RE NOT OUR SON. THERE'S NONE OF ME IN YOU. NONE OF YOUR FATHER.
YOU'RE NOTHING.

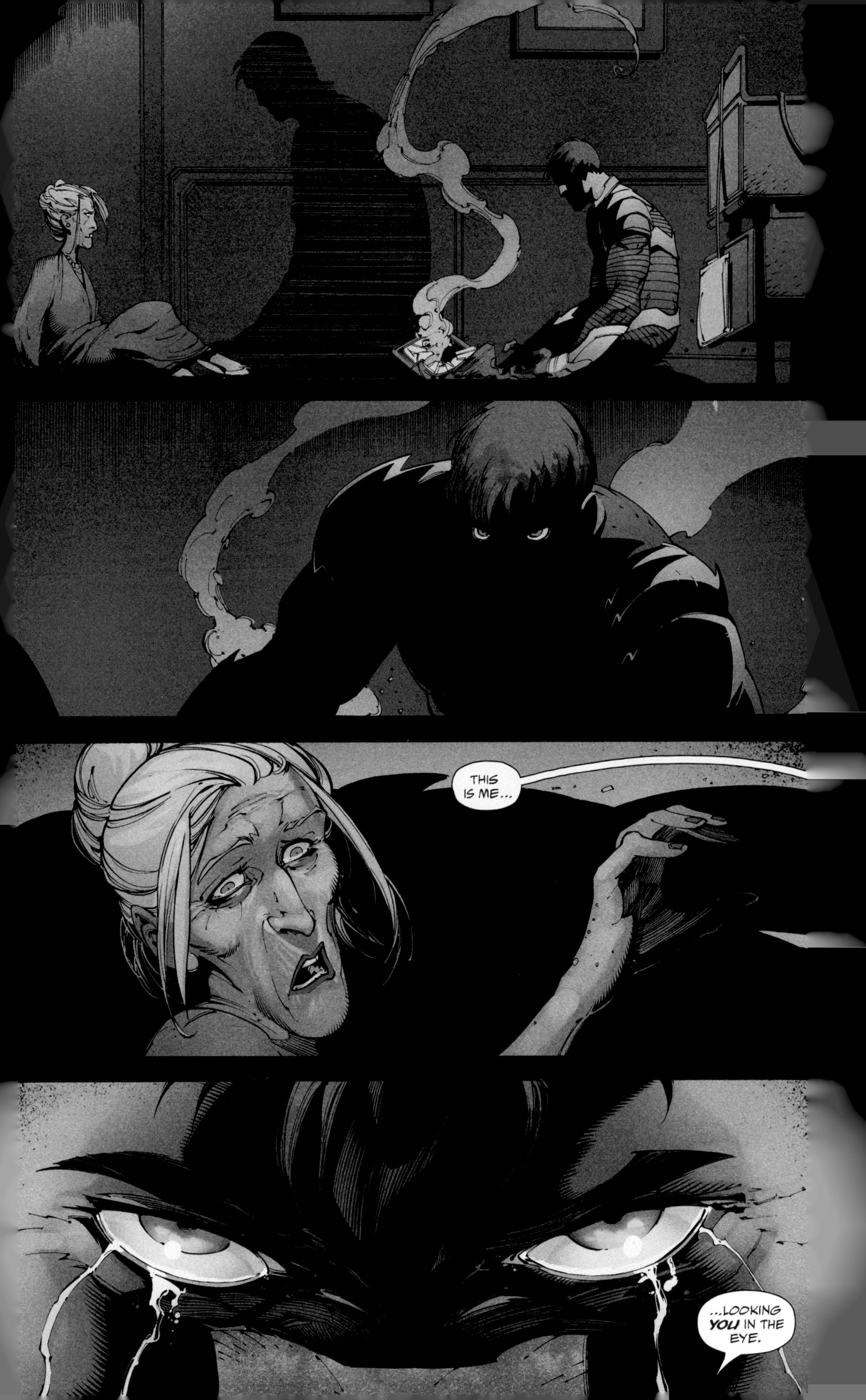
THIS IS ME...
...LOOKING YOU IN THE EYE.

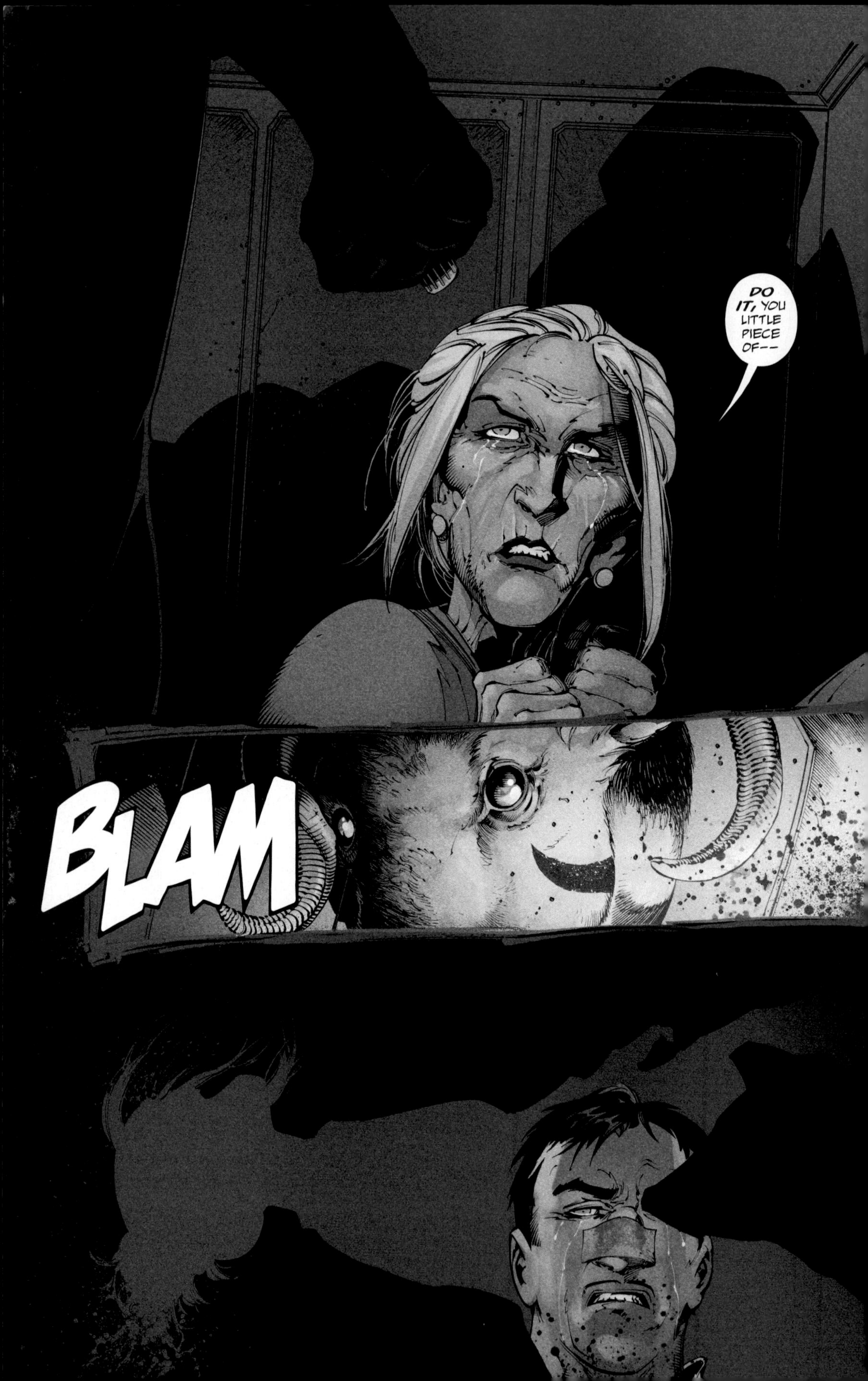
DO IT, YOU LITTLE PIECE OF--
BLAM

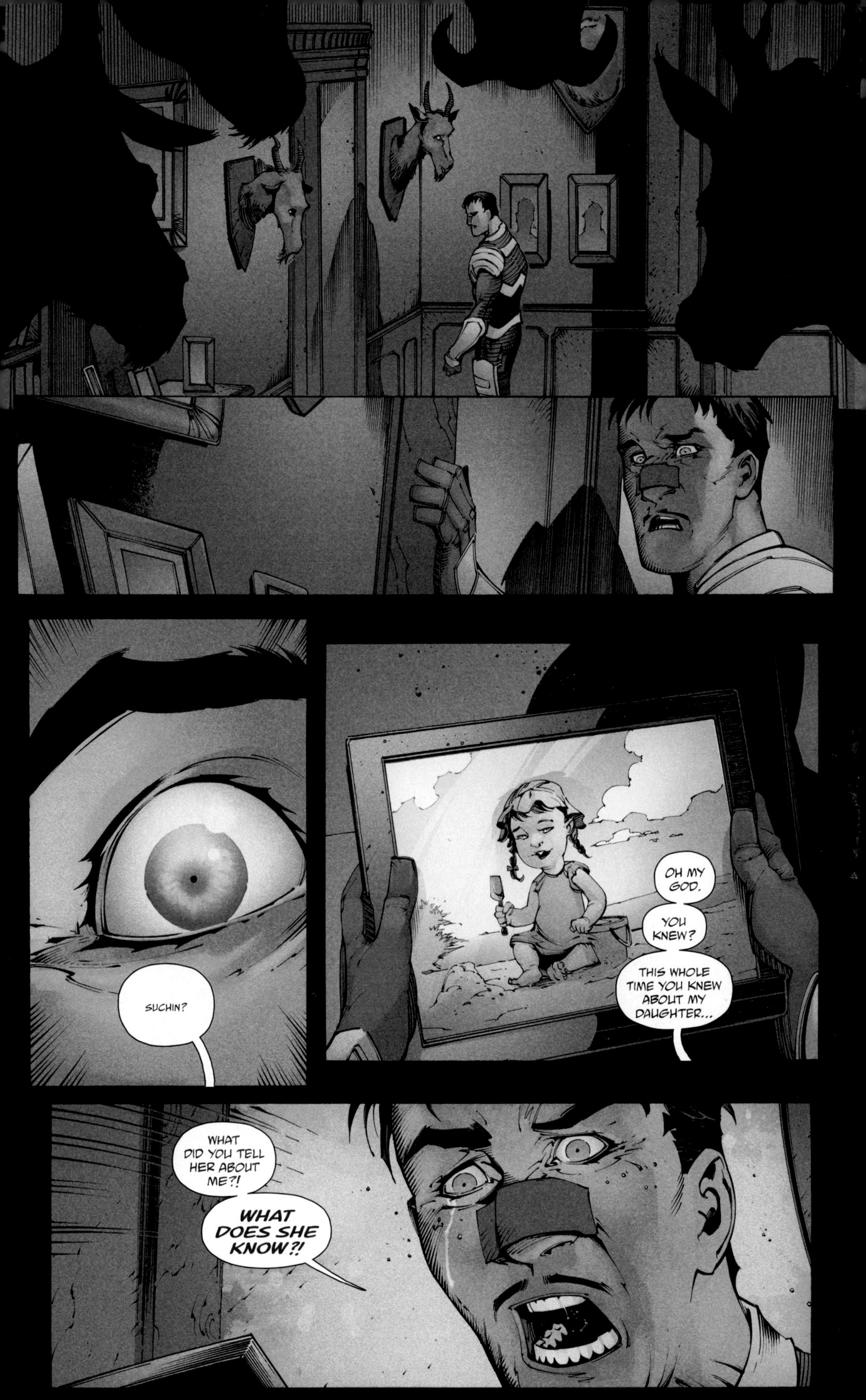
SUCHIN?
OH MY GOD.
YOU KNEW?
THIS WHOLE TIME YOU KNEW ABOUT MY DAUGHTER...
WHAT DID YOU TELL HER ABOUT ME?!
WHAT DOES SHE KNOW?!

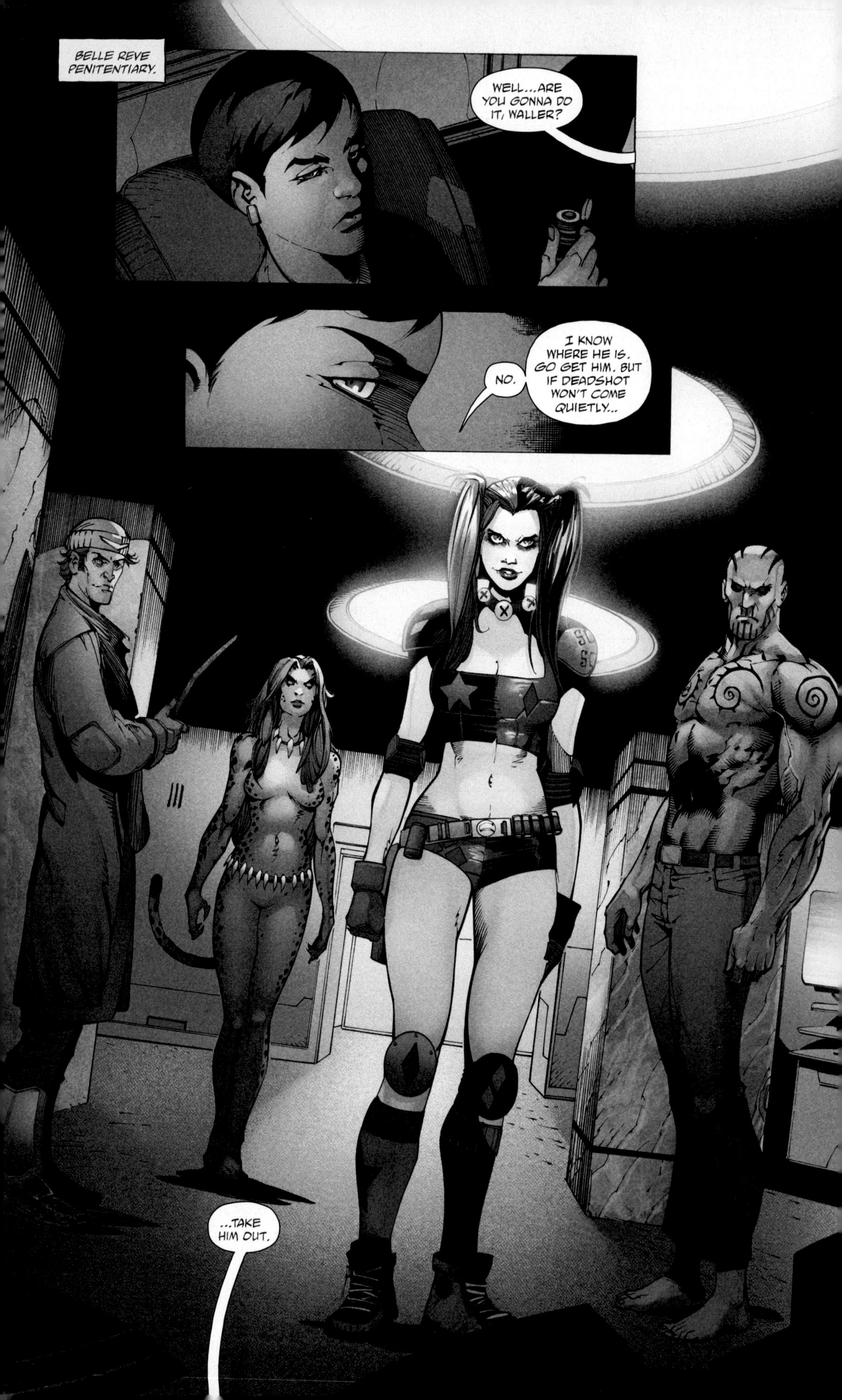
BELLE REVE PENITENTIARY.
WELL...ARE YOU GONNA DO IT, WALLER?
NO.
I KNOW WHERE HE IS. GO GET HIM. BUT IF DEADSHOT WON'T COME QUIETLY...
...TAKE HIM OUT.

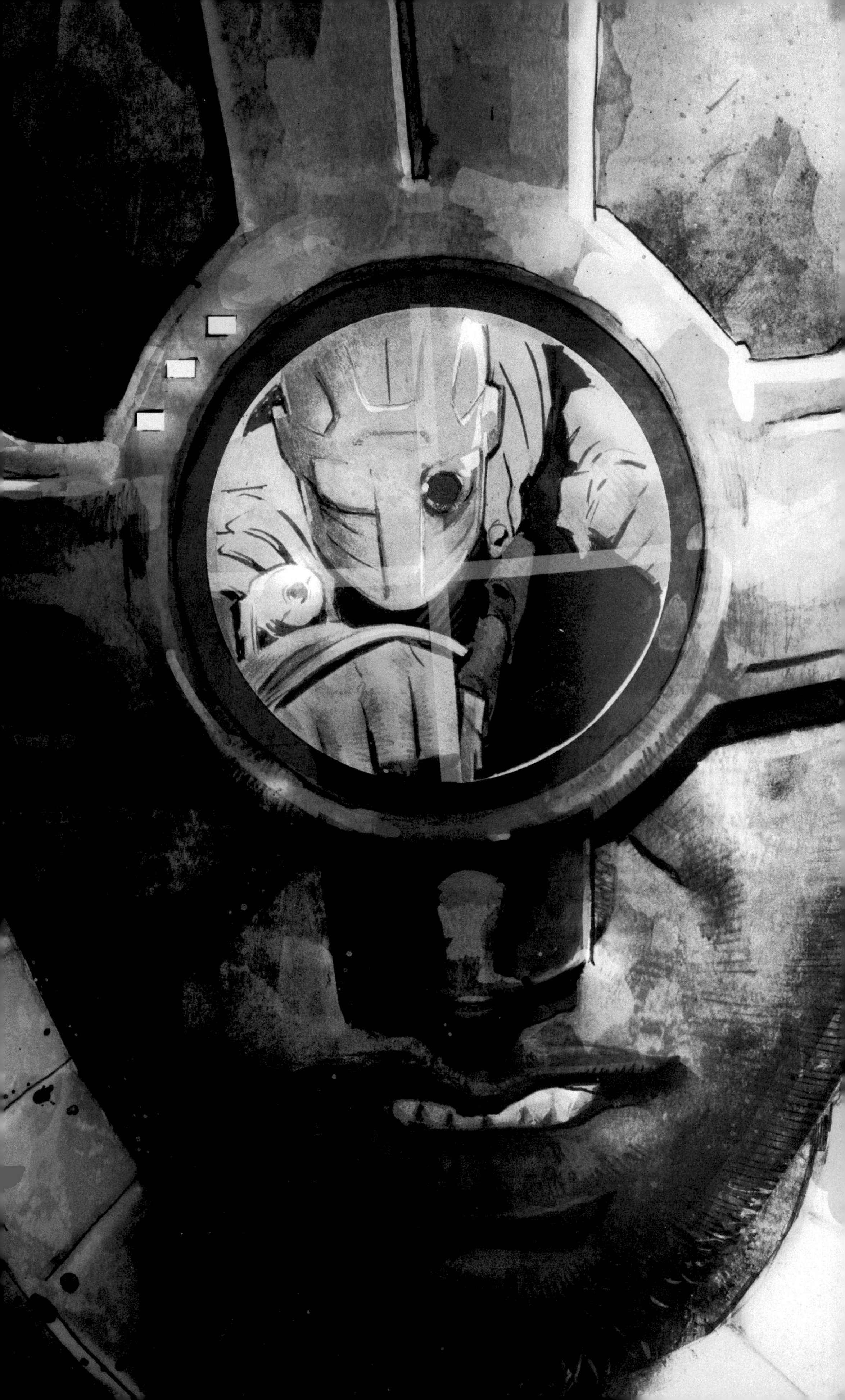

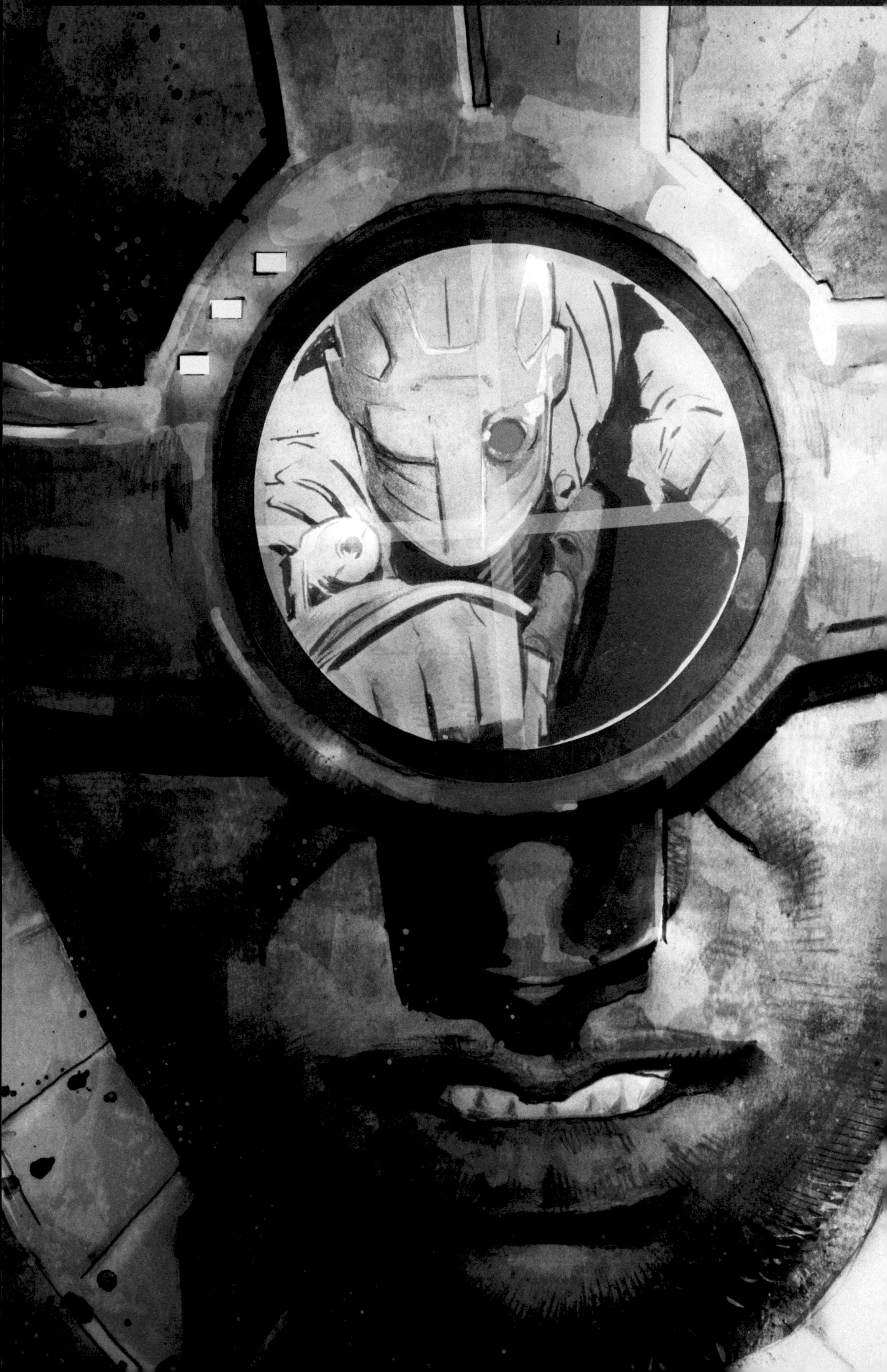

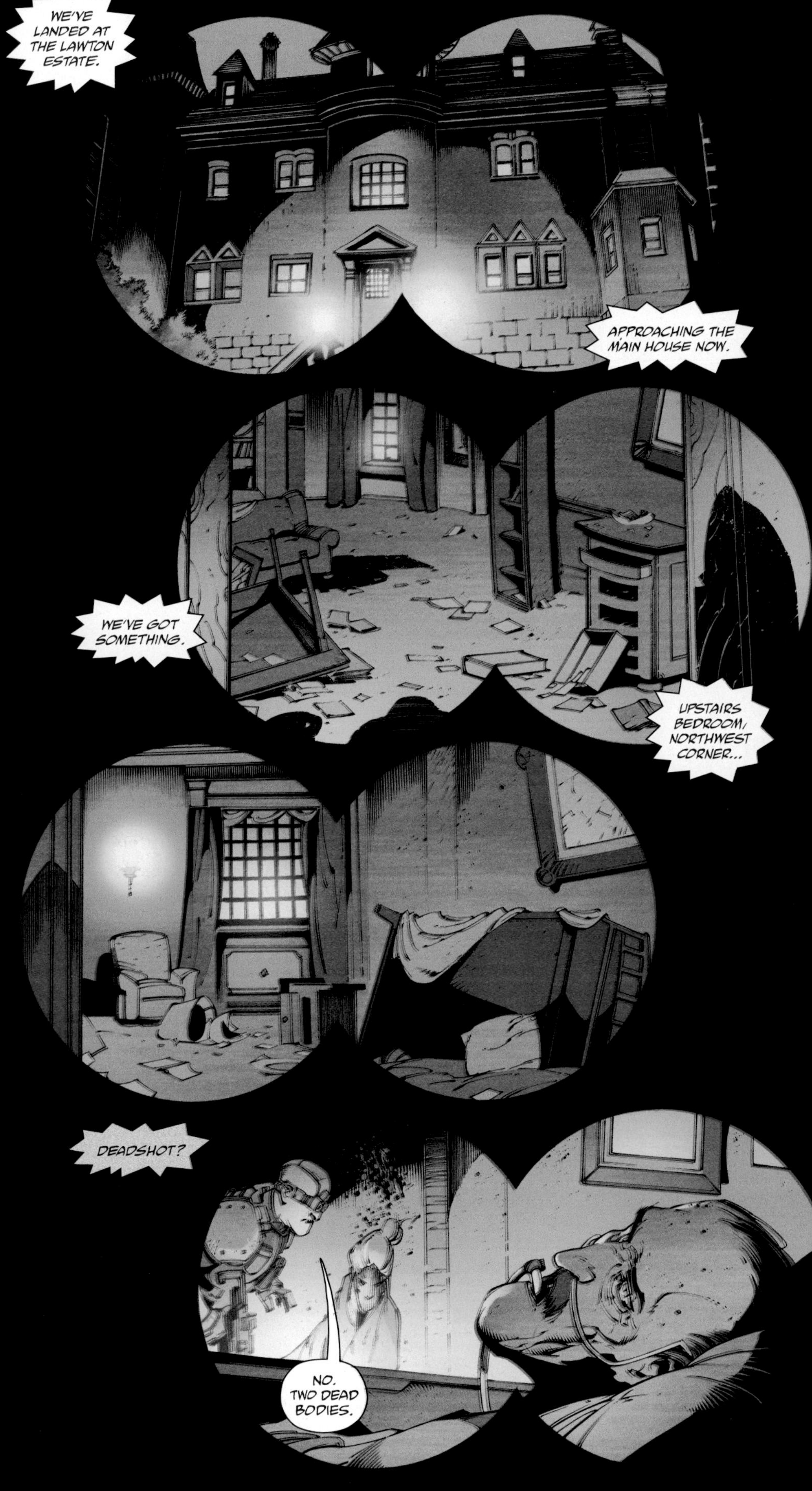
WE'VE LANDED AT THE LAWTON ESTATE.
APPROACHING THE MAIN HOUSE NOW.
WE'VE GOT SOMETHING.
UPSTAIRS BEDROOM, NORTHWEST CORNER...
DEADSHOT?
NO. TWO DEAD BODIES.

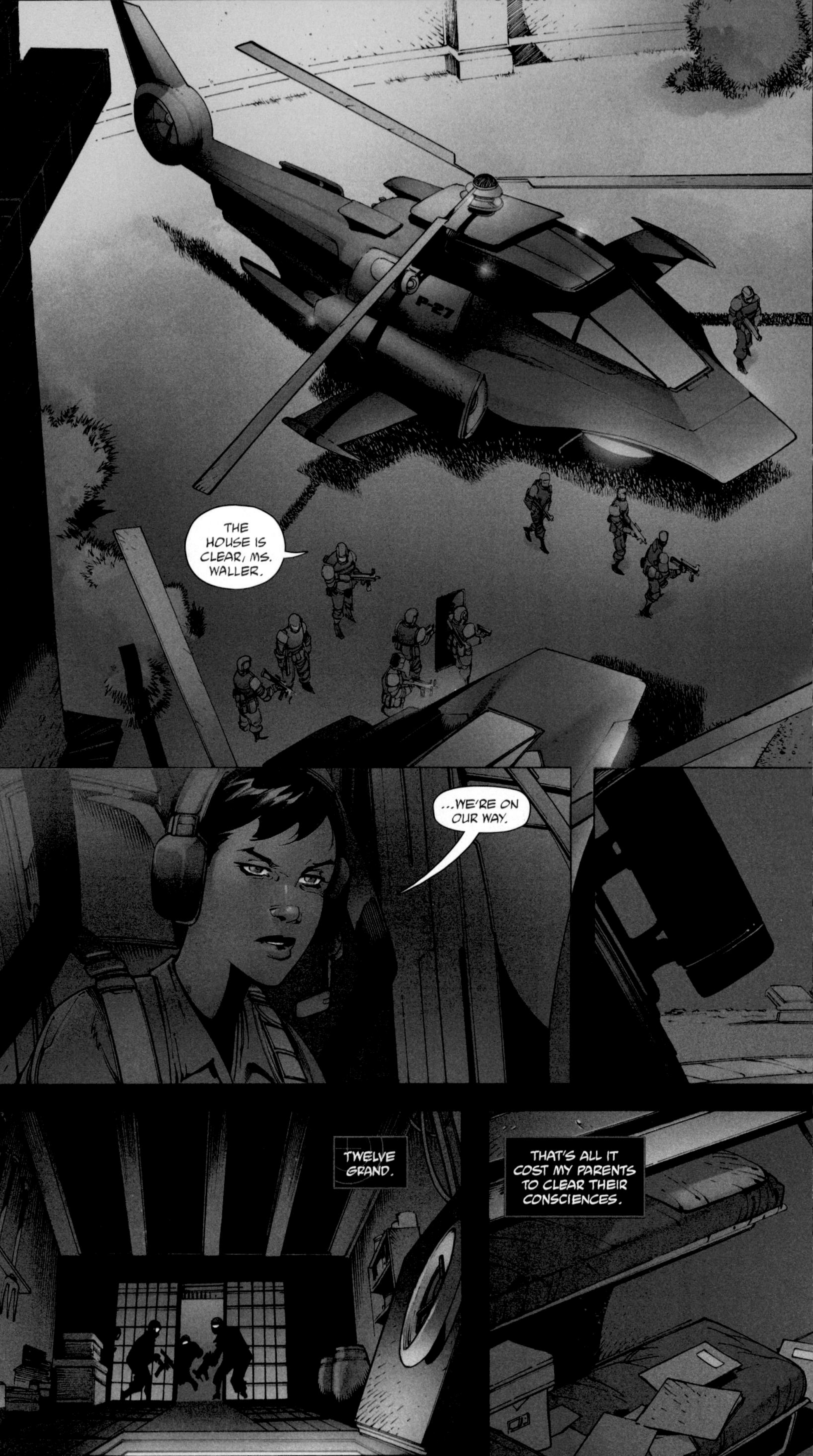
THE HOUSE IS CLEAR, MS. WALLER.
...WE'RE ON OUR WAY.
TWELVE GRAND.
THAT'S ALL IT COST MY PARENTS TO CLEAR THEIR CONSCIENCES.

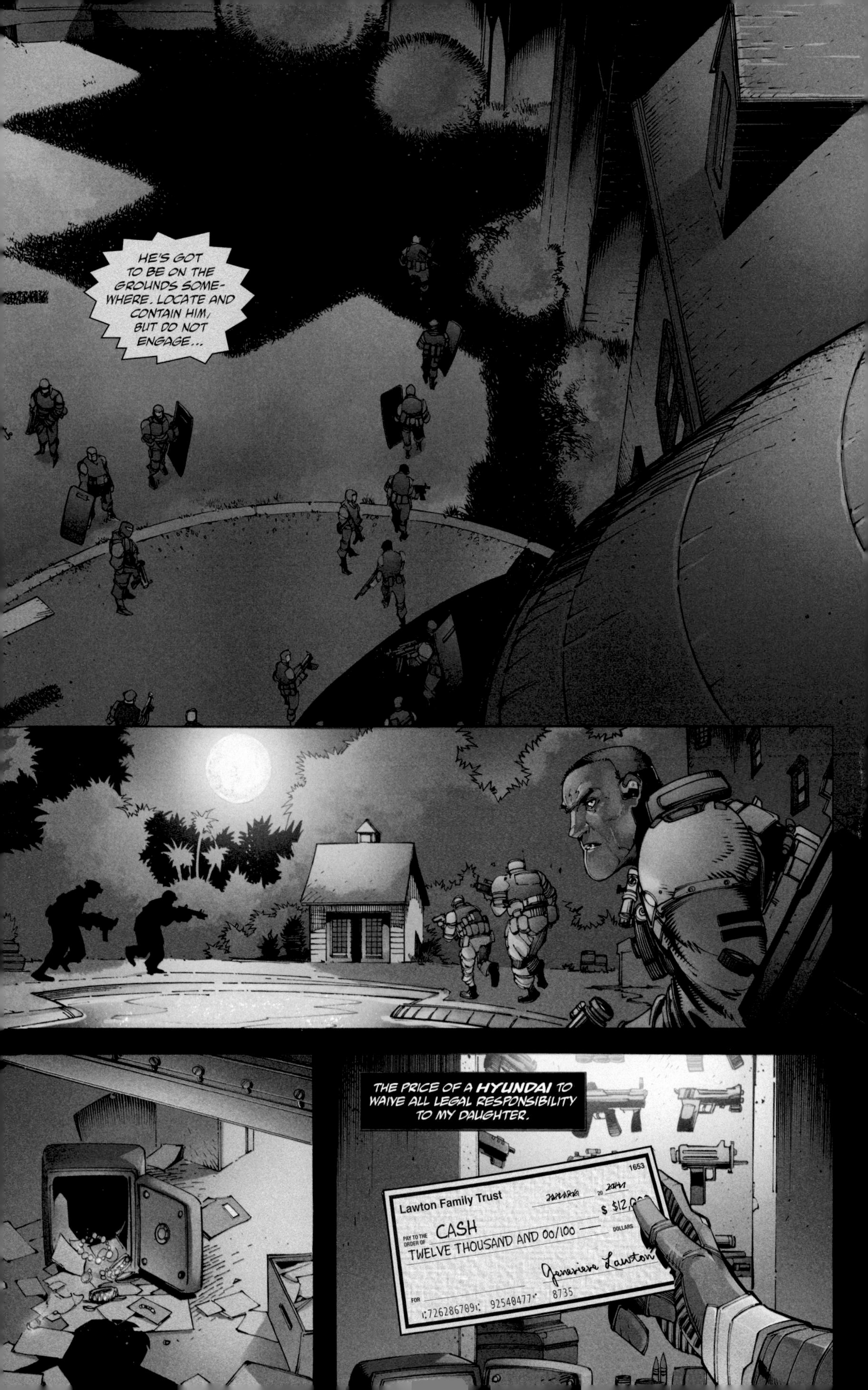
HE'S GOT TO BE ON THE GROUNDS SOME-WHERE. LOCATE AND CONTAIN HIM, BUT DO NOT ENGAGE...
THE PRICE OF A HYUNDAI TO WAIVE ALL LEGAL RESPONSIBILITY TO MY DAUGHTER.
1653
Lawton Family Trust
PAY TO THE ORDER OF CASH
DOLLARS
TWELVE THOUSAND AND 00/100
FOR
8735

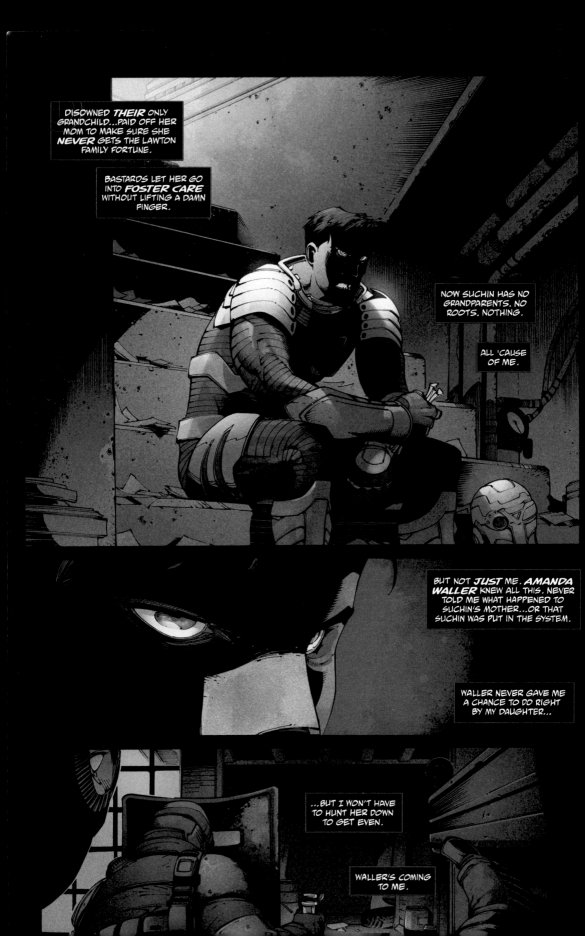

DISOWNED **THEIR** ONLY GRANDCHILD...PAID OFF HER MOM TO MAKE SURE SHE **NEVER** GETS THE LAWTON FAMILY FORTUNE.

BASTARDS LET HER GO INTO **FOSTER CARE** WITHOUT LIFTING A DAMN FINGER.

NOW SUCHIN HAS NO GRANDPARENTS. NO ROOTS. NOTHING.

ALL 'CAUSE OF ME.

BUT NOT **JUST** ME. **AMANDA WALLER** KNEW ALL THIS. NEVER TOLD ME WHAT HAPPENED TO SUCHIN'S MOTHER...OR THAT SUCHIN WAS PUT IN THE SYSTEM.

WALLER NEVER GAVE ME A CHANCE TO DO RIGHT BY MY DAUGHTER...

...BUT I WON'T HAVE TO HUNT HER DOWN TO GET EVEN.

WALLER'S COMING TO ME.

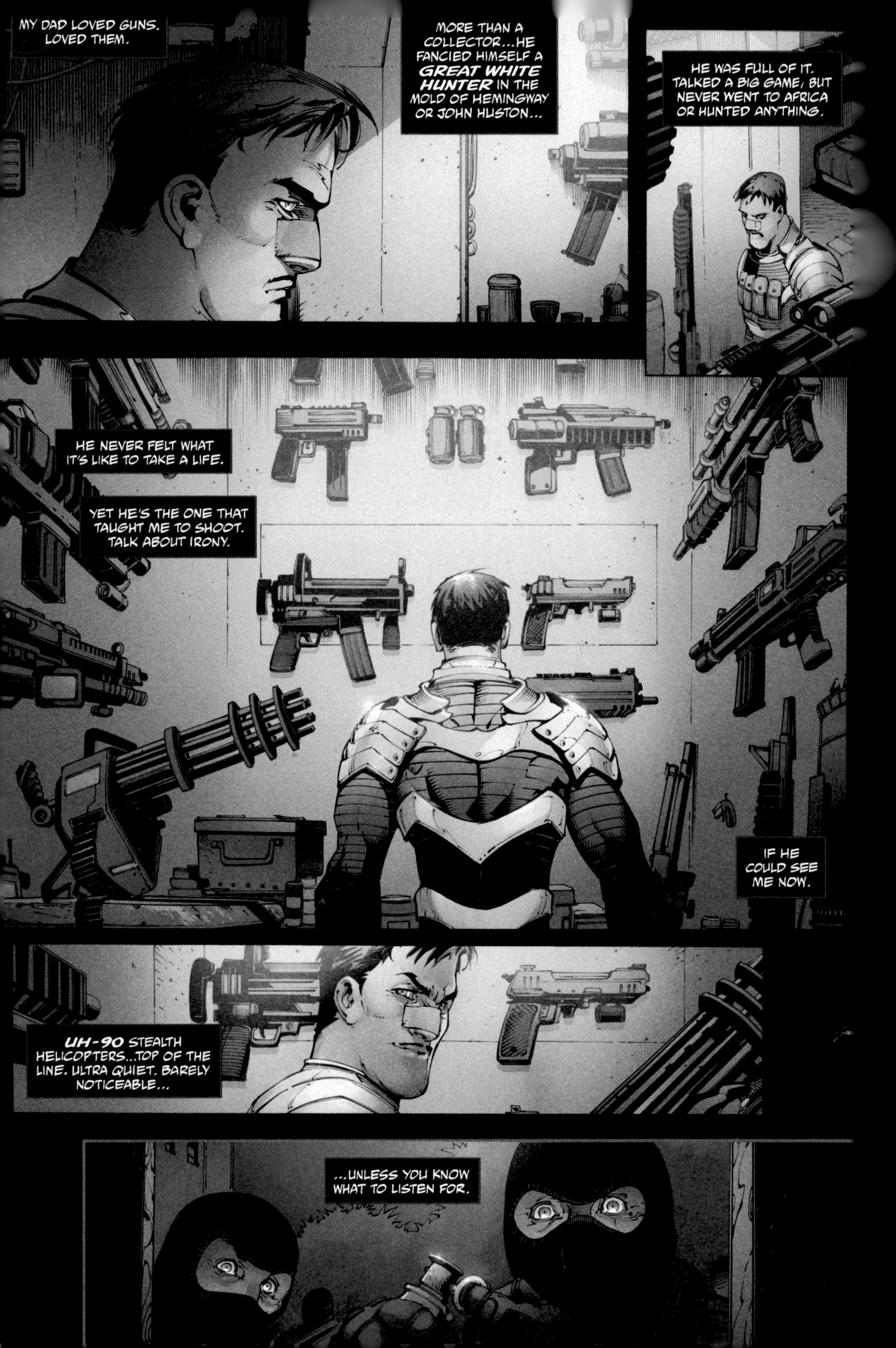
MY DAD LOVED GUNS. LOVED THEM.
MORE THAN A COLLECTOR...HE FANCIED HIMSELF A GREAT WHITE HUNTER IN THE MOLD OF HEMINGWAY OR JOHN HUSTON...
HE WAS FULL OF IT. TALKED A BIG GAME, BUT NEVER WENT TO AFRICA OR HUNTED ANYTHING.
HE NEVER FELT WHAT IT'S LIKE TO TAKE A LIFE.
YET HE'S THE ONE THAT TAUGHT ME TO SHOOT. TALK ABOUT IRONY.
IF HE COULD SEE ME NOW.
UH-90 STEALTH HELICOPTERS...TOP OF THE LINE. ULTRA QUIET. BARELY NOTICEABLE...
...UNLESS YOU KNOW WHAT TO LISTEN FOR.

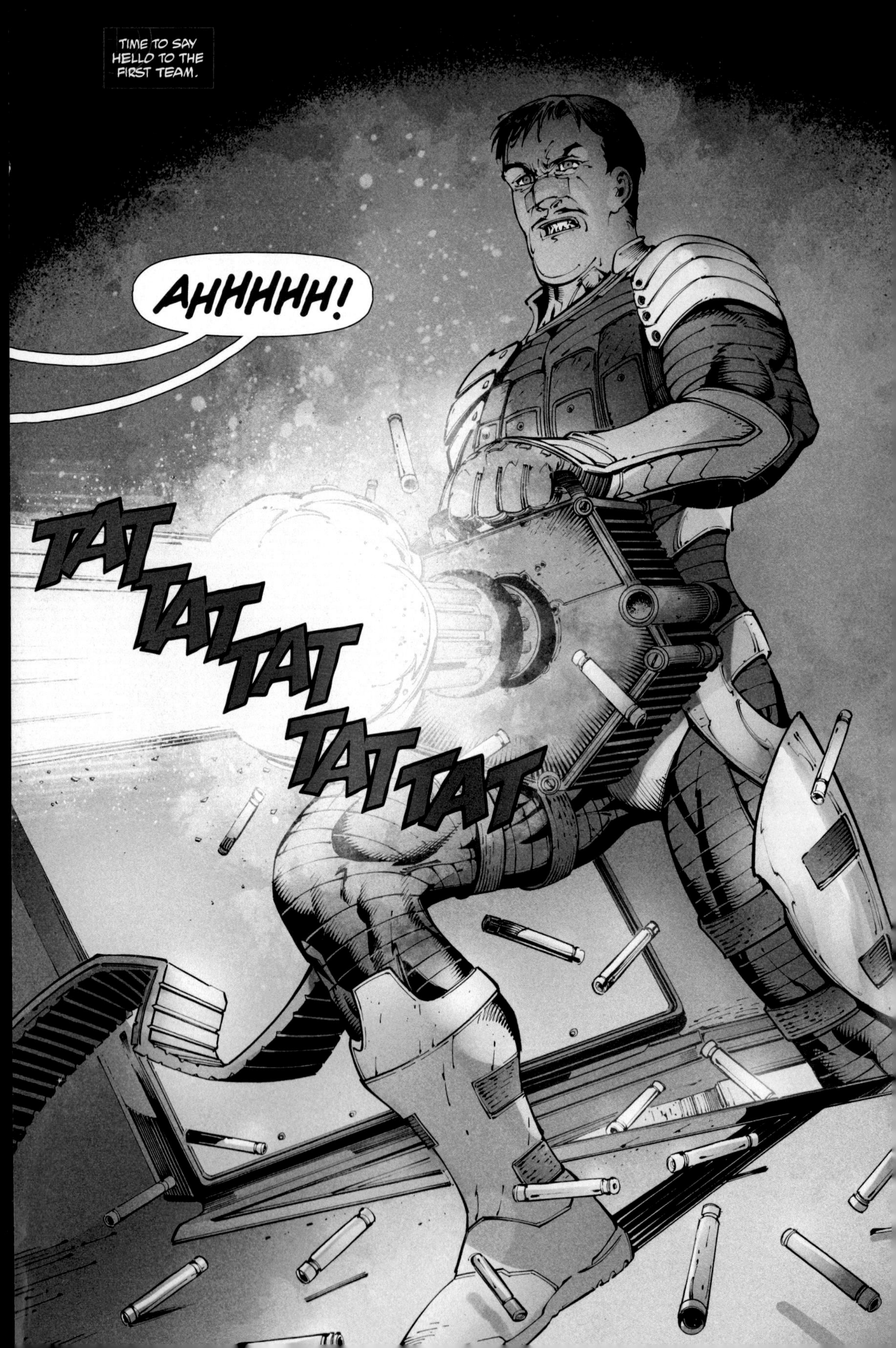
TIME TO SAY HELLO TO THE FIRST TEAM.
AHHHHH!
TAT TAT TAT TAT TAT

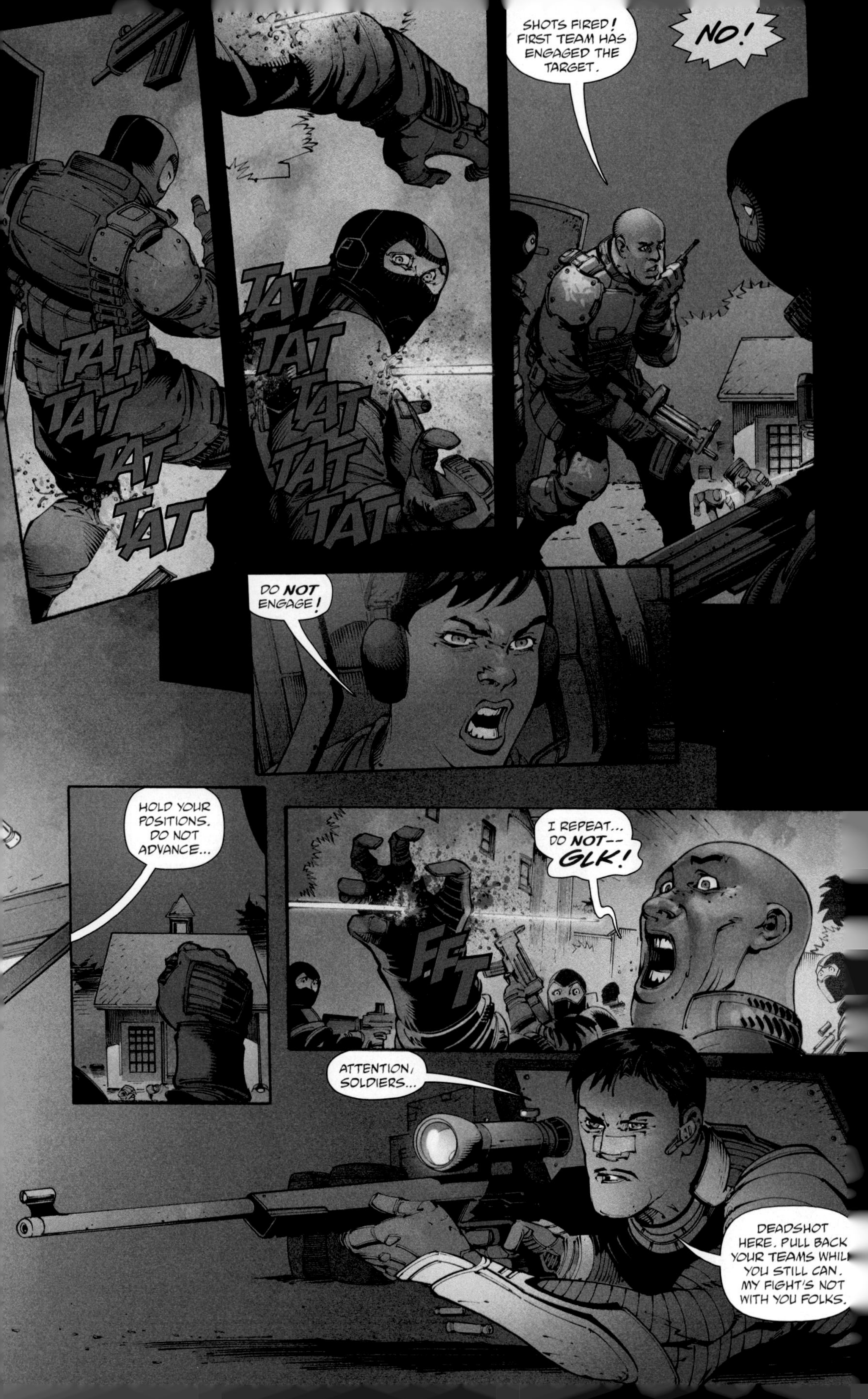
TAT TAT TAT TAT
TAT TAT TAT TAT TAT
SHOTS FIRED! FIRST TEAM HAS ENGAGED THE TARGET.
NO!
DO NOT ENGAGE!
HOLD YOUR POSITIONS. DO NOT ADVANCE...
I REPEAT... DO NOT-- GLK!
FFT
ATTENTION, SOLDIERS...
DEADSHOT HERE. PULL BACK YOUR TEAMS WHIL YOU STILL CAN. MY FIGHT'S NOT WITH YOU FOLKS.

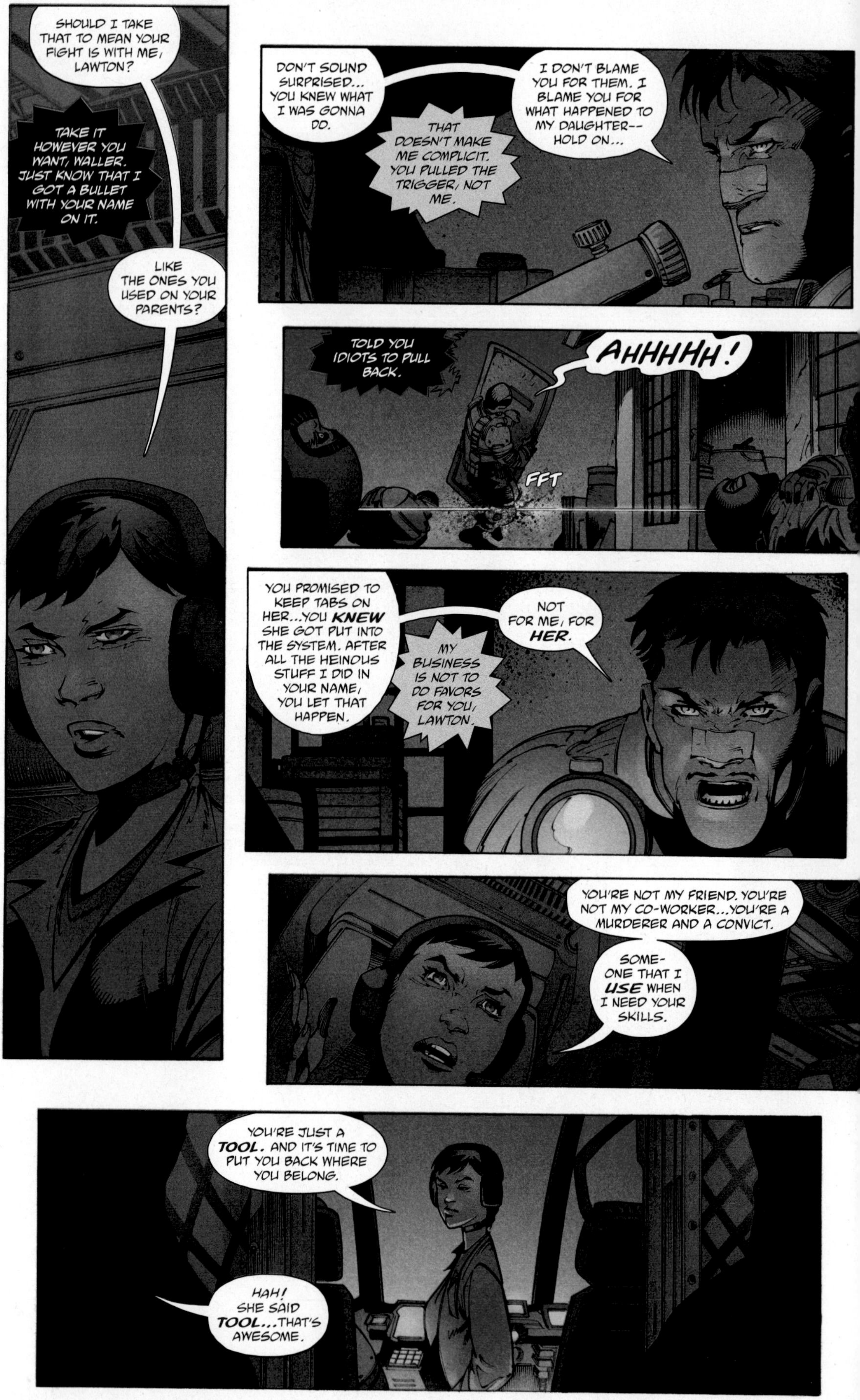
SHOULD I TAKE THAT TO MEAN YOUR FIGHT IS WITH ME, LAWTON?
TAKE IT HOWEVER YOU WANT, WALLER. JUST KNOW THAT I GOT A BULLET WITH YOUR NAME ON IT.
LIKE THE ONES YOU USED ON YOUR PARENTS?
DON'T SOUND SURPRISED... YOU KNEW WHAT I WAS GONNA DO.
THAT DOESN'T MAKE ME COMPLICIT. YOU PULLED THE TRIGGER, NOT ME.
I DON'T BLAME YOU FOR THEM. I BLAME YOU FOR WHAT HAPPENED TO MY DAUGHTER-- HOLD ON...
TOLD YOU IDIOTS TO PULL BACK.
AHHHHH!
FFT
YOU PROMISED TO KEEP TABS ON HER...YOU KNEW SHE GOT PUT INTO THE SYSTEM. AFTER ALL THE HEINOUS STUFF I DID IN YOUR NAME, YOU LET THAT HAPPEN.
MY BUSINESS IS NOT TO DO FAVORS FOR YOU, LAWTON.
NOT FOR ME, FOR HER.
YOU'RE NOT MY FRIEND. YOU'RE NOT MY CO-WORKER...YOU'RE A MURDERER AND A CONVICT.
SOME-ONE THAT I USE WHEN I NEED YOUR SKILLS.
YOU'RE JUST A TOOL. AND IT'S TIME TO PUT YOU BACK WHERE YOU BELONG.
HAH! SHE SAID TOOL...THAT'S AWESOME.

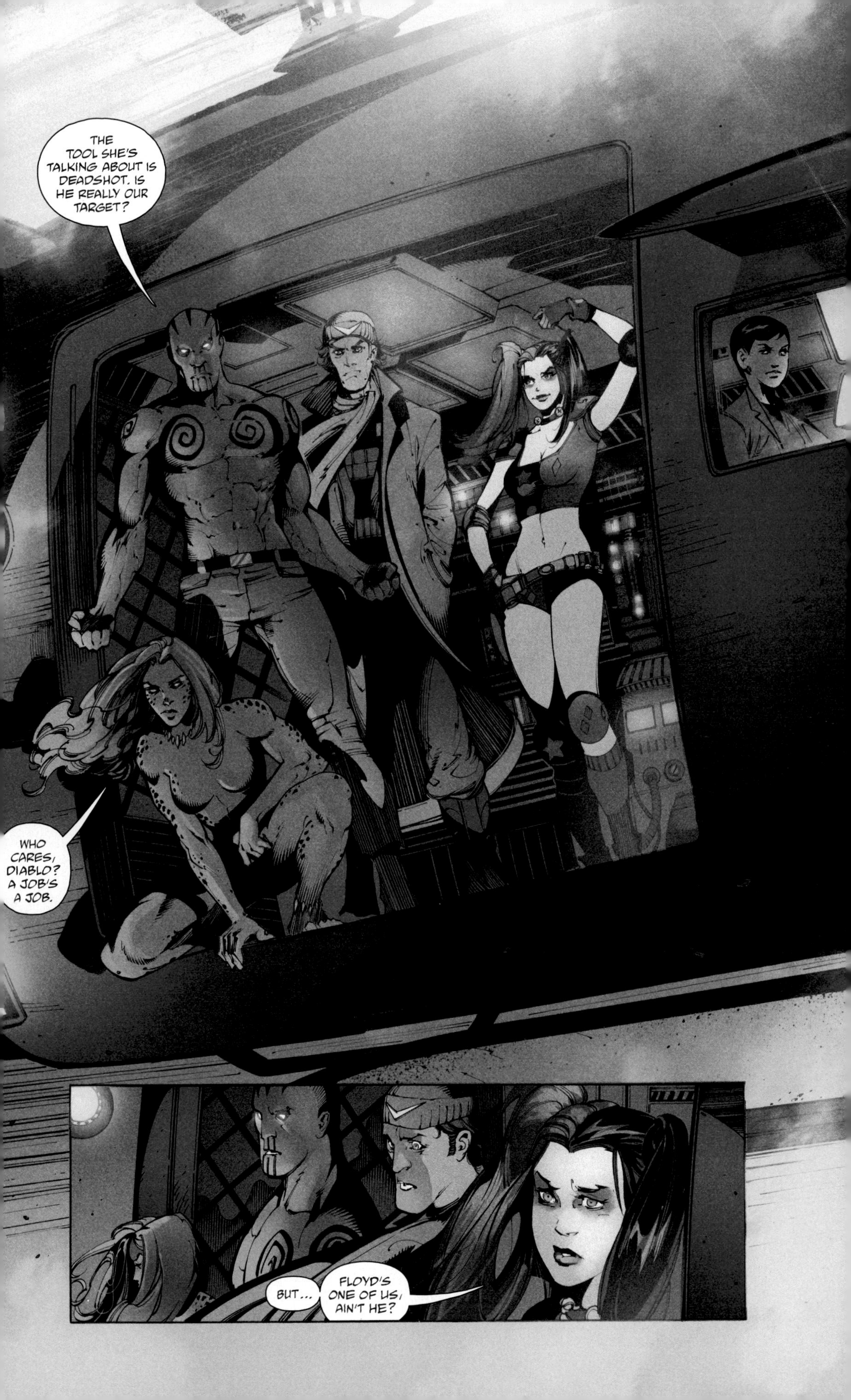
THE TOOL SHE'S TALKING ABOUT IS DEADSHOT. IS HE REALLY OUR TARGET?
WHO CARES, DIABLO? A JOB'S A JOB.
BUT...
FLOYD'S ONE OF US, AIN'T HE?

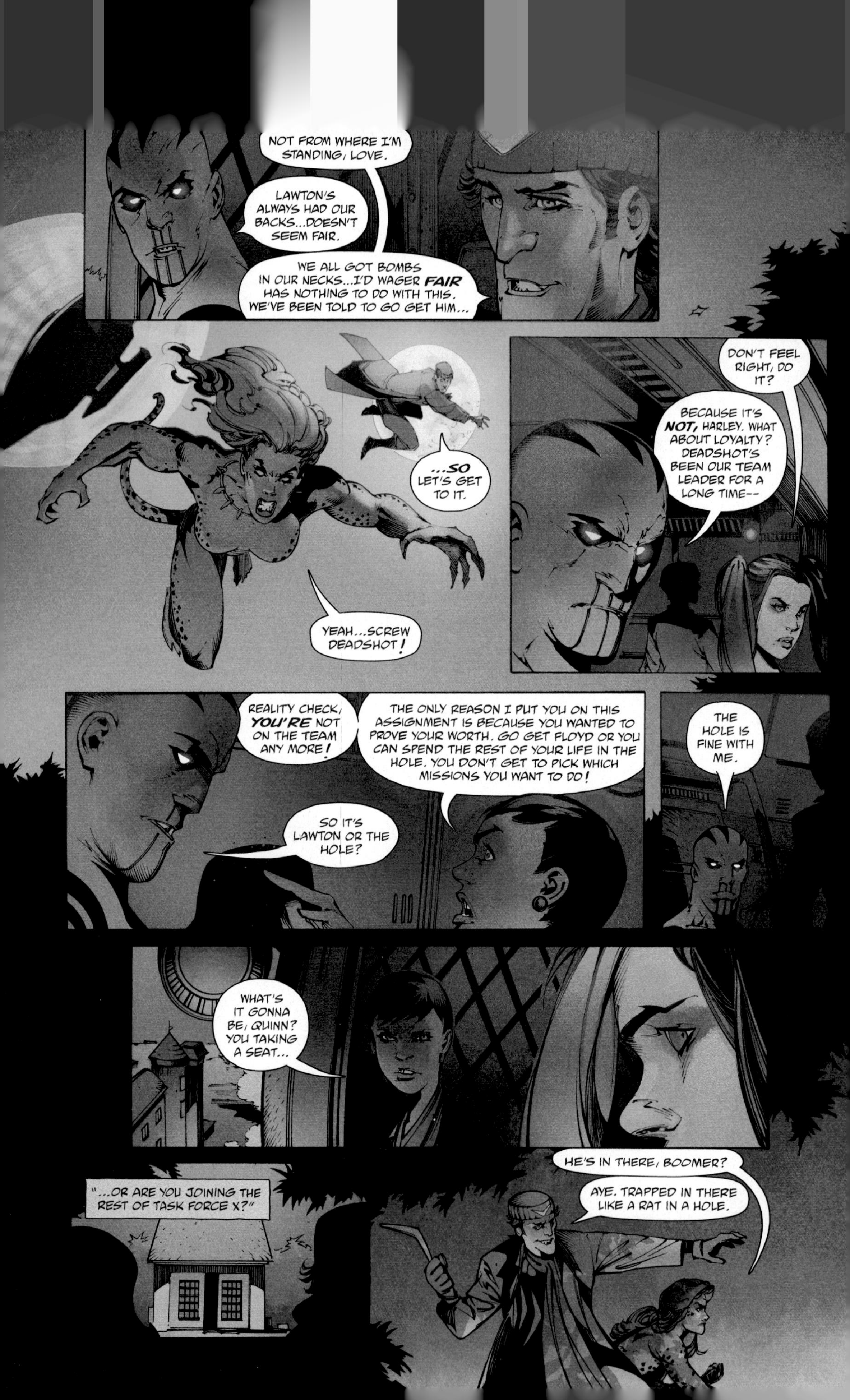

NOT FROM WHERE I'M STANDING, LOVE.
LAWTON'S ALWAYS HAD OUR BACKS...DOESN'T SEEM FAIR.
WE ALL GOT BOMBS IN OUR NECKS...I'D WAGER FAIR HAS NOTHING TO DO WITH THIS. WE'VE BEEN TOLD TO GO GET HIM...
...SO LET'S GET TO IT.
YEAH...SCREW DEADSHOT!
DON'T FEEL RIGHT, DO IT?
BECAUSE IT'S NOT, HARLEY. WHAT ABOUT LOYALTY? DEADSHOT'S BEEN OUR TEAM LEADER FOR A LONG TIME--
REALITY CHECK, YOU'RE NOT ON THE TEAM ANY MORE!
THE ONLY REASON I PUT YOU ON THIS ASSIGNMENT IS BECAUSE YOU WANTED TO PROVE YOUR WORTH. GO GET FLOYD OR YOU CAN SPEND THE REST OF YOUR LIFE IN THE HOLE. YOU DON'T GET TO PICK WHICH MISSIONS YOU WANT TO DO!
SO IT'S LAWTON OR THE HOLE?
THE HOLE IS FINE WITH ME.
WHAT'S IT GONNA BE, QUINN? YOU TAKING A SEAT...
"...OR ARE YOU JOINING THE REST OF TASK FORCE X?"
HE'S IN THERE, BOOMER?
AYE. TRAPPED IN THERE LIKE A RAT IN A HOLE.

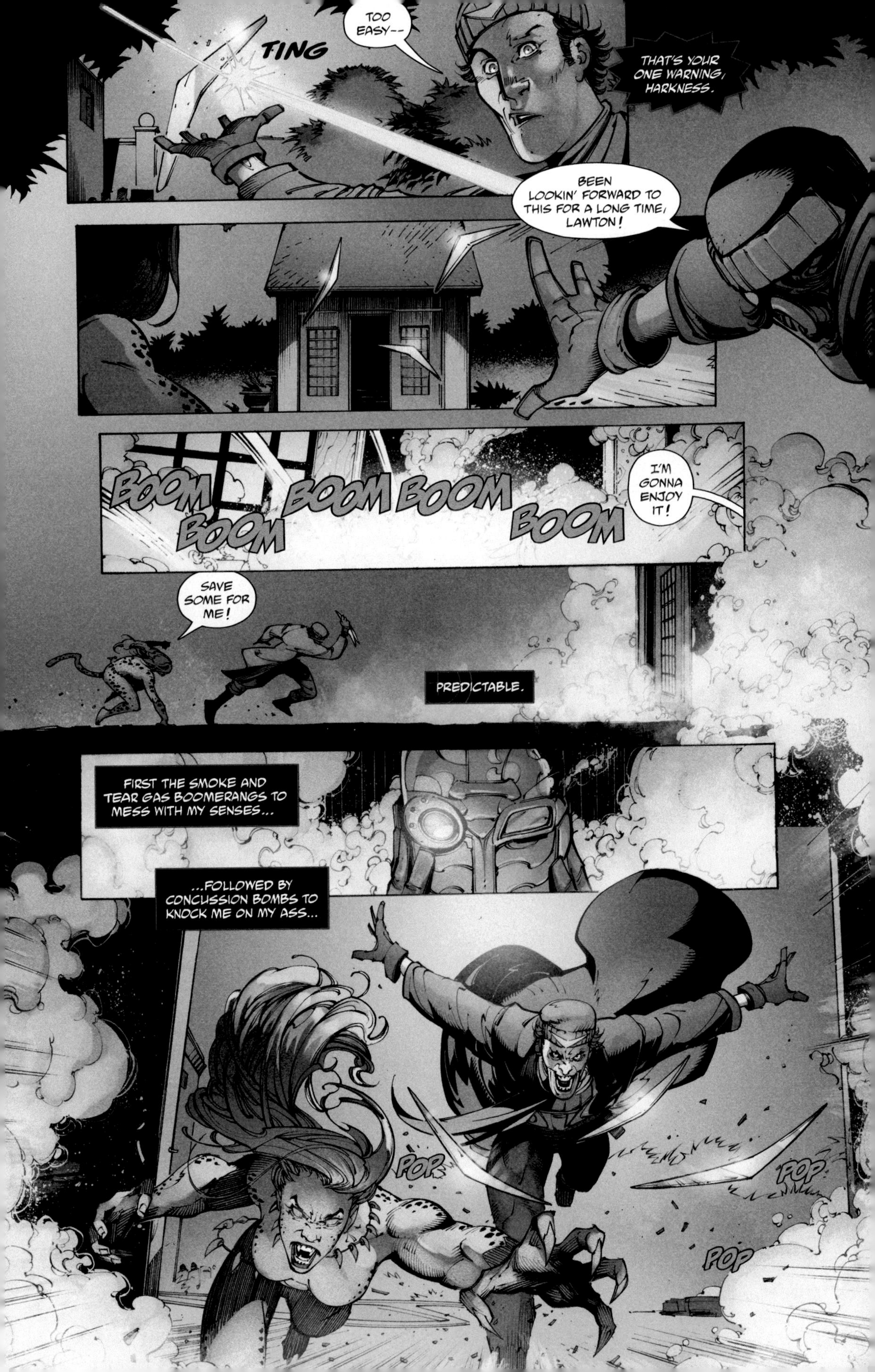
TOO EASY--
TING
THAT'S YOUR ONE WARNING, HARKNESS.
BEEN LOOKIN' FORWARD TO THIS FOR A LONG TIME, LAWTON!
BOOM
BOOM
BOOM
BOOM
BOOM
I'M GONNA ENJOY IT!
SAVE SOME FOR ME!
PREDICTABLE.
FIRST THE SMOKE AND TEAR GAS BOOMERANGS TO MESS WITH MY SENSES...
...FOLLOWED BY CONCUSSION BOMBS TO KNOCK ME ON MY ASS...
POP
POP
POP

THOOOM

.700 NITRO EXPRESS...**DOUBLE BARREL.** MY DAD'S *ELEPHANT GUN.* FOR ALL THAT BIG GAME HUNTING HE NEVER DID.

BOOM

CHEETAH'S STRONG BUT THIS OUGHT'A SL HER DOWN FOR A B

LAWTON... YA FARG'N BASTAGE--

AHHH!

POP

BE THANKFUL I DIDN'T USE THE ELEPHANT GUN ON *YOU.*

WALLER! STOP COWERING BEHIND THE SQUAD. COME OUT AND LET'S SETTLE THIS ONCE AND FOR ALL...

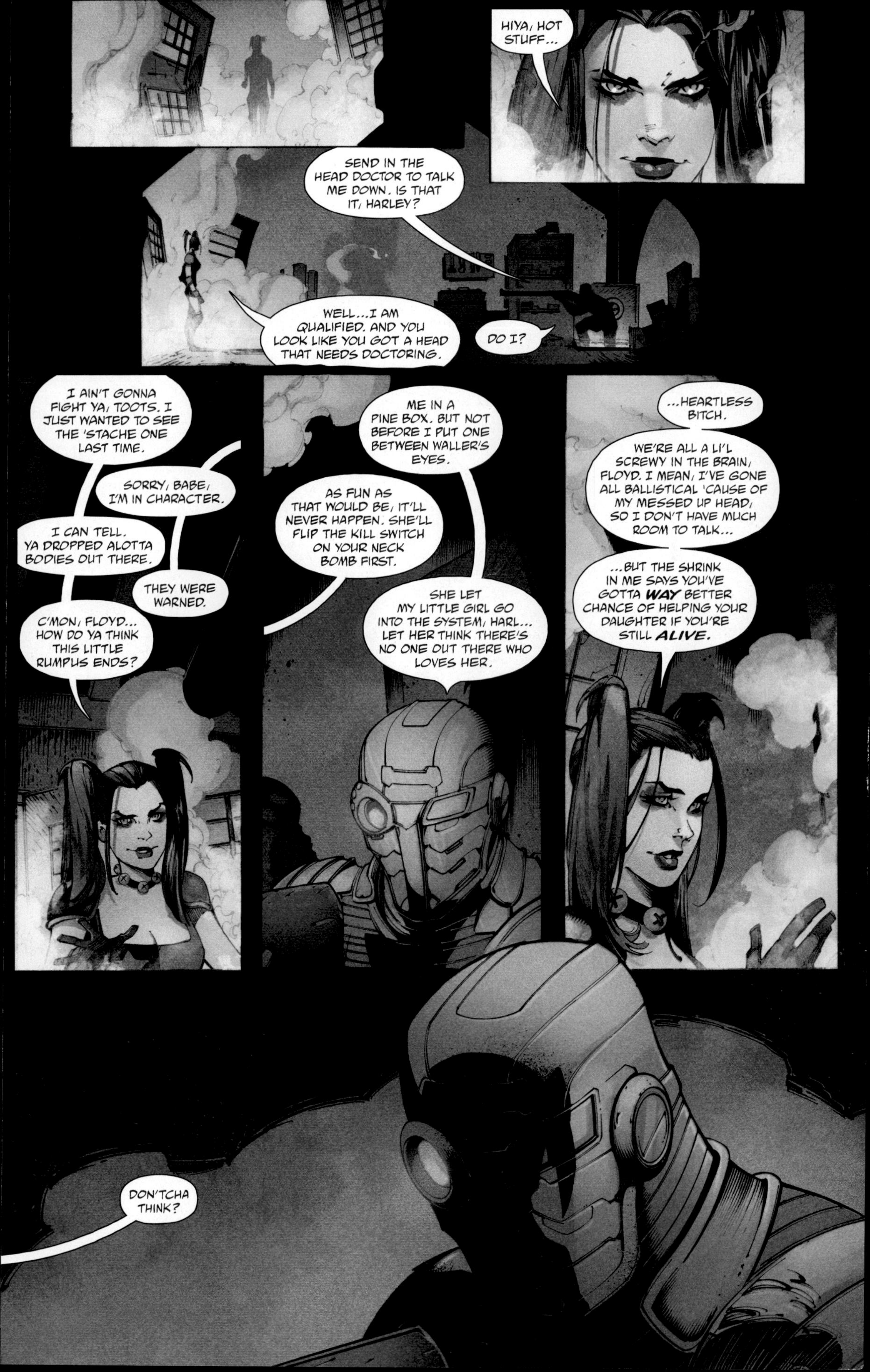
HIYA, HOT STUFF...
SEND IN THE HEAD DOCTOR TO TALK ME DOWN. IS THAT IT, HARLEY?
WELL...I AM QUALIFIED. AND YOU LOOK LIKE YOU GOT A HEAD THAT NEEDS DOCTORING.
DO I?
I AIN'T GONNA FIGHT YA, TOOTS. I JUST WANTED TO SEE THE 'STACHE ONE LAST TIME.
SORRY, BABE, I'M IN CHARACTER.
I CAN TELL. YA DROPPED ALOTTA BODIES OUT THERE.
THEY WERE WARNED.
C'MON, FLOYD... HOW DO YA THINK THIS LITTLE RUMPUS ENDS?
ME IN A PINE BOX. BUT NOT BEFORE I PUT ONE BETWEEN WALLER'S EYES.
AS FUN AS THAT WOULD BE, IT'LL NEVER HAPPEN. SHE'LL FLIP THE KILL SWITCH ON YOUR NECK BOMB FIRST.
SHE LET MY LITTLE GIRL GO INTO THE SYSTEM, HARL... LET HER THINK THERE'S NO ONE OUT THERE WHO LOVES HER.
...HEARTLESS BITCH.
WE'RE ALL A LI'L SCREWY IN THE BRAIN, FLOYD. I MEAN, I'VE GONE ALL BALLISTICAL 'CAUSE OF MY MESSED UP HEAD, SO I DON'T HAVE MUCH ROOM TO TALK...
...BUT THE SHRINK IN ME SAYS YOU'VE GOTTA WAY BETTER CHANCE OF HELPING YOUR DAUGHTER IF YOU'RE STILL ALIVE.
DON'TCHA THINK?

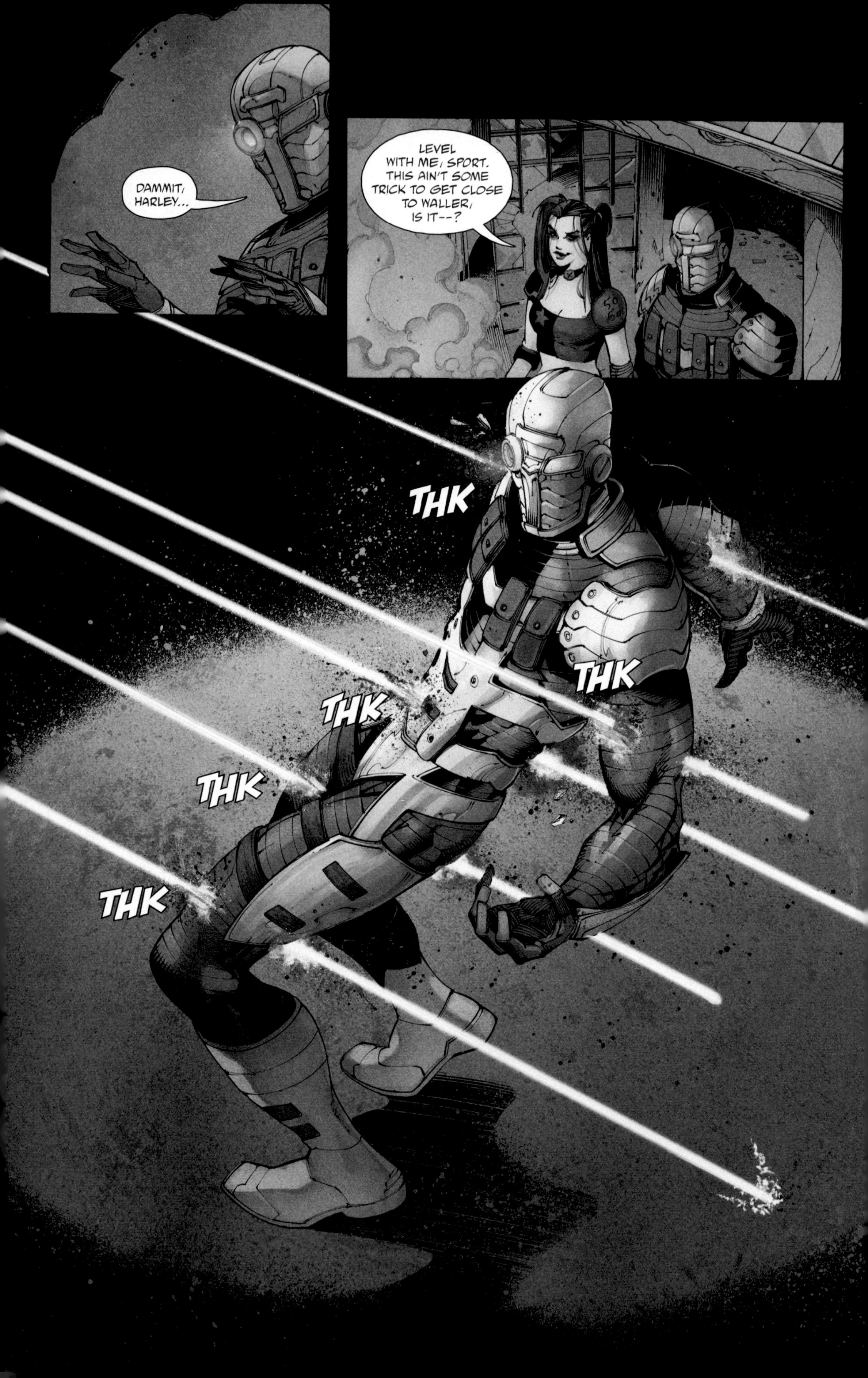
DAMMIT, HARLEY...
LEVEL WITH ME, SPORT. THIS AIN'T SOME TRICK TO GET CLOSE TO WALLER, IS IT--?
THK
THK
THK
THK
THK

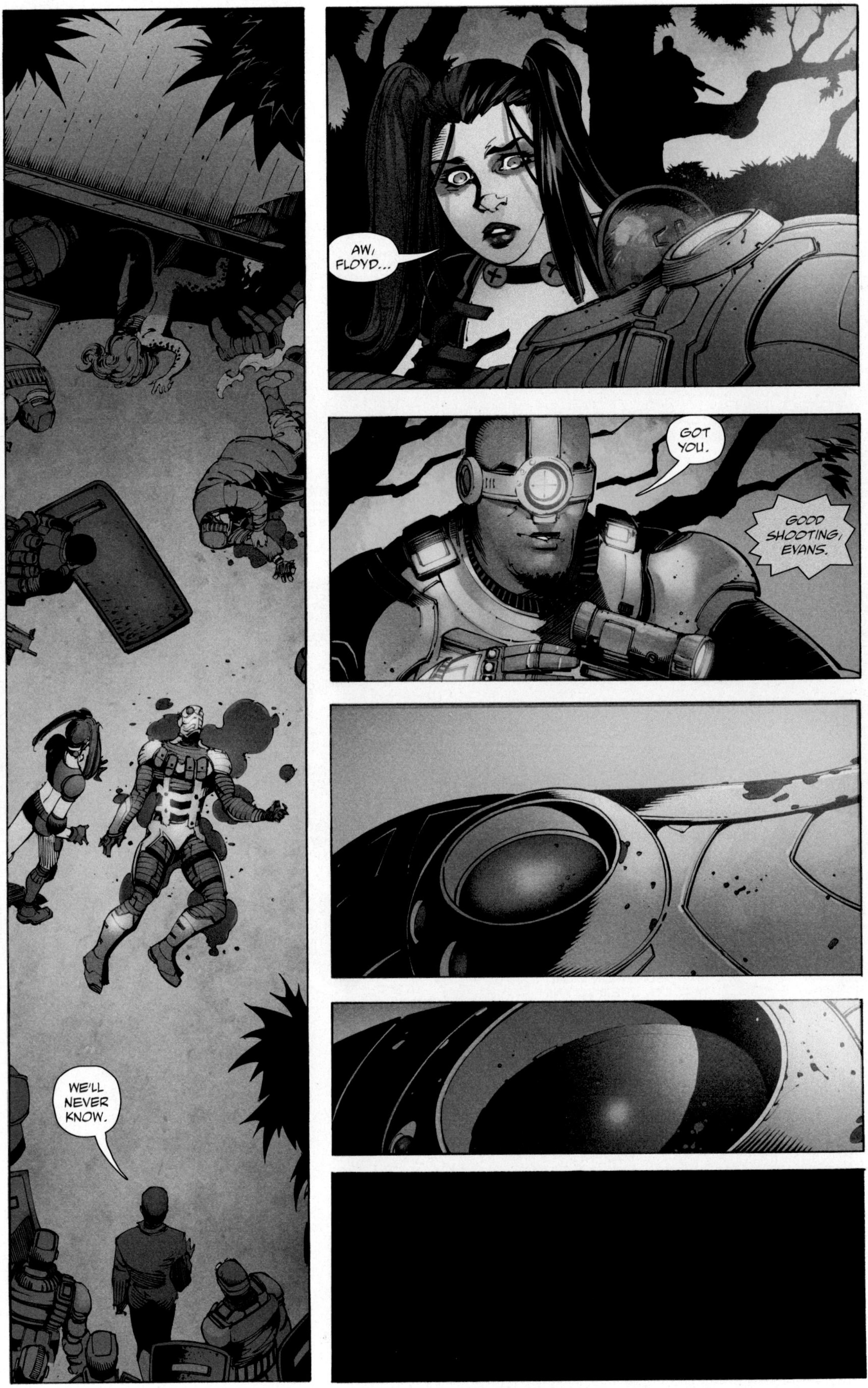
WE'LL NEVER KNOW.
AW, FLOYD...
GOT YOU.
GOOD SHOOTING, EVANS.

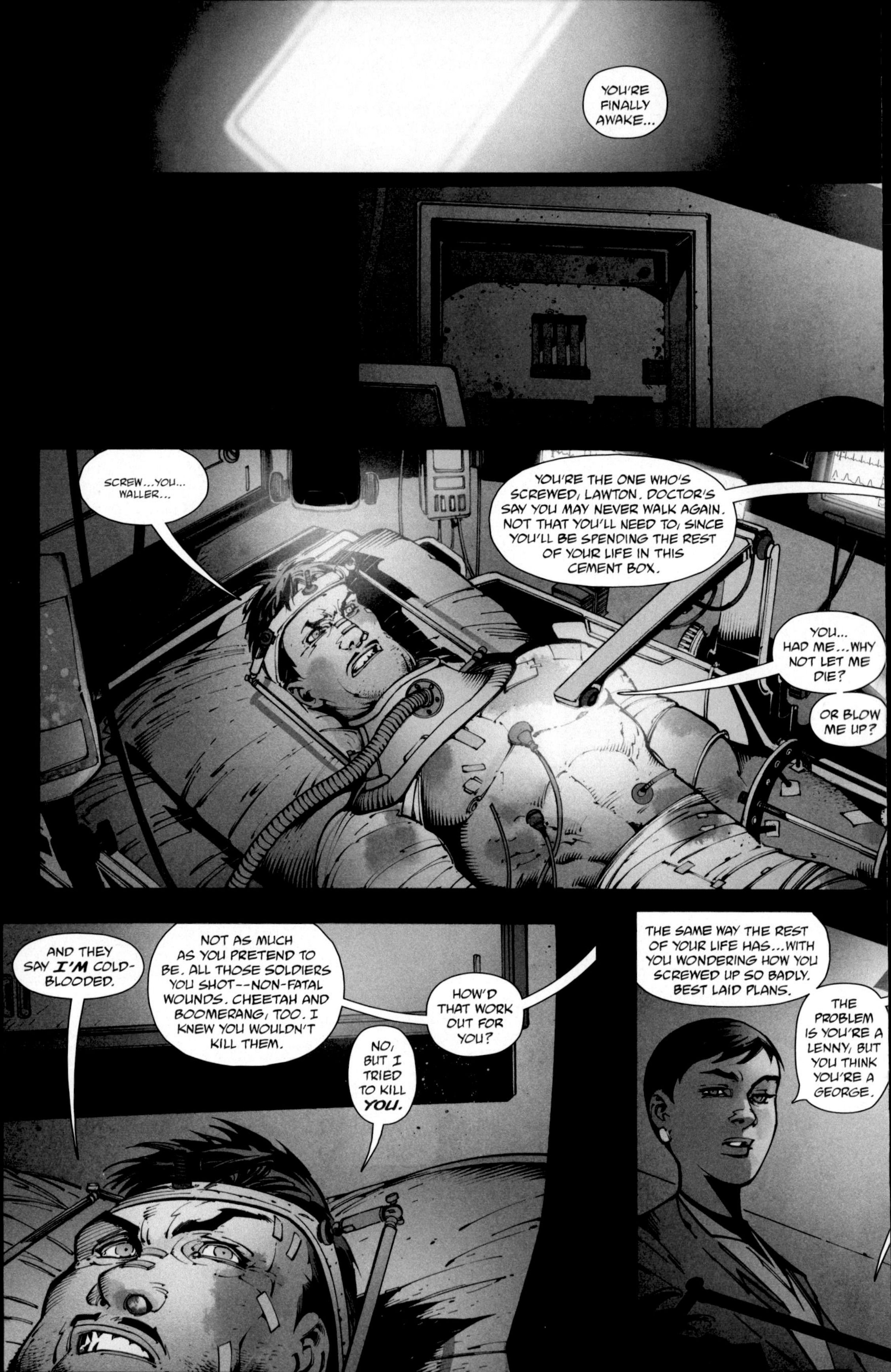

YOU'RE FINALLY AWAKE...
SCREW...YOU... WALLER...
YOU'RE THE ONE WHO'S SCREWED, LAWTON. DOCTOR'S SAY YOU MAY NEVER WALK AGAIN. NOT THAT YOU'LL NEED TO, SINCE YOU'LL BE SPENDING THE REST OF YOUR LIFE IN THIS CEMENT BOX.
YOU... HAD ME...WHY NOT LET ME DIE?
OR BLOW ME UP?
AND THEY SAY I'M COLD-BLOODED.
NOT AS MUCH AS YOU PRETEND TO BE. ALL THOSE SOLDIERS YOU SHOT--NON-FATAL WOUNDS. CHEETAH AND BOOMERANG, TOO. I KNEW YOU WOULDN'T KILL THEM.
HOW'D THAT WORK OUT FOR YOU?
NO, BUT I TRIED TO KILL YOU.
THE SAME WAY THE REST OF YOUR LIFE HAS...WITH YOU WONDERING HOW YOU SCREWED UP SO BADLY. BEST LAID PLANS.
THE PROBLEM IS YOU'RE A LENNY, BUT YOU THINK YOU'RE A GEORGE.

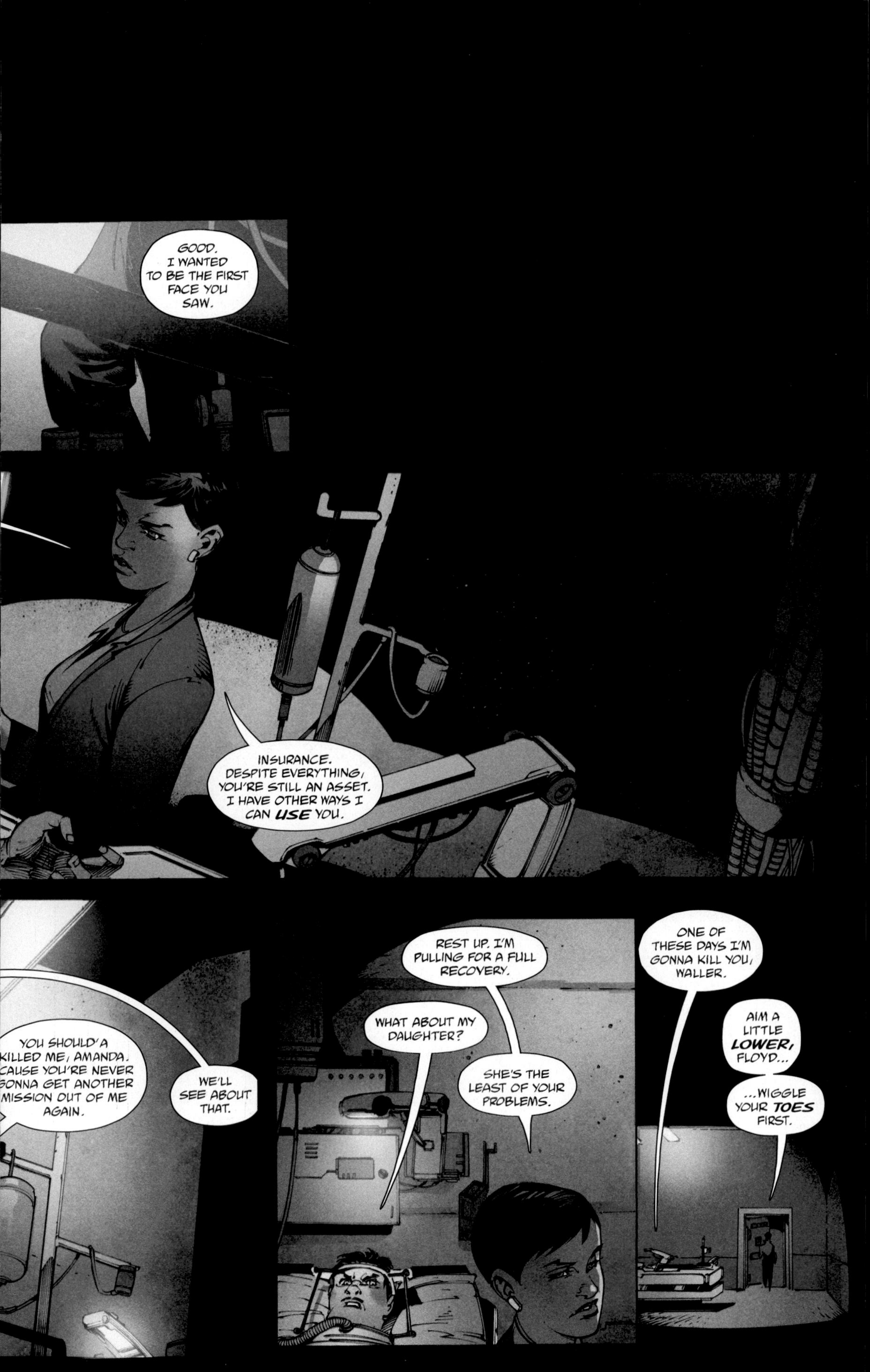
GOOD. I WANTED TO BE THE FIRST FACE YOU SAW.
INSURANCE. DESPITE EVERYTHING, YOU'RE STILL AN ASSET. I HAVE OTHER WAYS I CAN USE YOU.
YOU SHOULD'A KILLED ME, AMANDA. CAUSE YOU'RE NEVER GONNA GET ANOTHER MISSION OUT OF ME AGAIN.
WE'LL SEE ABOUT THAT.
WHAT ABOUT MY DAUGHTER?
SHE'S THE LEAST OF YOUR PROBLEMS.
REST UP. I'M PULLING FOR A FULL RECOVERY.
ONE OF THESE DAYS I'M GONNA KILL YOU, WALLER.
AIM A LITTLE LOWER, FLOYD...
...WIGGLE YOUR TOES FIRST.

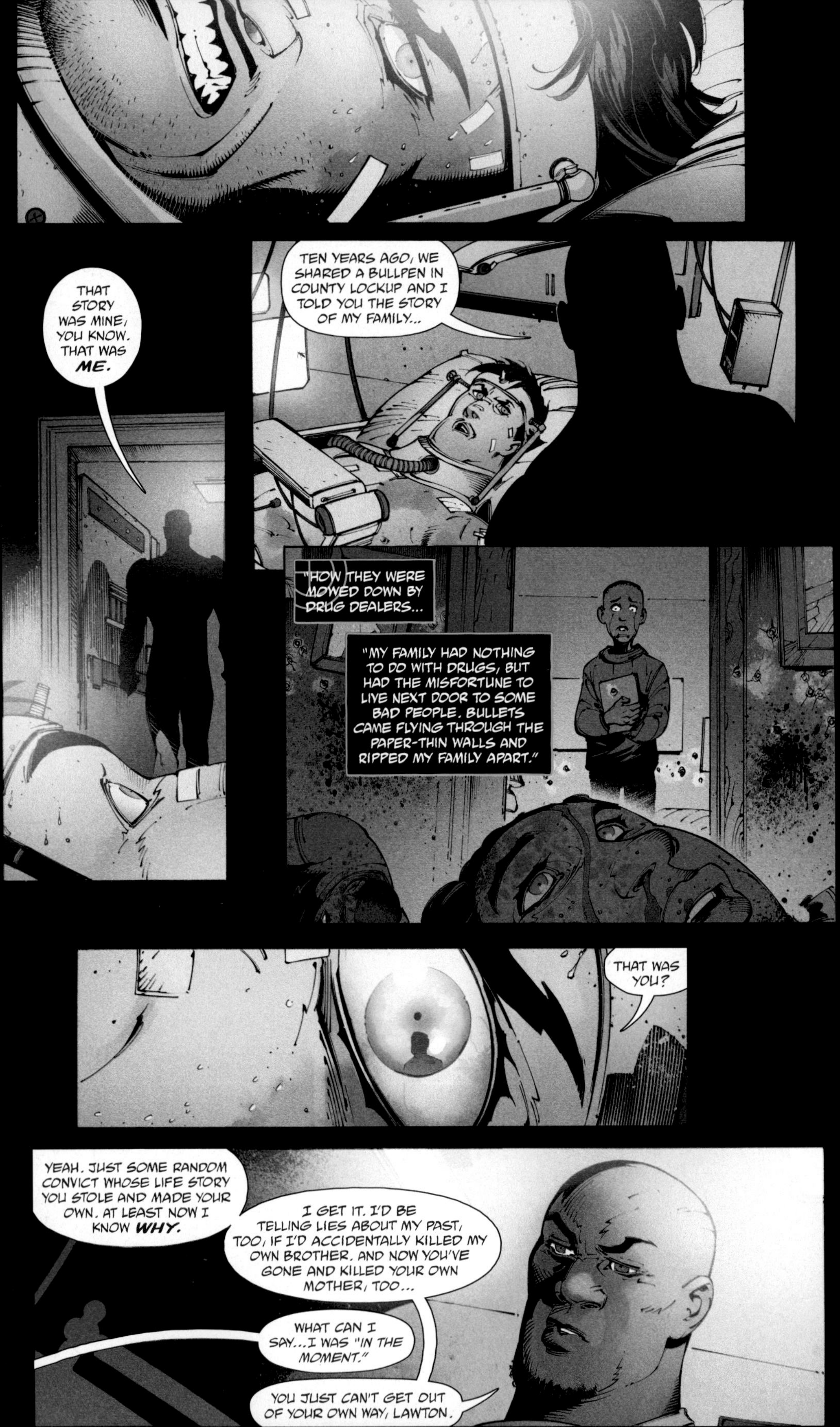
THAT STORY WAS MINE, YOU KNOW. THAT WAS *ME.*
TEN YEARS AGO, WE SHARED A BULLPEN IN COUNTY LOCKUP AND I TOLD YOU THE STORY OF MY FAMILY...
"HOW THEY WERE MOWED DOWN BY DRUG DEALERS...
"MY FAMILY HAD NOTHING TO DO WITH DRUGS, BUT HAD THE MISFORTUNE TO LIVE NEXT DOOR TO SOME BAD PEOPLE. BULLETS CAME FLYING THROUGH THE PAPER-THIN WALLS AND RIPPED MY FAMILY APART."
THAT WAS YOU?
YEAH. JUST SOME RANDOM CONVICT WHOSE LIFE STORY YOU STOLE AND MADE YOUR OWN. AT LEAST NOW I KNOW *WHY.*
I GET IT. I'D BE TELLING LIES ABOUT MY PAST, TOO, IF I'D ACCIDENTALLY KILLED MY OWN BROTHER. AND NOW YOU'VE GONE AND KILLED YOUR OWN MOTHER, TOO...
WHAT CAN I SAY...I WAS "IN THE MOMENT."
YOU JUST CAN'T GET OUT OF YOUR OWN WAY, LAWTON.

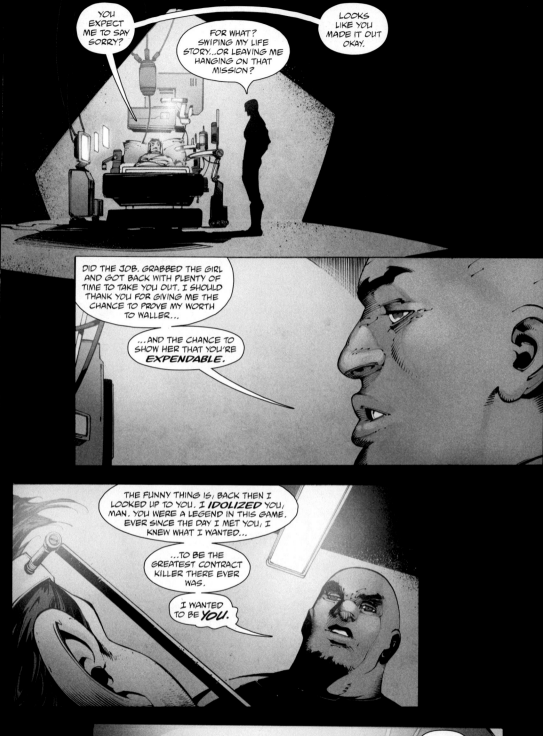

YOU EXPECT ME TO SAY SORRY?

FOR WHAT? SWIPING MY LIFE STORY...OR LEAVING ME HANGING ON THAT MISSION?

LOOKS LIKE YOU MADE IT OUT OKAY.

DID THE JOB. GRABBED THE GIRL AND GOT BACK WITH PLENTY OF TIME TO TAKE YOU OUT. I SHOULD THANK YOU FOR GIVING ME THE CHANCE TO PROVE MY WORTH TO WALLER...

...AND THE CHANCE TO SHOW HER THAT YOU'RE *EXPENDABLE*.

THE FUNNY THING IS, BACK THEN I LOOKED UP TO YOU. I *IDOLIZED* YOU, MAN. YOU WERE A LEGEND IN THIS GAME. EVER SINCE THE DAY I MET YOU, I KNEW WHAT I WANTED...

...TO BE THE GREATEST CONTRACT KILLER THERE EVER WAS.

I WANTED TO BE *YOU.*

EVANS...

YOU WERE ALWAYS GONNA BE MY REPLACEMENT, WEREN'T YOU?

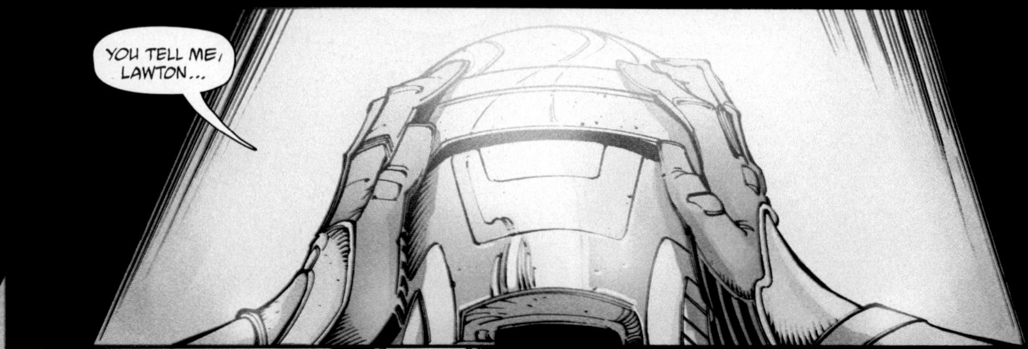
YOU TELL ME, LAWTON...
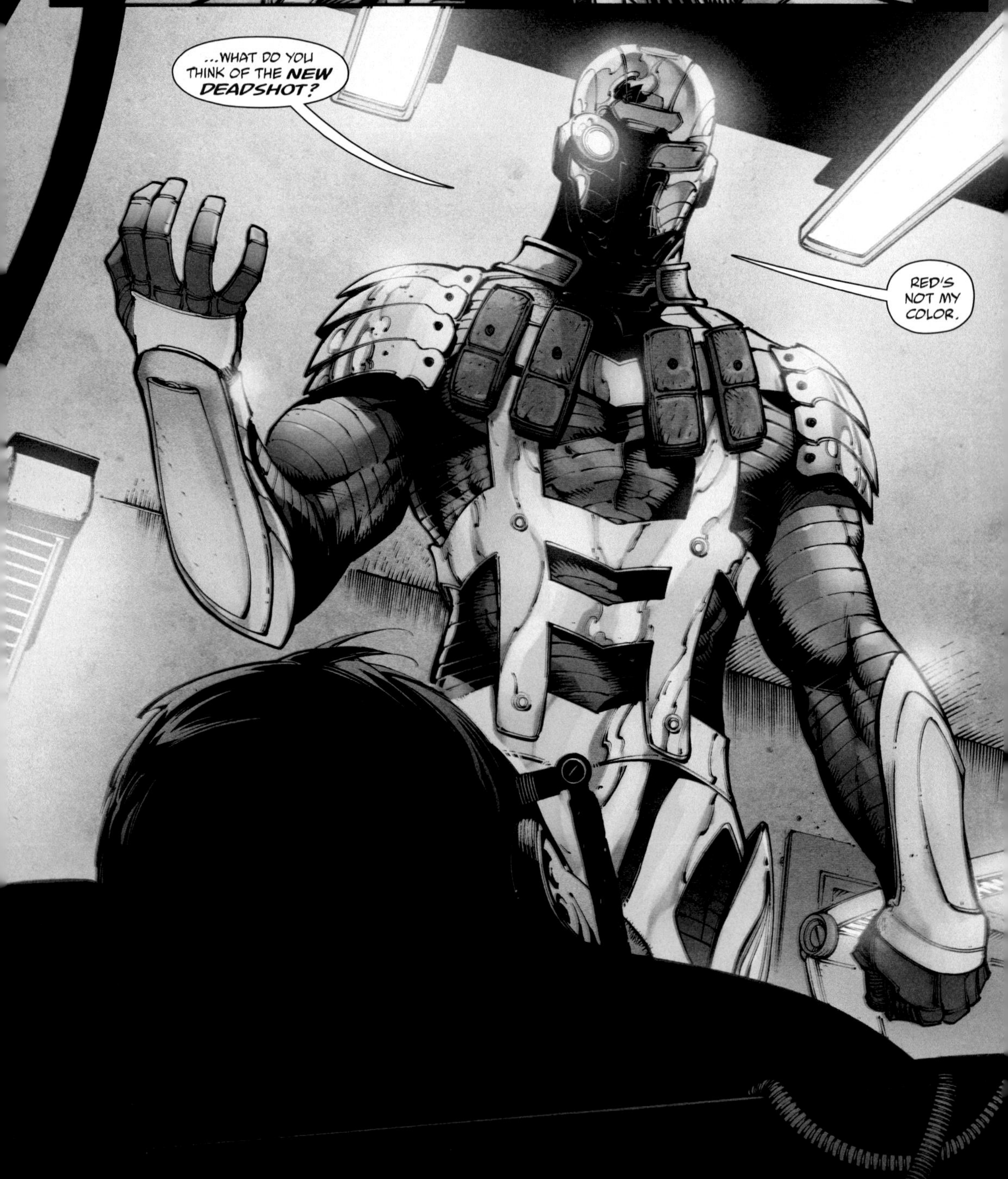
...WHAT DO YOU THINK OF THE NEW DEADSHOT?
RED'S NOT MY COLOR.

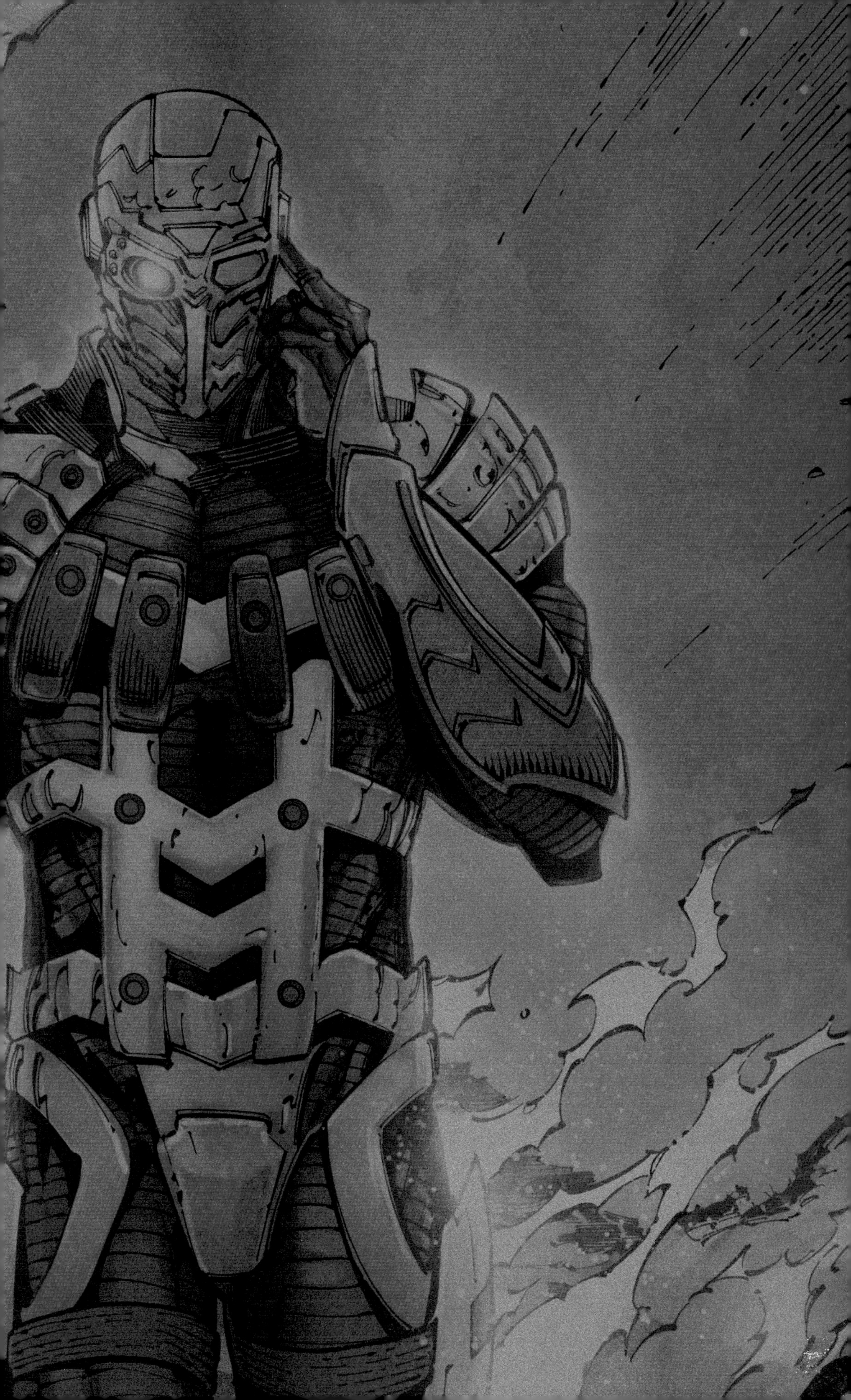

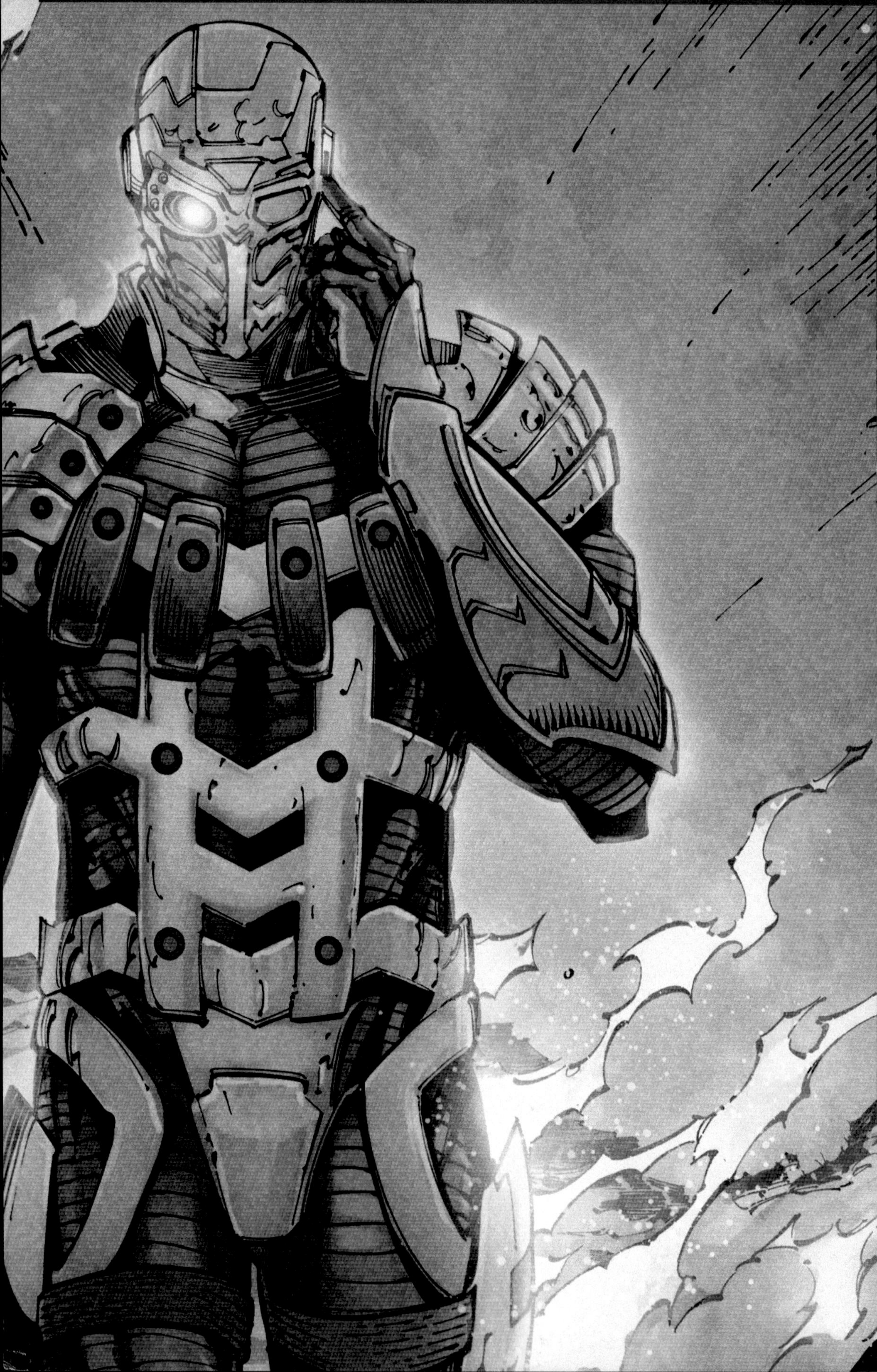

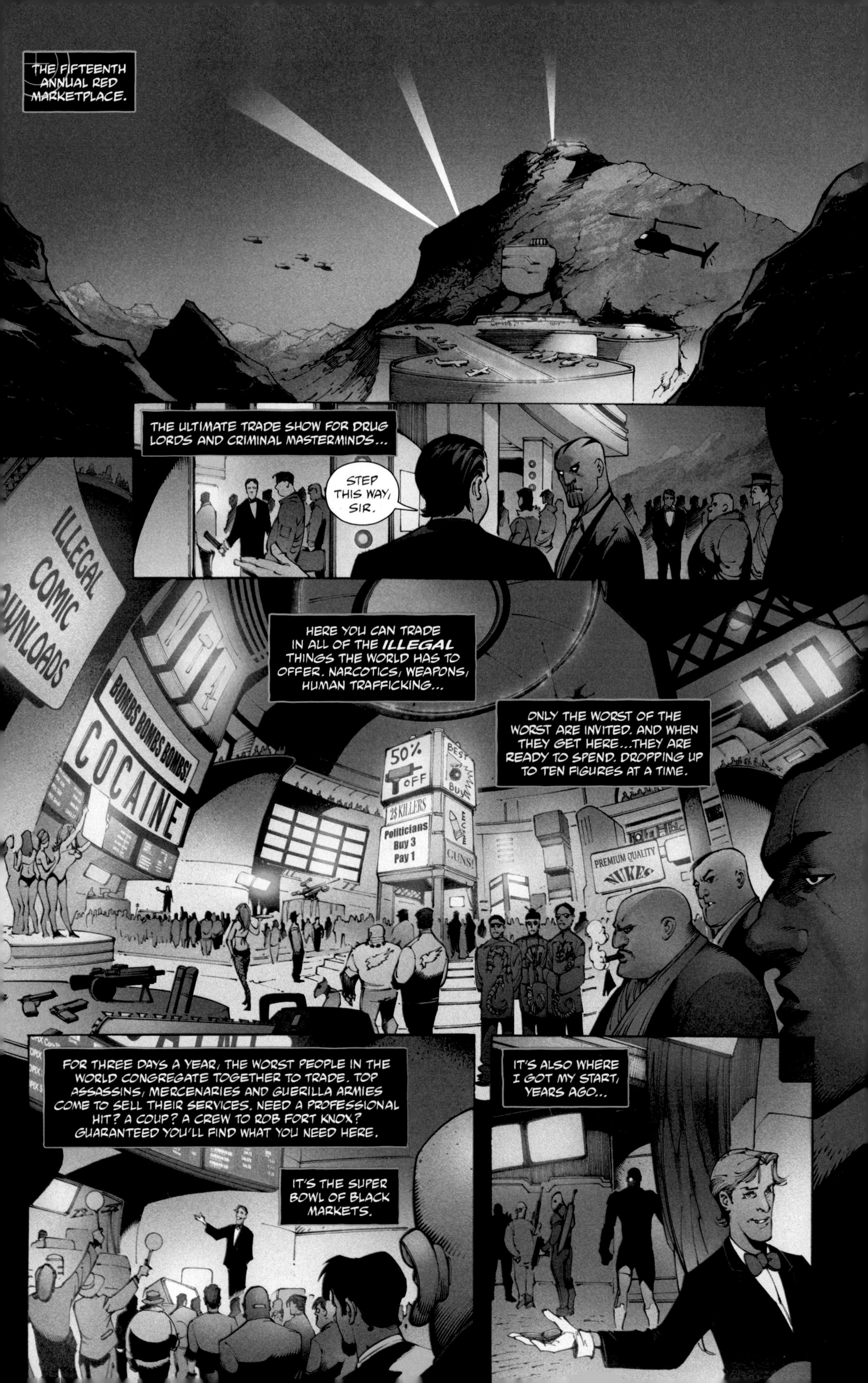
THE FIFTEENTH ANNUAL RED MARKETPLACE.
THE ULTIMATE TRADE SHOW FOR DRUG LORDS AND CRIMINAL MASTERMINDS...
STEP THIS WAY, SIR.
HERE YOU CAN TRADE IN ALL OF THE ILLEGAL THINGS THE WORLD HAS TO OFFER. NARCOTICS, WEAPONS, HUMAN TRAFFICKING...
ONLY THE WORST OF THE WORST ARE INVITED. AND WHEN THEY GET HERE...THEY ARE READY TO SPEND. DROPPING UP TO TEN FIGURES AT A TIME.
ILLEGAL COMIC DOWNLOADS
BOMBS BOMBS BOMBS!
COCAINE
50% OFF
BEST BUY
2$ KILLERS
Politicians Buy 3 Pay 1
GUNS!
PREMIUM QUALITY NUKES
FOR THREE DAYS A YEAR, THE WORST PEOPLE IN THE WORLD CONGREGATE TOGETHER TO TRADE. TOP ASSASSINS, MERCENARIES AND GUERILLA ARMIES COME TO SELL THEIR SERVICES. NEED A PROFESSIONAL HIT? A COUP? A CREW TO ROB FORT KNOX? GUARANTEED YOU'LL FIND WHAT YOU NEED HERE.
IT'S THE SUPER BOWL OF BLACK MARKETS.
IT'S ALSO WHERE I GOT MY START, YEARS AGO...

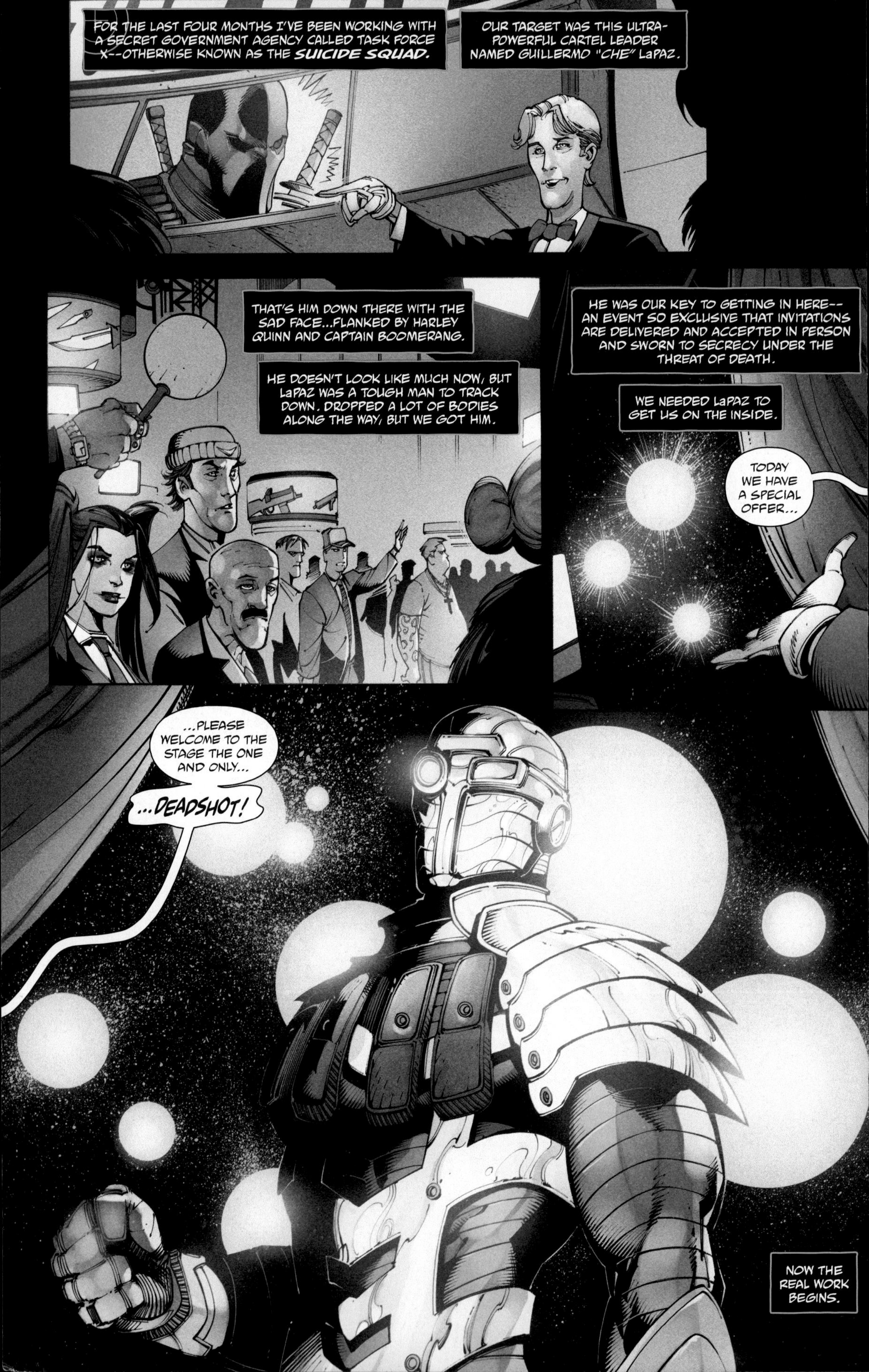
FOR THE LAST FOUR MONTHS I'VE BEEN WORKING WITH A SECRET GOVERNMENT AGENCY CALLED TASK FORCE X--OTHERWISE KNOWN AS THE *SUICIDE SQUAD.*
OUR TARGET WAS THIS ULTRA-POWERFUL CARTEL LEADER NAMED GUILLERMO *"CHE"* LaPAZ.
THAT'S HIM DOWN THERE WITH THE SAD FACE...FLANKED BY HARLEY QUINN AND CAPTAIN BOOMERANG.
HE DOESN'T LOOK LIKE MUCH NOW, BUT LaPAZ WAS A TOUGH MAN TO TRACK DOWN. DROPPED A LOT OF BODIES ALONG THE WAY, BUT WE GOT HIM.
HE WAS OUR KEY TO GETTING IN HERE-- AN EVENT SO EXCLUSIVE THAT INVITATIONS ARE DELIVERED AND ACCEPTED IN PERSON AND SWORN TO SECRECY UNDER THE THREAT OF DEATH.
WE NEEDED LaPAZ TO GET US ON THE INSIDE.
TODAY WE HAVE A SPECIAL OFFER...
...PLEASE WELCOME TO THE STAGE THE ONE AND ONLY...
...DEADSHOT!
NOW THE REAL WORK BEGINS.

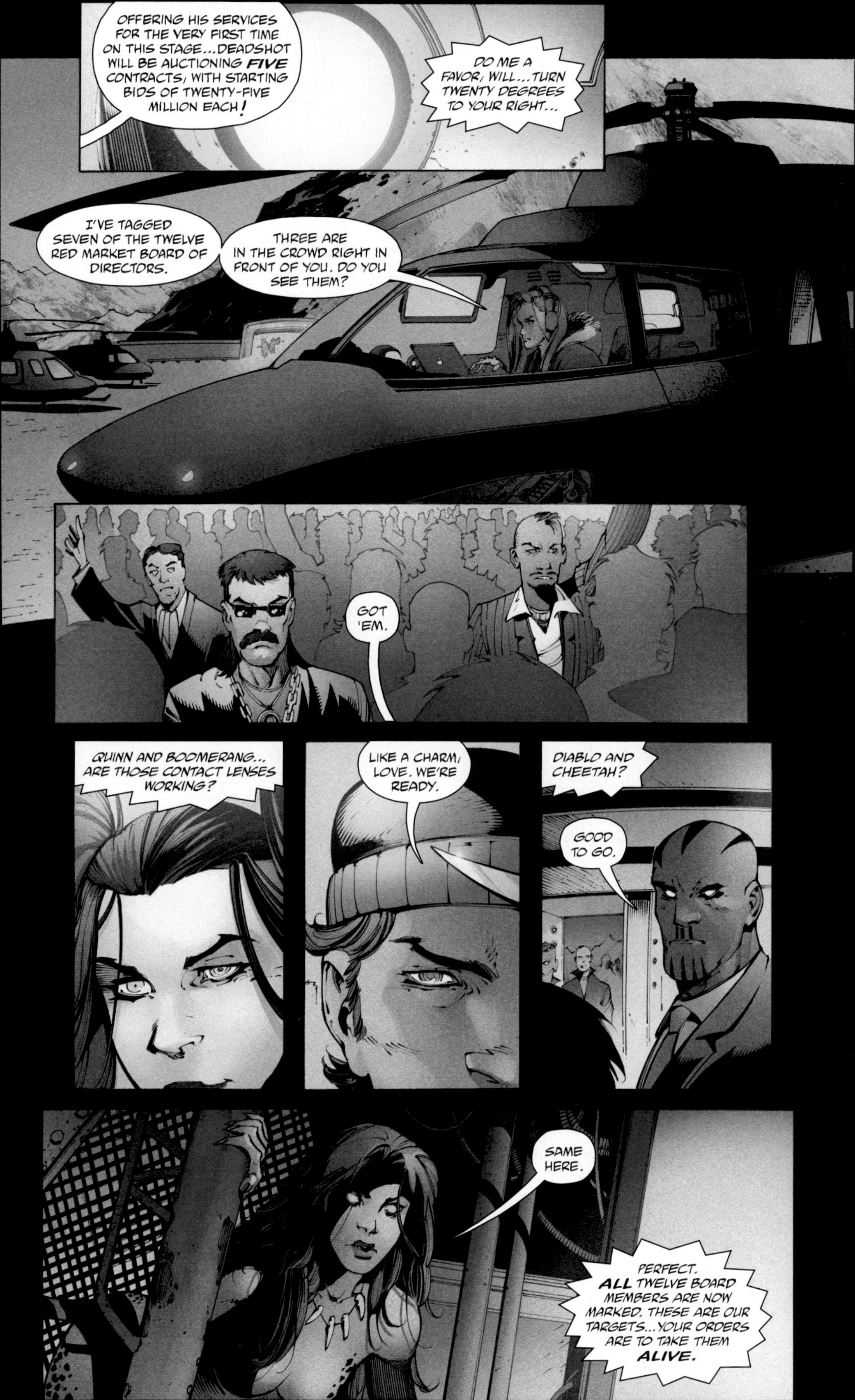
OFFERING HIS SERVICES FOR THE VERY FIRST TIME ON THIS STAGE...DEADSHOT WILL BE AUCTIONING FIVE CONTRACTS, WITH STARTING BIDS OF TWENTY-FIVE MILLION EACH!
DO ME A FAVOR, WILL...TURN TWENTY DEGREES TO YOUR RIGHT...
I'VE TAGGED SEVEN OF THE TWELVE RED MARKET BOARD OF DIRECTORS.
THREE ARE IN THE CROWD RIGHT IN FRONT OF YOU. DO YOU SEE THEM?
GOT 'EM.
QUINN AND BOOMERANG... ARE THOSE CONTACT LENSES WORKING?
LIKE A CHARM, LOVE. WE'RE READY.
DIABLO AND CHEETAH?
GOOD TO GO.
SAME HERE.
PERFECT. ALL TWELVE BOARD MEMBERS ARE NOW MARKED. THESE ARE OUR TARGETS...YOUR ORDERS ARE TO TAKE THEM ALIVE.

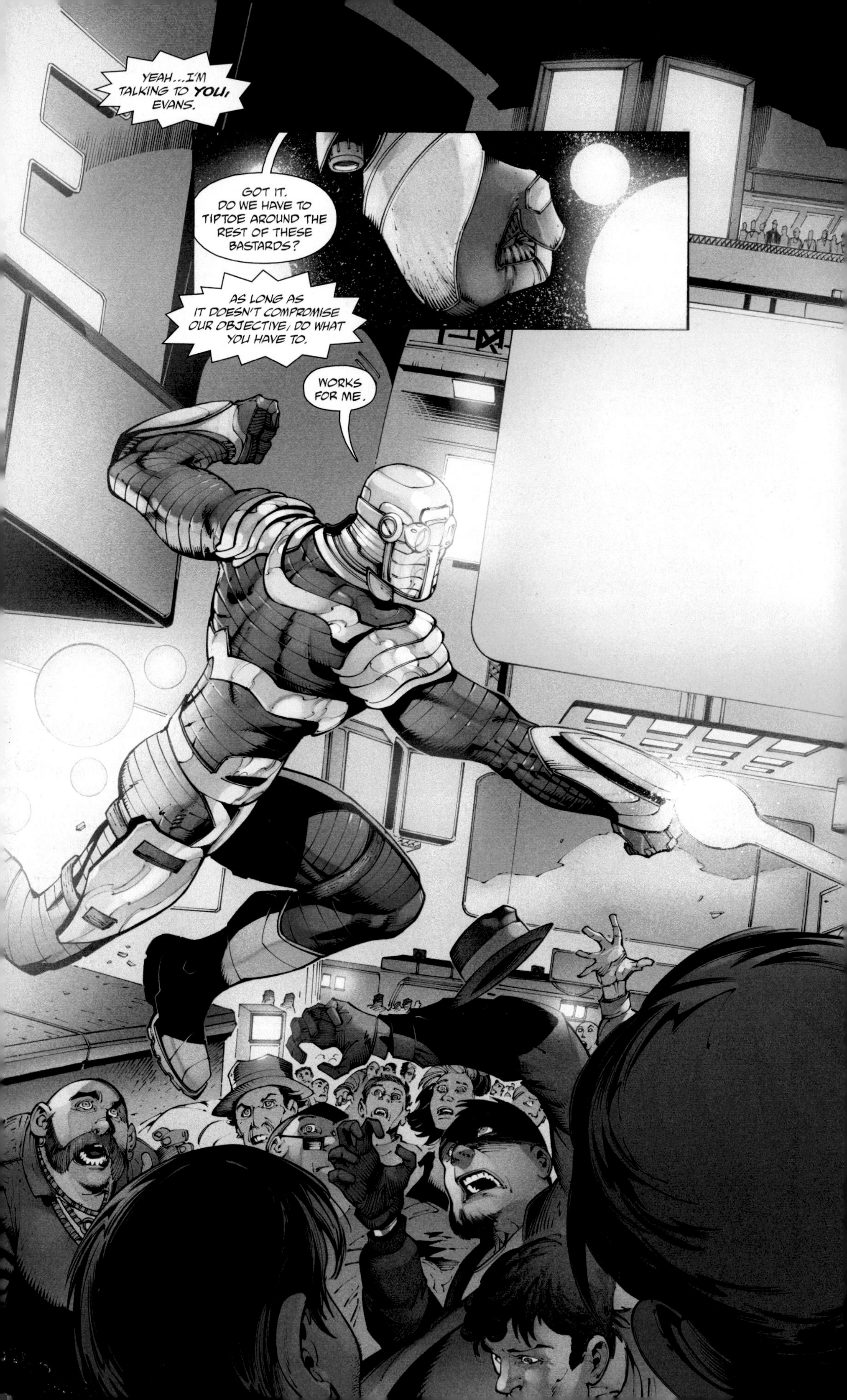
YEAH...I'M TALKING TO YOU, EVANS.
GOT IT. DO WE HAVE TO TIPTOE AROUND THE REST OF THESE BASTARDS?
AS LONG AS IT DOESN'T COMPROMISE OUR OBJECTIVE, DO WHAT YOU HAVE TO.
WORKS FOR ME.

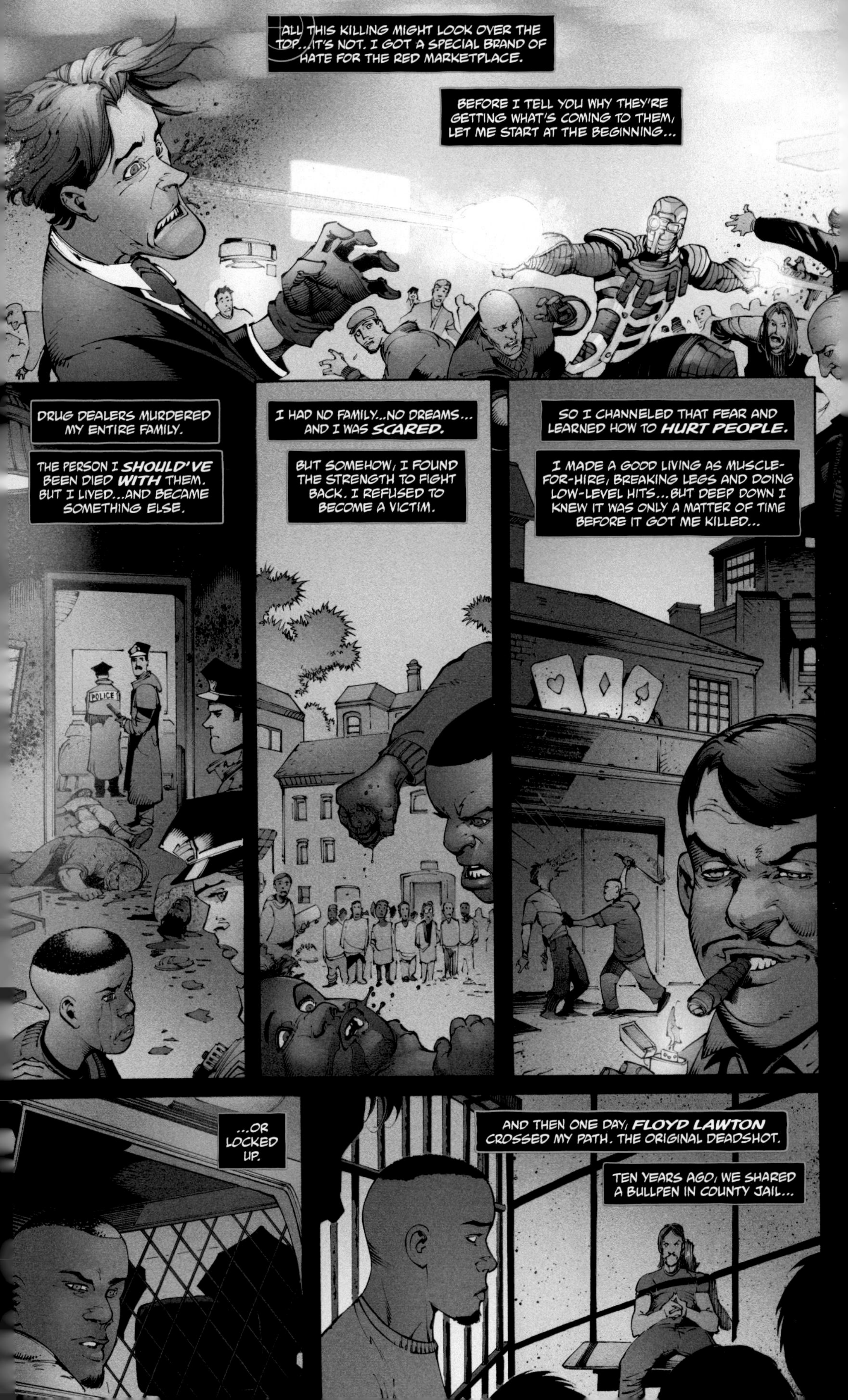

ALL THIS KILLING MIGHT LOOK OVER THE TOP... IT'S NOT. I GOT A SPECIAL BRAND OF HATE FOR THE RED MARKETPLACE.
BEFORE I TELL YOU WHY THEY'RE GETTING WHAT'S COMING TO THEM, LET ME START AT THE BEGINNING...
DRUG DEALERS MURDERED MY ENTIRE FAMILY.
THE PERSON I SHOULD'VE BEEN DIED WITH THEM. BUT I LIVED...AND BECAME SOMETHING ELSE.
POLICE
I HAD NO FAMILY...NO DREAMS... AND I WAS SCARED.
BUT SOMEHOW, I FOUND THE STRENGTH TO FIGHT BACK. I REFUSED TO BECOME A VICTIM.
SO I CHANNELED THAT FEAR AND LEARNED HOW TO HURT PEOPLE.
I MADE A GOOD LIVING AS MUSCLE-FOR-HIRE, BREAKING LEGS AND DOING LOW-LEVEL HITS...BUT DEEP DOWN I KNEW IT WAS ONLY A MATTER OF TIME BEFORE IT GOT ME KILLED...
...OR LOCKED UP.
AND THEN ONE DAY, FLOYD LAWTON CROSSED MY PATH. THE ORIGINAL DEADSHOT.
TEN YEARS AGO, WE SHARED A BULLPEN IN COUNTY JAIL...

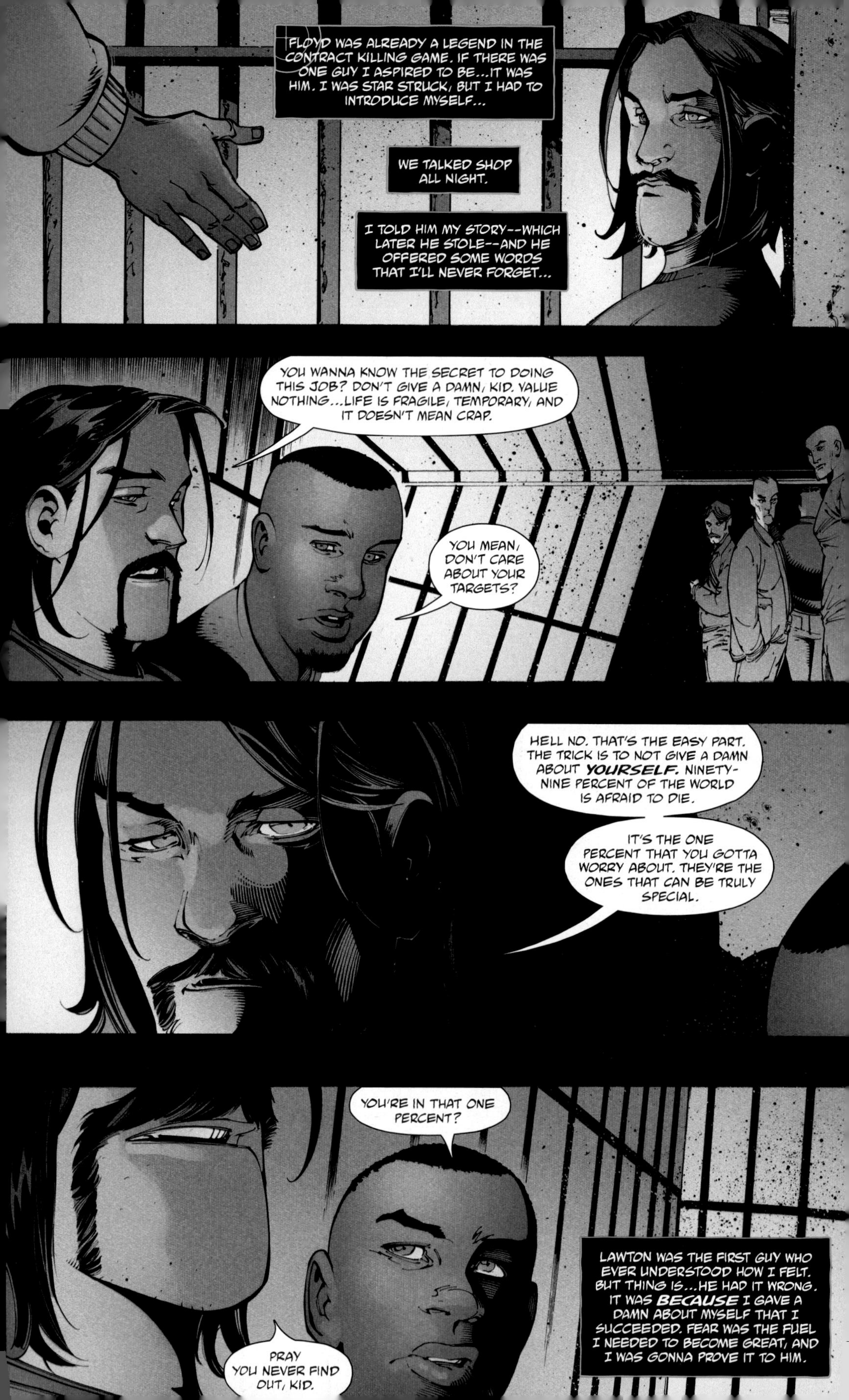

FLOYD WAS ALREADY A LEGEND IN THE CONTRACT KILLING GAME. IF THERE WAS ONE GUY I ASPIRED TO BE...IT WAS HIM. I WAS STAR STRUCK, BUT I HAD TO INTRODUCE MYSELF...
WE TALKED SHOP ALL NIGHT.
I TOLD HIM MY STORY--WHICH LATER HE STOLE--AND HE OFFERED SOME WORDS THAT I'LL NEVER FORGET...
YOU WANNA KNOW THE SECRET TO DOING THIS JOB? DON'T GIVE A DAMN, KID. VALUE NOTHING...LIFE IS FRAGILE, TEMPORARY, AND IT DOESN'T MEAN CRAP.
YOU MEAN, DON'T CARE ABOUT YOUR TARGETS?
HELL NO. THAT'S THE EASY PART. THE TRICK IS TO NOT GIVE A DAMN ABOUT **YOURSELF.** NINETY-NINE PERCENT OF THE WORLD IS AFRAID TO DIE.
IT'S THE ONE PERCENT THAT YOU GOTTA WORRY ABOUT. THEY'RE THE ONES THAT CAN BE TRULY SPECIAL.
YOU'RE IN THAT ONE PERCENT?
PRAY YOU NEVER FIND OUT, KID.
LAWTON WAS THE FIRST GUY WHO EVER UNDERSTOOD HOW I FELT. BUT THING IS...HE HAD IT WRONG. IT WAS ***BECAUSE*** I GAVE A DAMN ABOUT MYSELF THAT I SUCCEEDED. FEAR WAS THE FUEL I NEEDED TO BECOME GREAT, AND I WAS GONNA PROVE IT TO HIM.

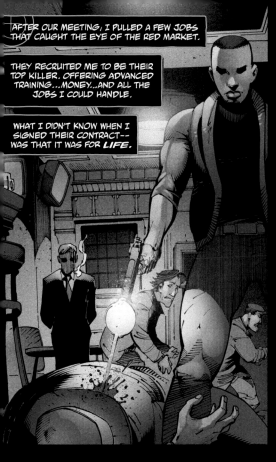

AFTER OUR MEETING, I PULLED A FEW JOBS THAT CAUGHT THE EYE OF THE RED MARKET.

THEY RECRUITED ME TO BE THEIR TOP KILLER, OFFERING ADVANCED TRAINING...MONEY...AND ALL THE JOBS I COULD HANDLE.

WHAT I DIDN'T KNOW WHEN I SIGNED THEIR CONTRACT-- WAS THAT IT WAS FOR *LIFE.*

AFTER TWO YEARS OF TRAINING AND ANOTHER SEVEN PROVING THAT I'M THE BEST DAMN KILLER IN THE WORLD, I WANTED TO STRIKE OUT ON MY OWN.

I ALSO NEEDED TO MAKE DEADSHOT PAY FOR STEALING MY FAMILY TRAGEDY AND PAWNING IT OFF AS HIS. HE MUST'VE THOUGHT I WAS SOME KIND OF PUNK. I WAS GONNA SHOW HIM DIFFERENT.

THE RED MARKET REFUSED TO RELEASE MY CONTRACT AND I DIDN'T TAKE NO FOR AN ANSWER.

THEY TRIED TO KILL ME. I TRIED TO KILL THEM...

ONE YEAR AND DOZENS OF BODIES LATER, I MET AMANDA WALLER...WHO WAS LOOKING TO REPLACE THE MIGHTY DEADSHOT--WHO TURNED OUT TO BE A GOVERNMENT STOOGE.

TALK ABOUT SERENDIPITY.

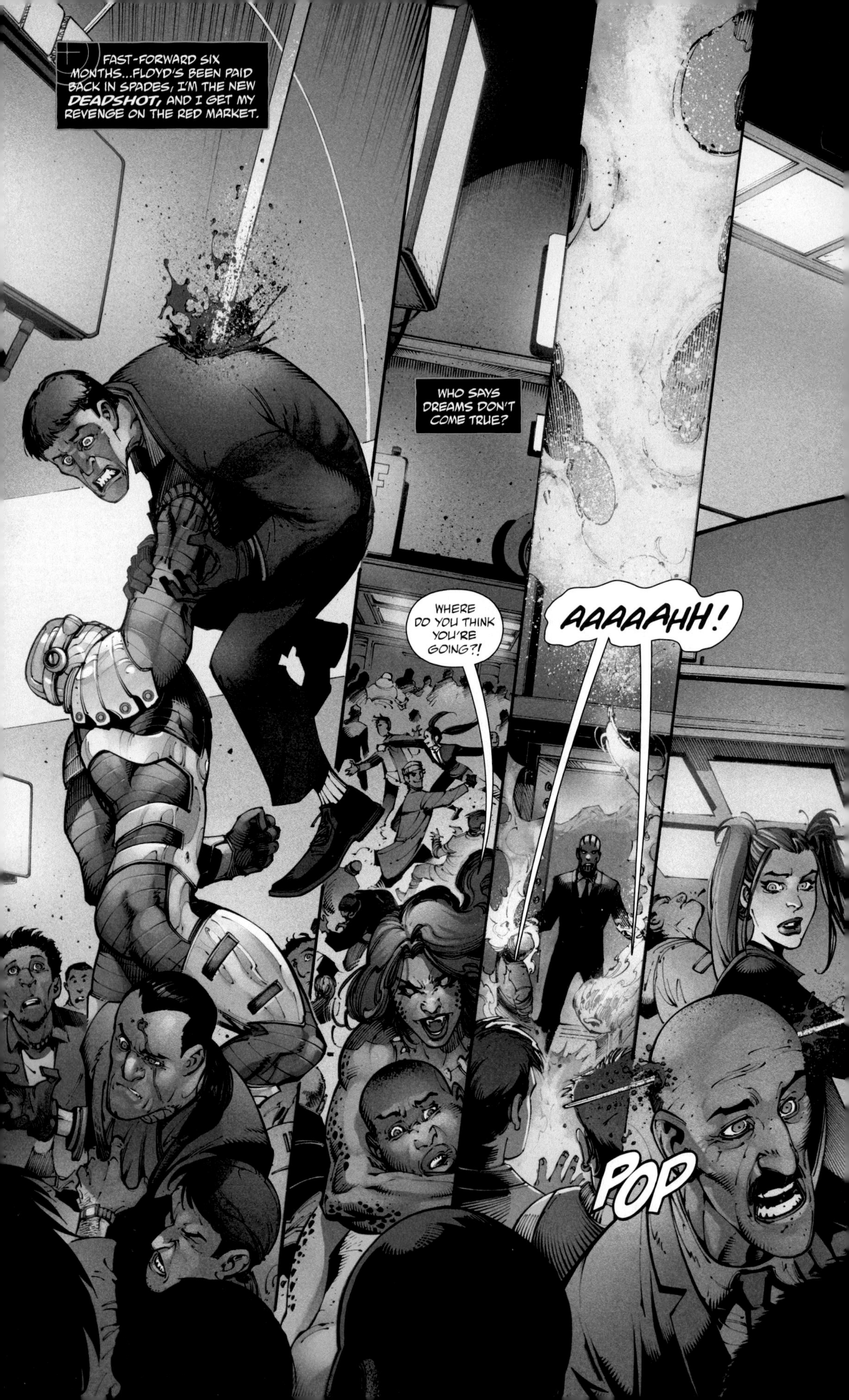
FAST-FORWARD SIX MONTHS...FLOYD'S BEEN PAID BACK IN SPADES, I'M THE NEW **DEADSHOT,** AND I GET MY REVENGE ON THE RED MARKET.
WHO SAYS DREAMS DON'T COME TRUE?
WHERE DO YOU THINK YOU'RE GOING?!
AAAAAHH!
POP

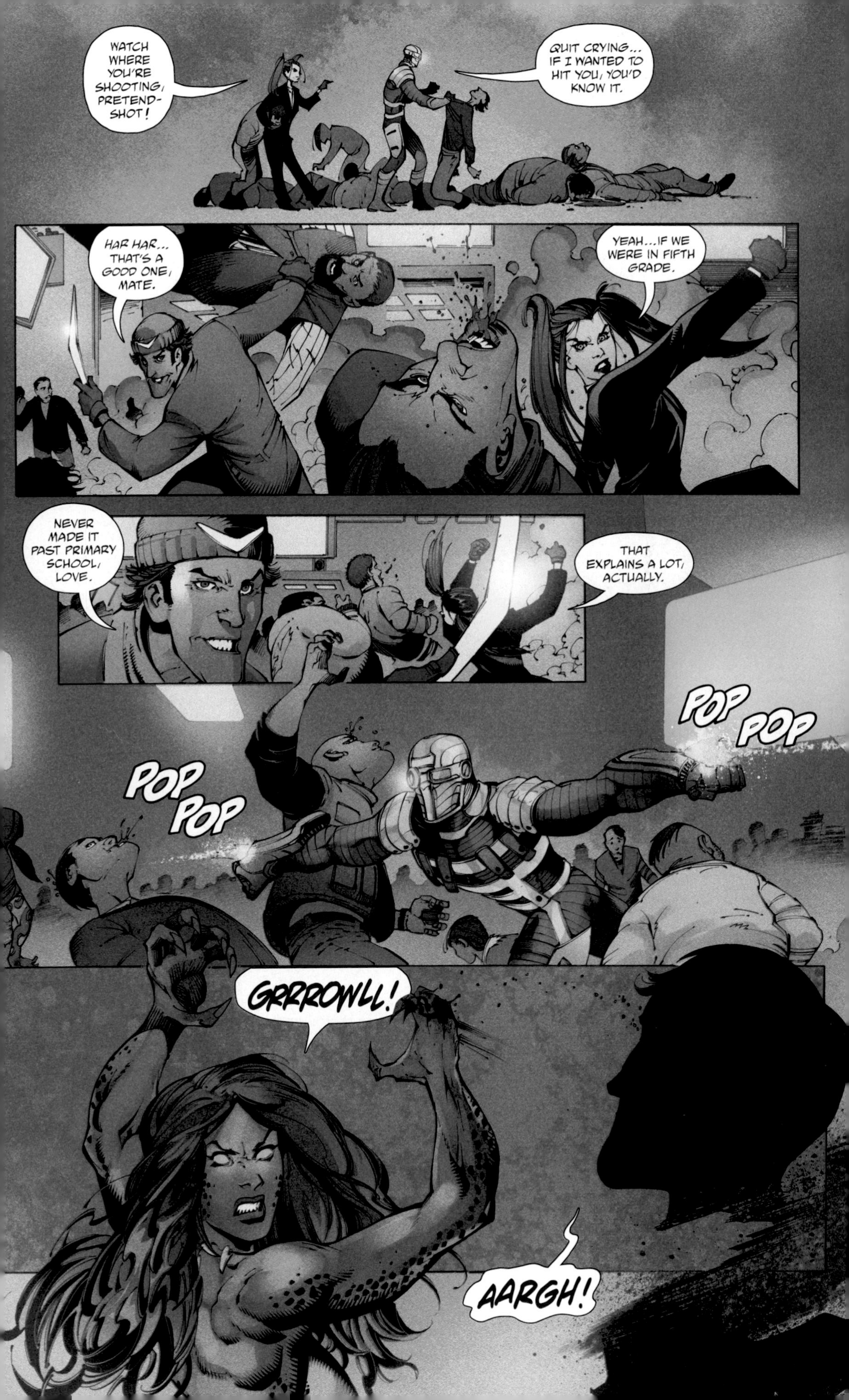
WATCH WHERE YOU'RE SHOOTING, PRETEND-SHOT!
QUIT CRYING... IF I WANTED TO HIT YOU, YOU'D KNOW IT.
HAR HAR... THAT'S A GOOD ONE, MATE.
YEAH...IF WE WERE IN FIFTH GRADE.
NEVER MADE IT PAST PRIMARY SCHOOL, LOVE.
THAT EXPLAINS A LOT, ACTUALLY.
POP POP
POP POP
GRRROWLL!
AARGH!

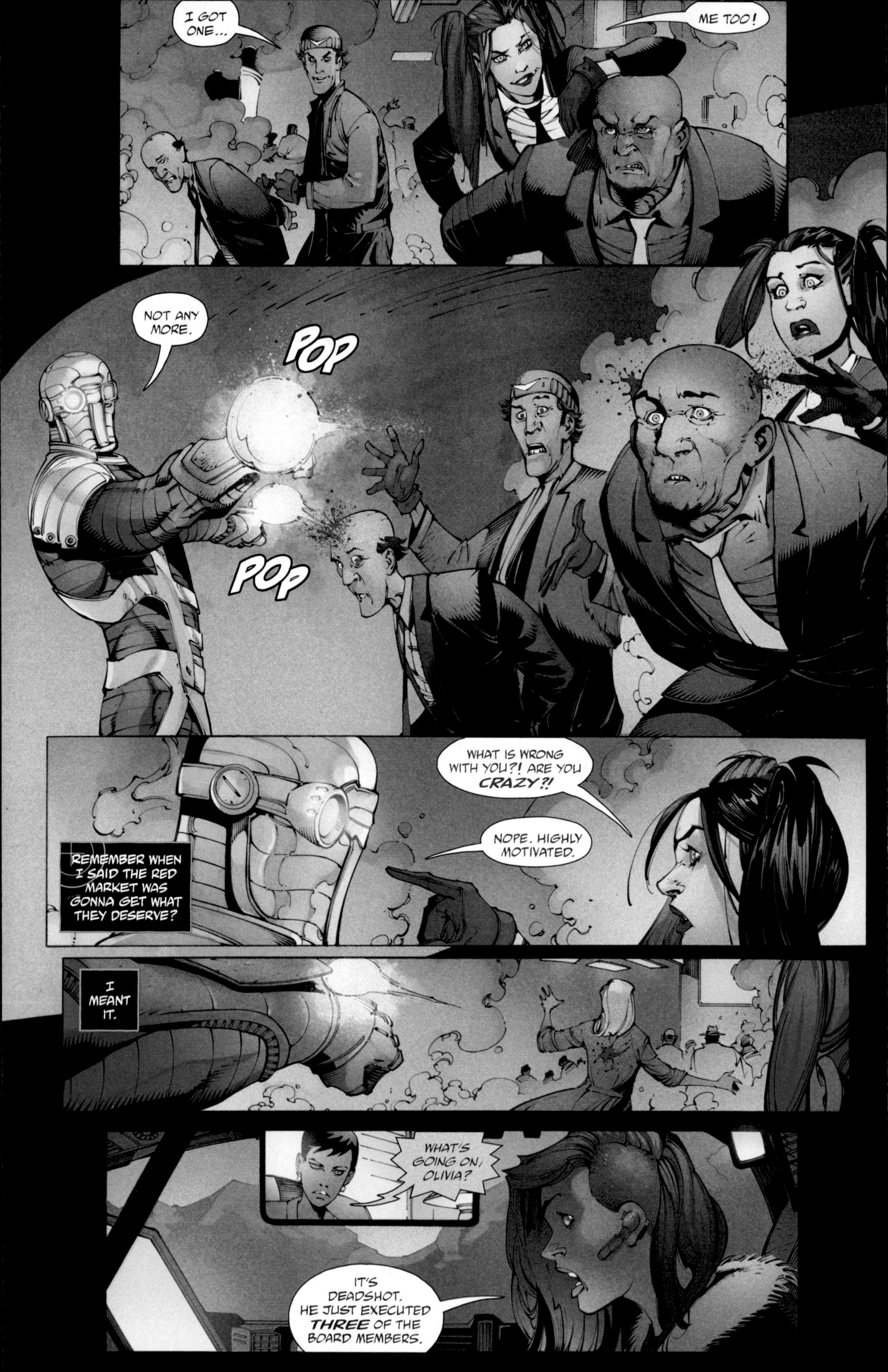
I GOT ONE...
ME TOO!
NOT ANY MORE.
POP
POP
WHAT IS WRONG WITH YOU?! ARE YOU CRAZY?!
NOPE. HIGHLY MOTIVATED.
REMEMBER WHEN I SAID THE RED MARKET WAS GONNA GET WHAT THEY DESERVE?
I MEANT IT.
WHAT'S GOING ON, OLIVIA?
IT'S DEADSHOT. HE JUST EXECUTED THREE OF THE BOARD MEMBERS.

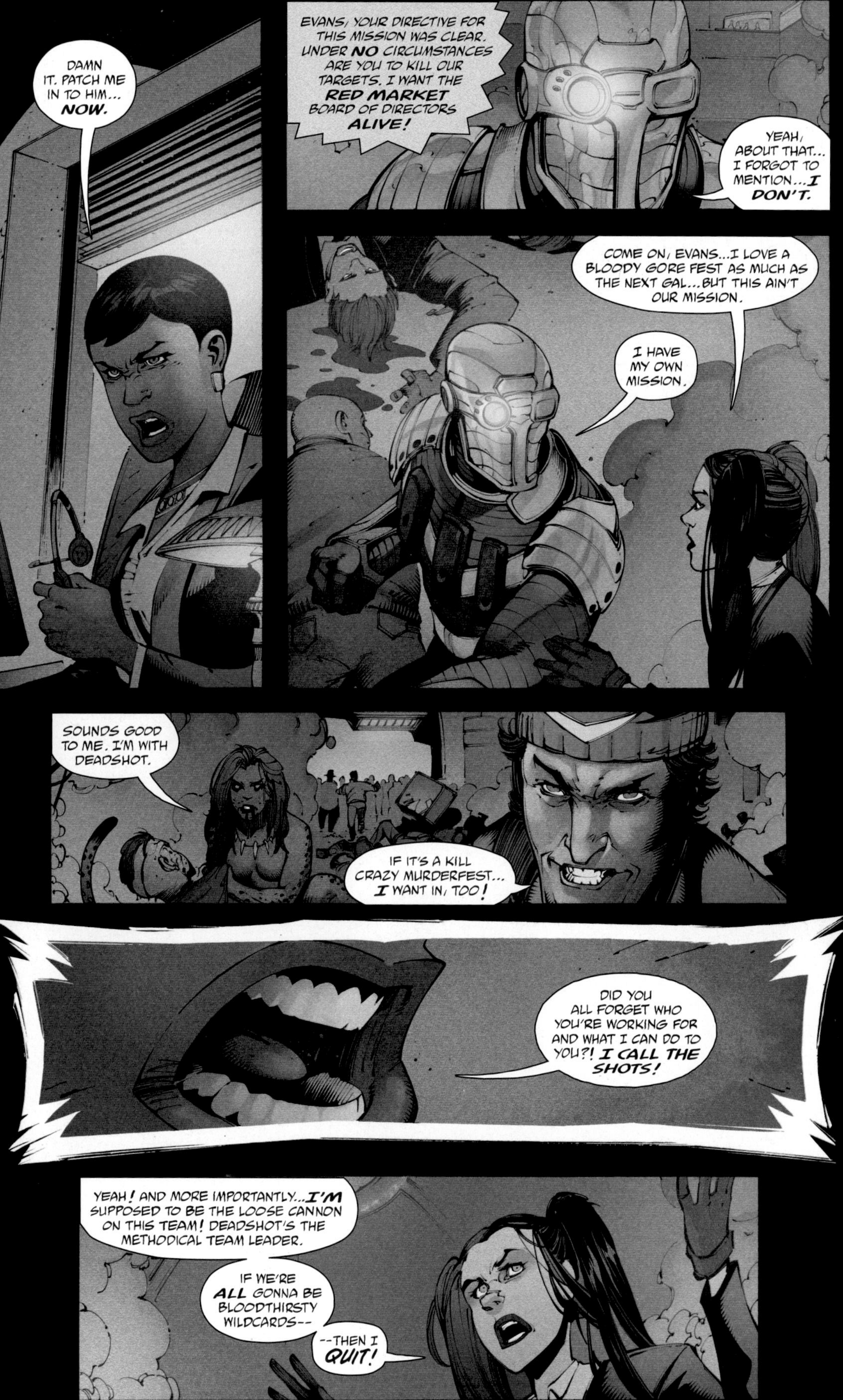
DAMN IT. PATCH ME IN TO HIM... NOW.
EVANS, YOUR DIRECTIVE FOR THIS MISSION WAS CLEAR. UNDER NO CIRCUMSTANCES ARE YOU TO KILL OUR TARGETS. I WANT THE RED MARKET BOARD OF DIRECTORS ALIVE!
YEAH, ABOUT THAT... I FORGOT TO MENTION... I DON'T.
COME ON, EVANS...I LOVE A BLOODY GORE FEST AS MUCH AS THE NEXT GAL...BUT THIS AIN'T OUR MISSION.
I HAVE MY OWN MISSION.
SOUNDS GOOD TO ME. I'M WITH DEADSHOT.
IF IT'S A KILL CRAZY MURDERFEST... I WANT IN, TOO!
DID YOU ALL FORGET WHO YOU'RE WORKING FOR AND WHAT I CAN DO TO YOU?! I CALL THE SHOTS!
YEAH! AND MORE IMPORTANTLY...I'M SUPPOSED TO BE THE LOOSE CANNON ON THIS TEAM! DEADSHOT'S THE METHODICAL TEAM LEADER.
IF WE'RE ALL GONNA BE BLOODTHIRSTY WILDCARDS--
--THEN I QUIT!

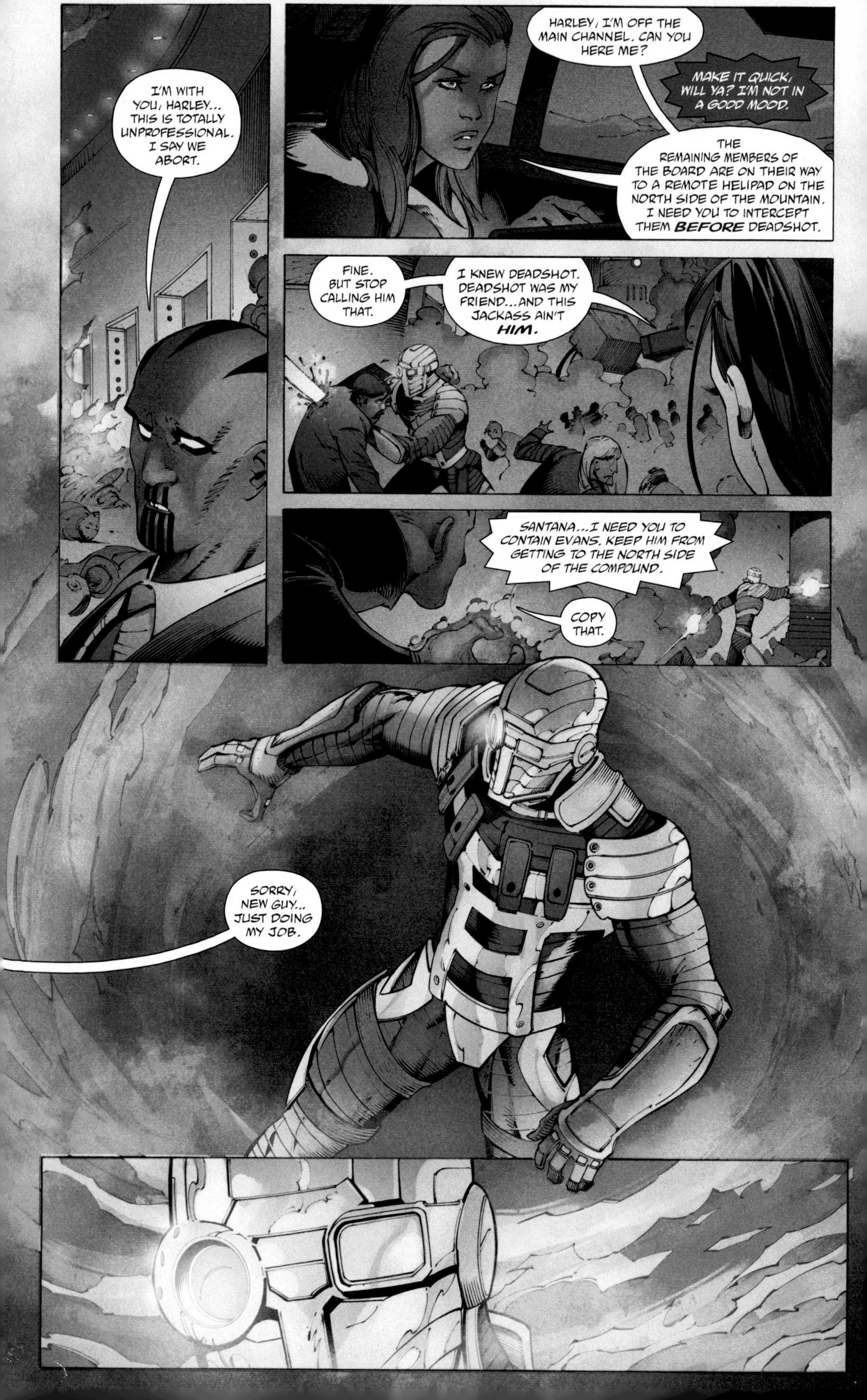
I'M WITH YOU, HARLEY... THIS IS TOTALLY UNPROFESSIONAL. I SAY WE ABORT.
HARLEY, I'M OFF THE MAIN CHANNEL. CAN YOU HERE ME?
MAKE IT QUICK, WILL YA? I'M NOT IN A GOOD MOOD.
THE REMAINING MEMBERS OF THE BOARD ARE ON THEIR WAY TO A REMOTE HELIPAD ON THE NORTH SIDE OF THE MOUNTAIN. I NEED YOU TO INTERCEPT THEM BEFORE DEADSHOT.
I KNEW DEADSHOT. DEADSHOT WAS MY FRIEND...AND THIS JACKASS AIN'T HIM.
FINE. BUT STOP CALLING HIM THAT.
SANTANA...I NEED YOU TO CONTAIN EVANS. KEEP HIM FROM GETTING TO THE NORTH SIDE OF THE COMPOUND.
COPY THAT.
SORRY, NEW GUY... JUST DOING MY JOB.

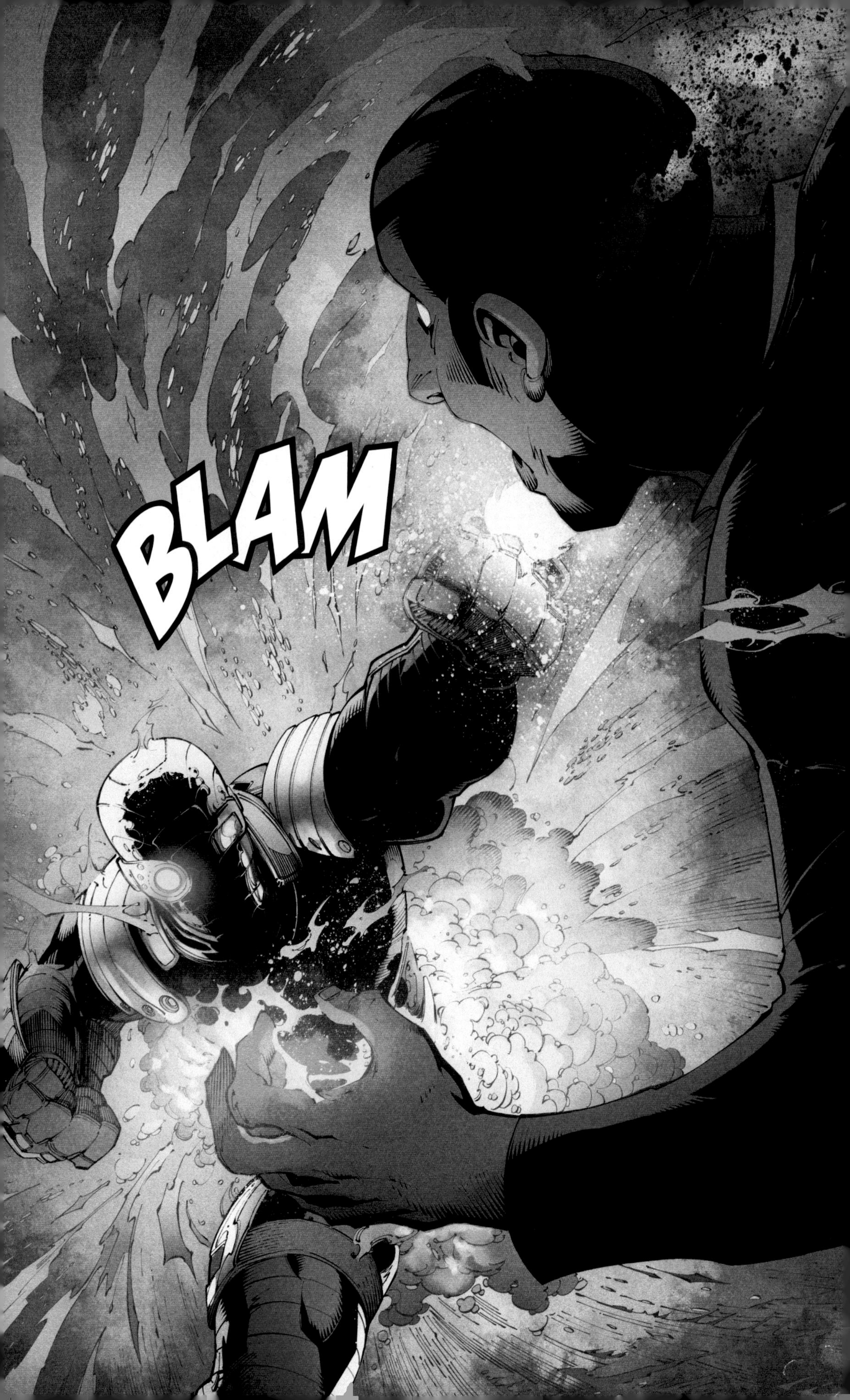
BLAM

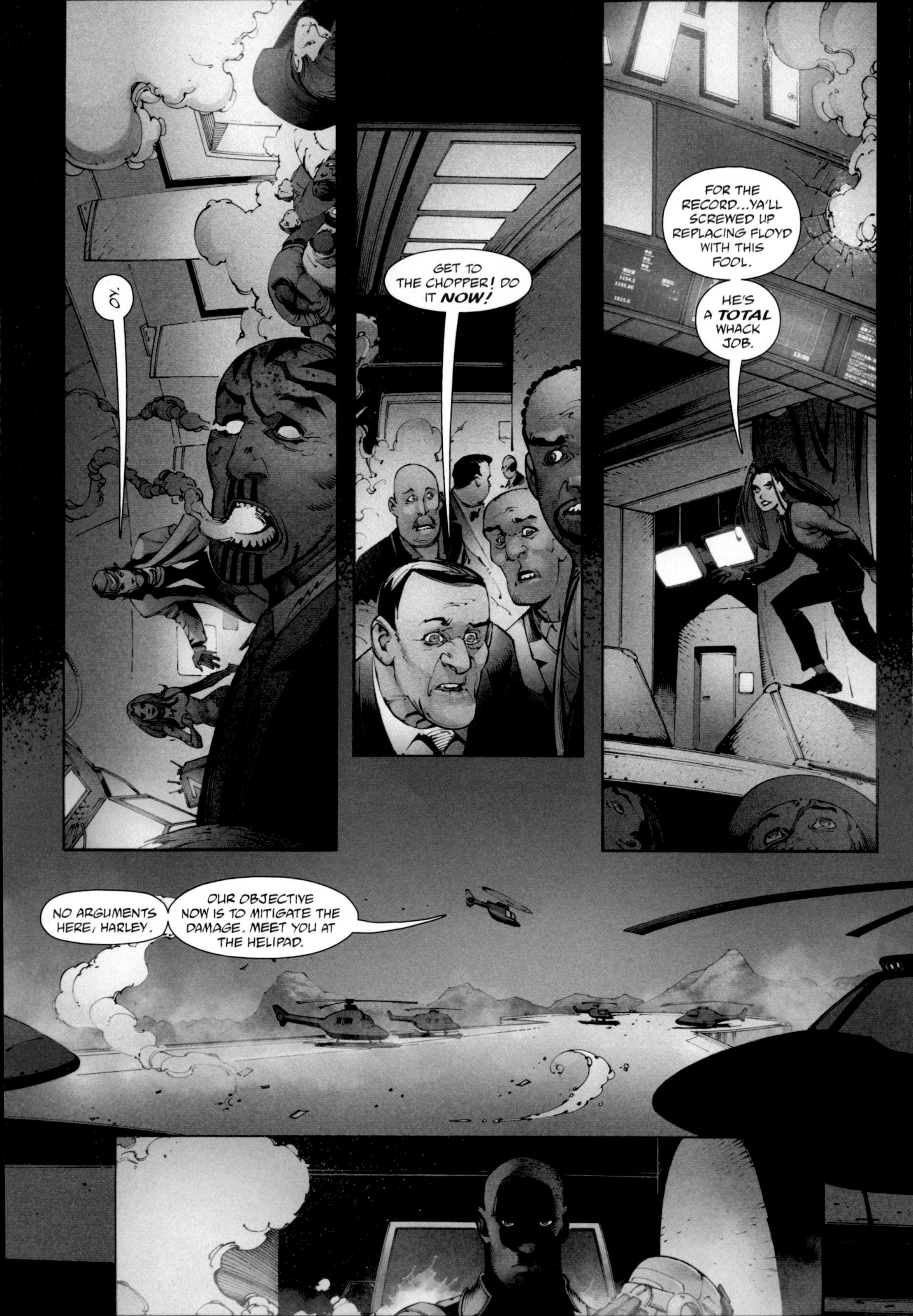

OY.
GET TO THE CHOPPER! DO IT **NOW!**
FOR THE RECORD...YA'LL SCREWED UP REPLACING FLOYD WITH THIS FOOL.
HE'S A **TOTAL** WHACK JOB.
NO ARGUMENTS HERE, HARLEY.
OUR OBJECTIVE NOW IS TO MITIGATE THE DAMAGE. MEET YOU AT THE HELIPAD.

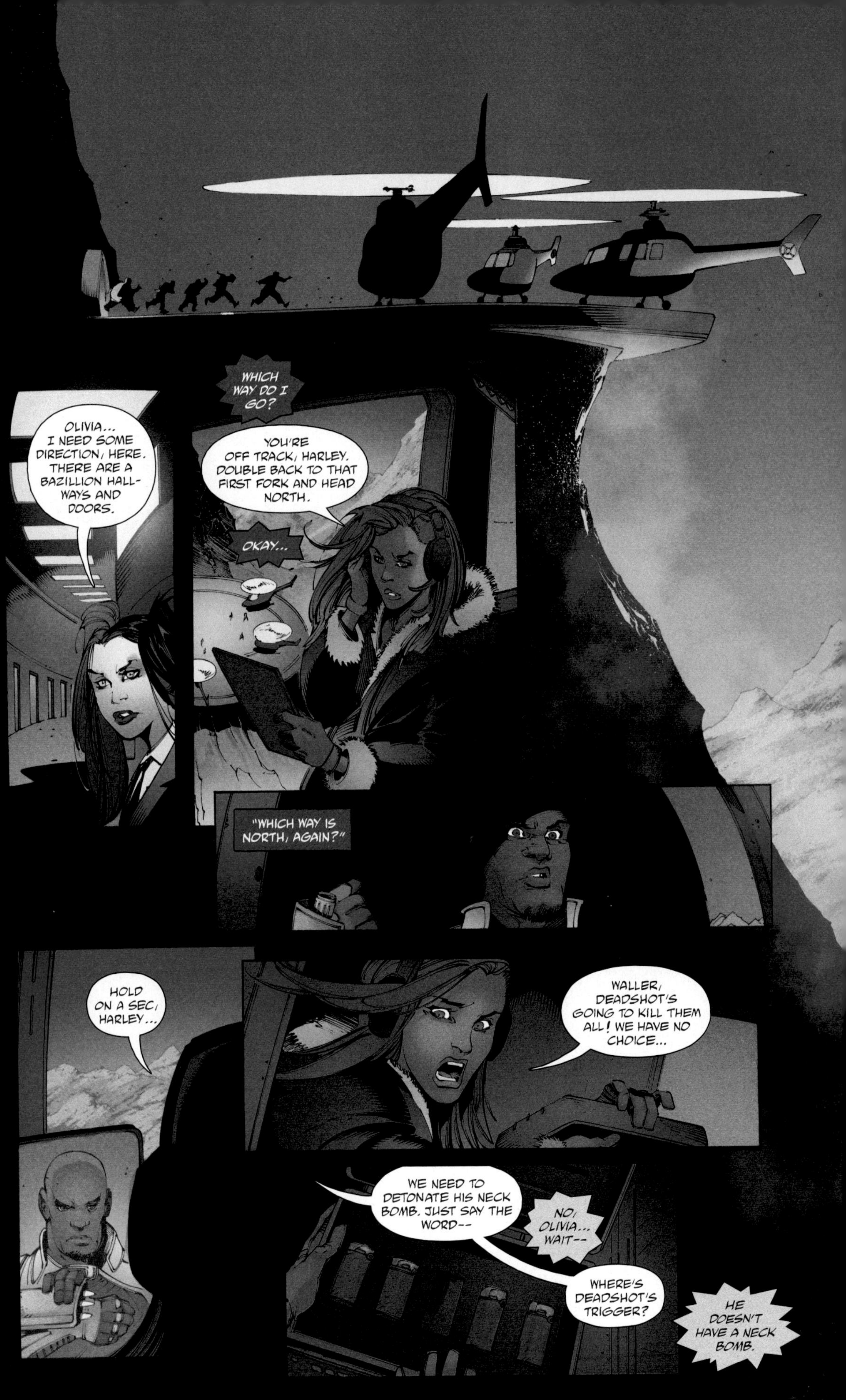
WHICH WAY DO I GO?
OLIVIA... I NEED SOME DIRECTION, HERE. THERE ARE A BAZILLION HALL-WAYS AND DOORS.
YOU'RE OFF TRACK, HARLEY. DOUBLE BACK TO THAT FIRST FORK AND HEAD NORTH.
OKAY...
"WHICH WAY IS NORTH, AGAIN?"
HOLD ON A SEC, HARLEY...
WALLER, DEADSHOT'S GOING TO KILL THEM ALL! WE HAVE NO CHOICE...
WE NEED TO DETONATE HIS NECK BOMB. JUST SAY THE WORD--
NO, OLIVIA... WAIT--
WHERE'S DEADSHOT'S TRIGGER?
HE DOESN'T HAVE A NECK BOMB.

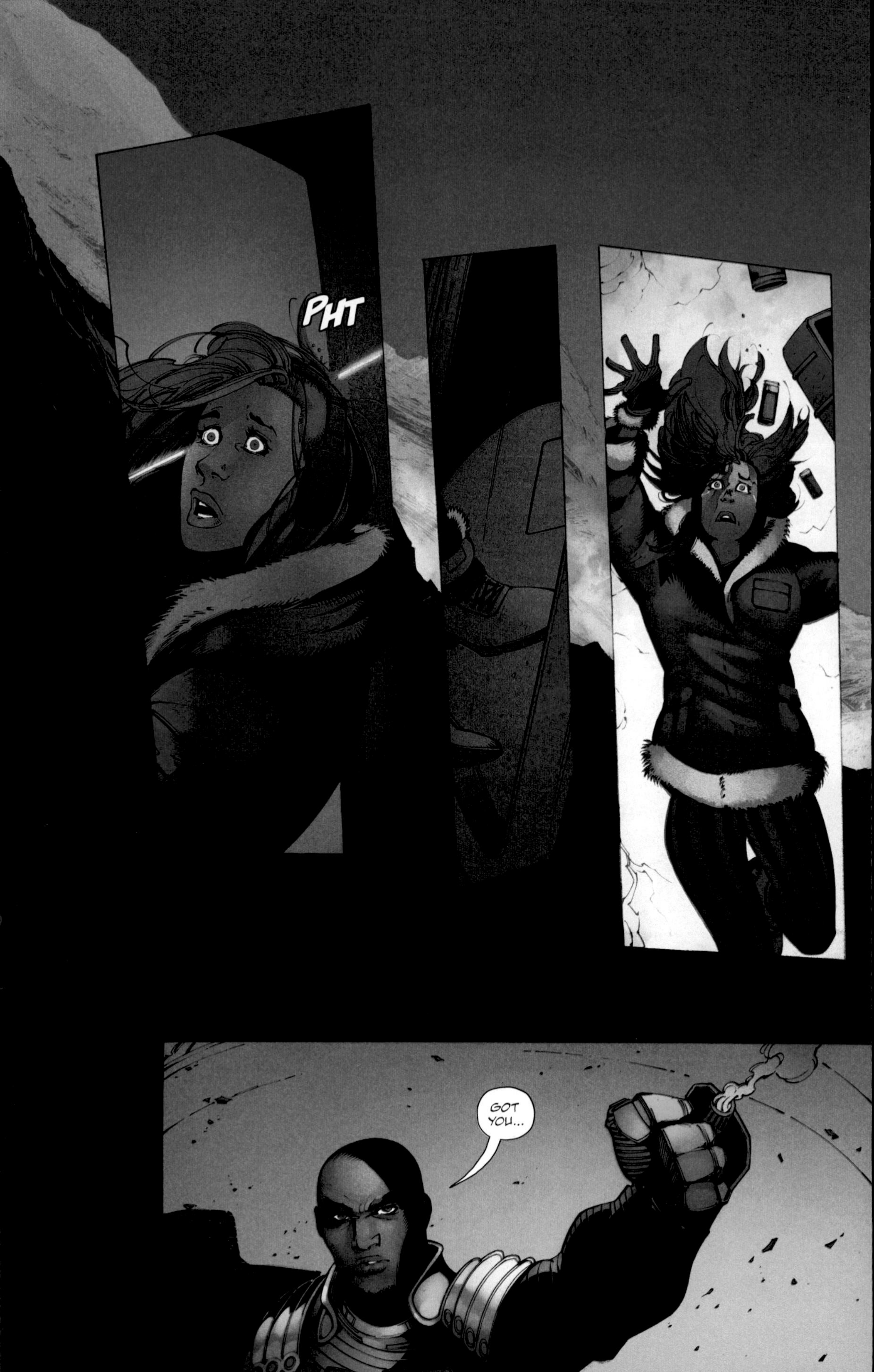
PHT
GOT YOU...

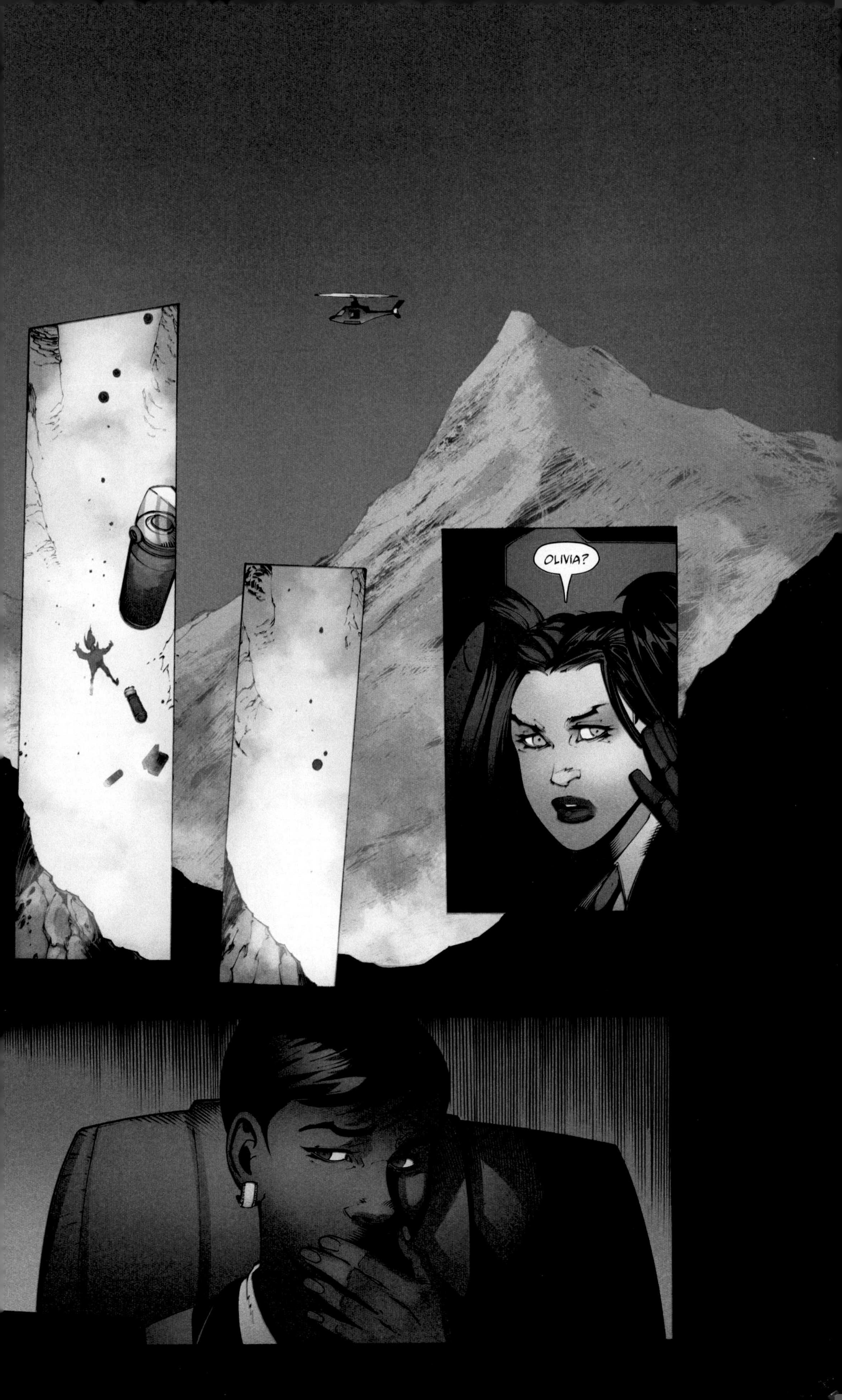
OLIVIA?

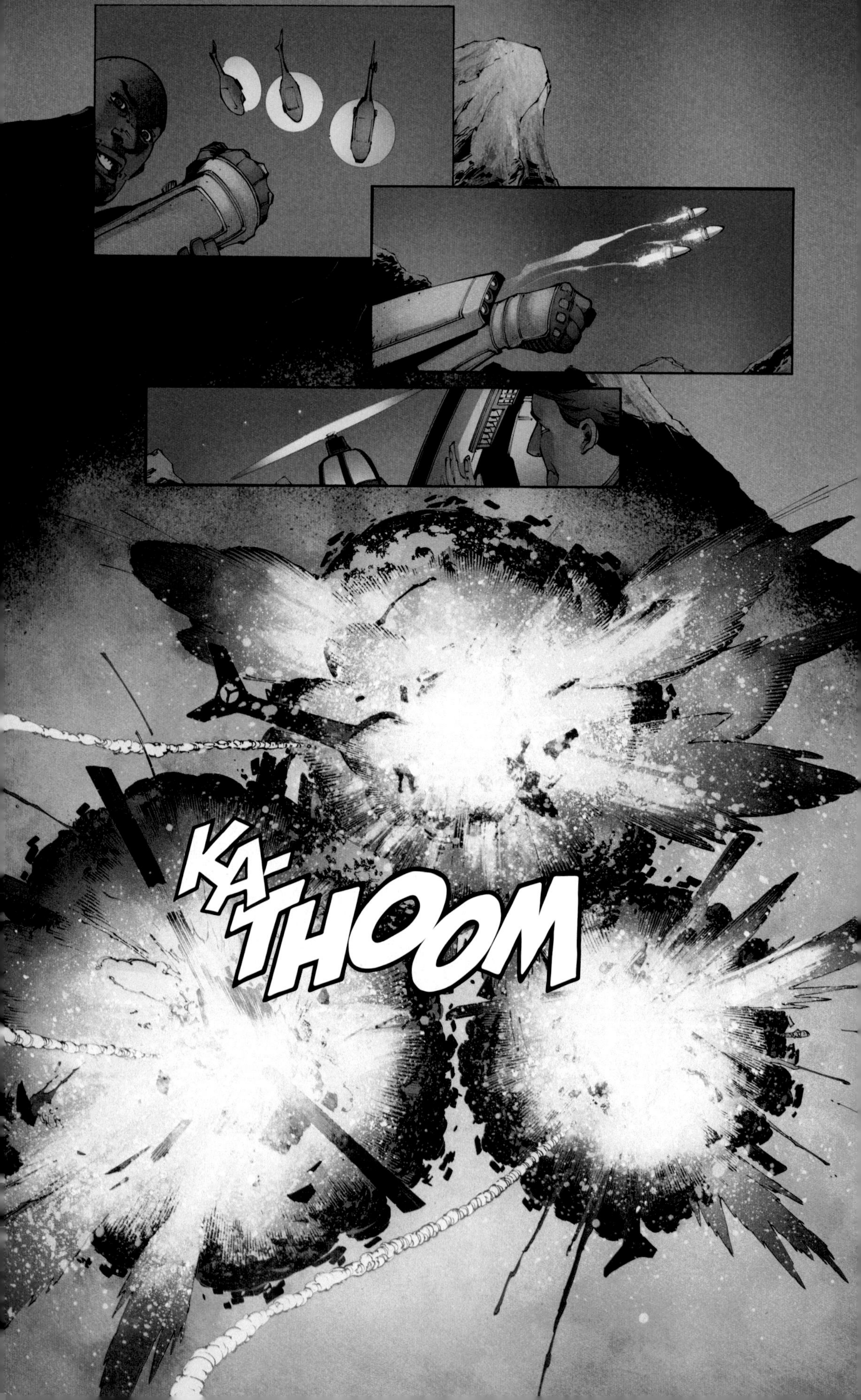
KA-THOOM

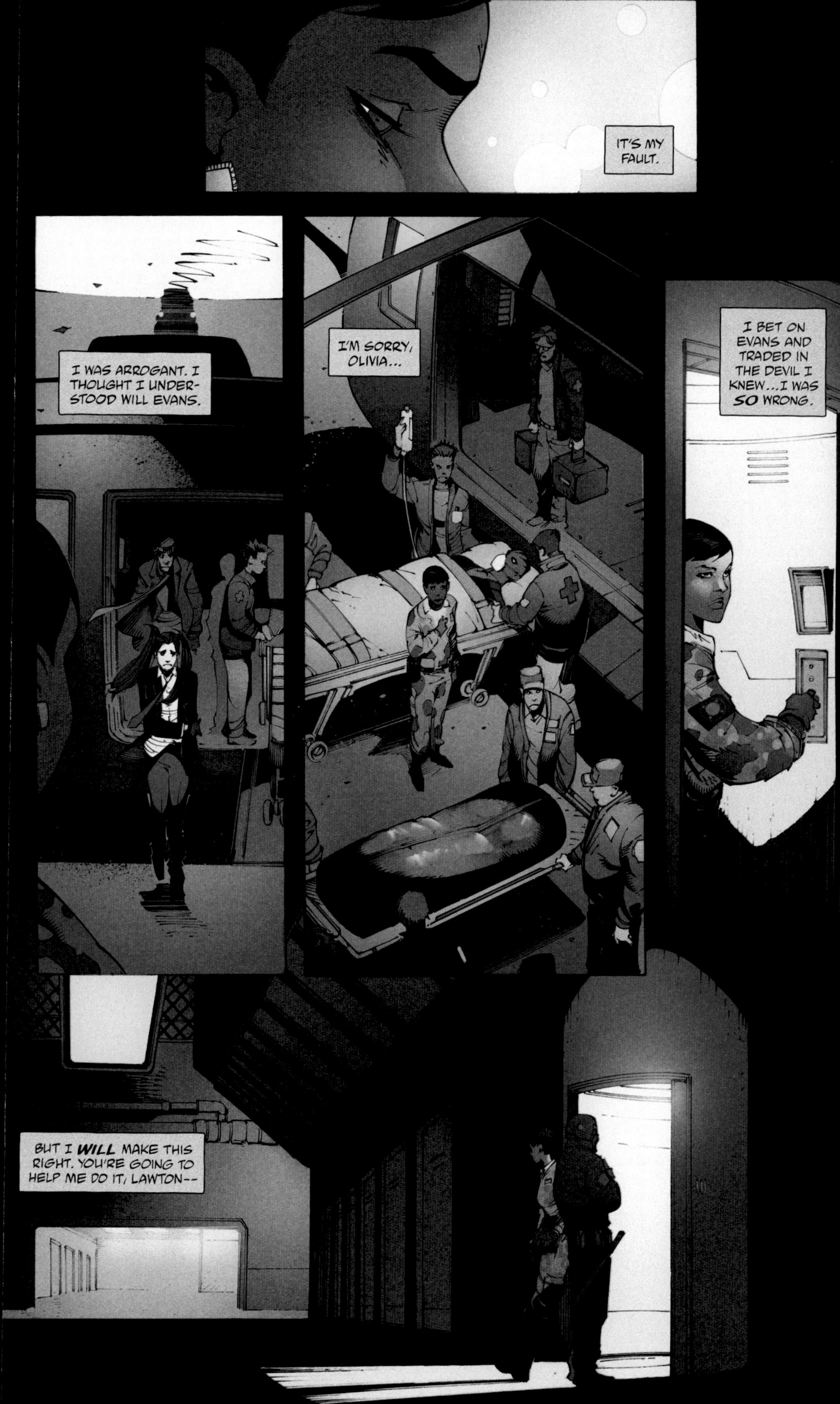
IT'S MY FAULT.
I WAS ARROGANT. I THOUGHT I UNDER-STOOD WILL EVANS.
I'M SORRY, OLIVIA...
I BET ON EVANS AND TRADED IN THE DEVIL I KNEW...I WAS SO WRONG.
BUT I WILL MAKE THIS RIGHT. YOU'RE GOING TO HELP ME DO IT, LAWTON--

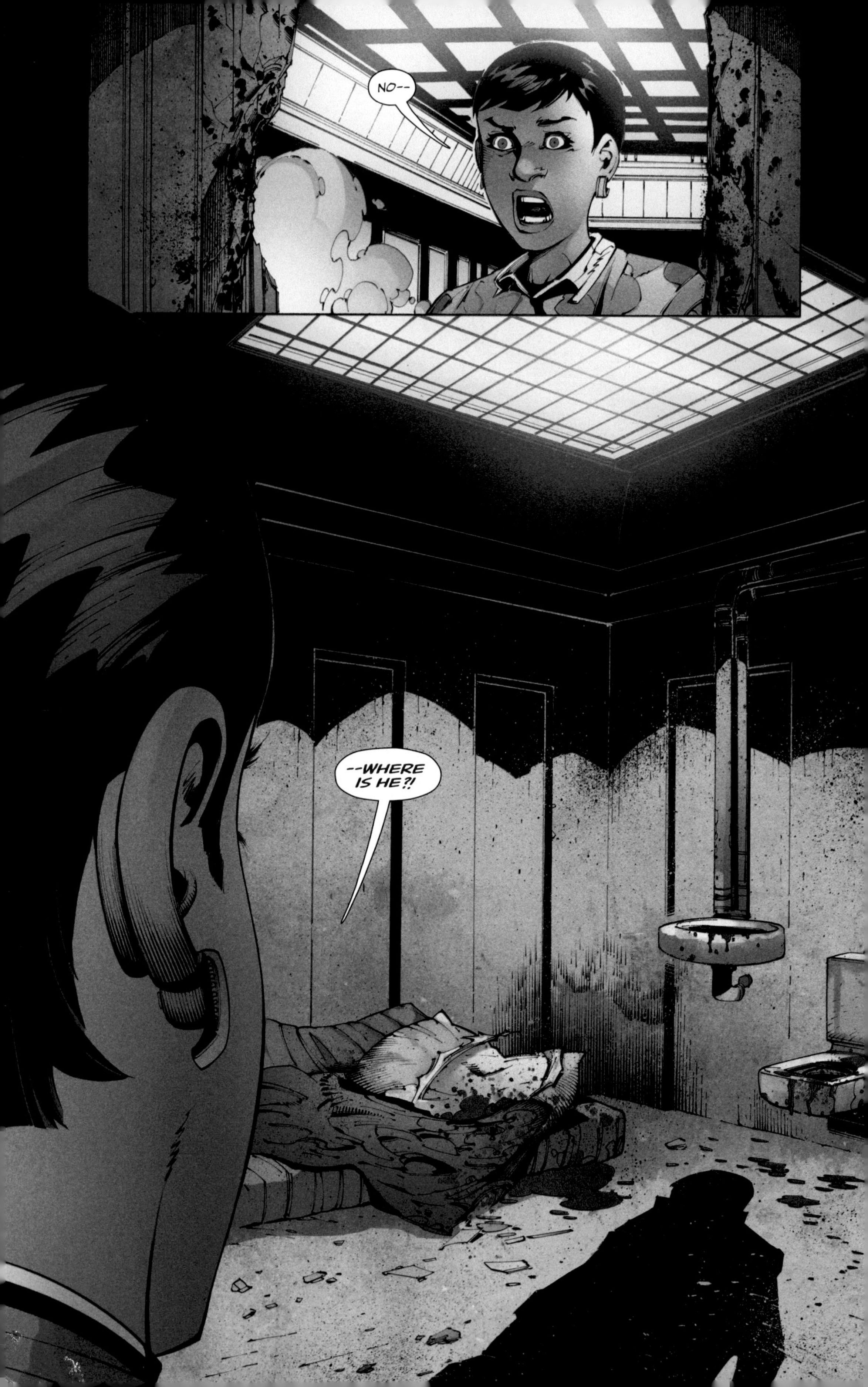
NO--
--WHERE IS HE?!

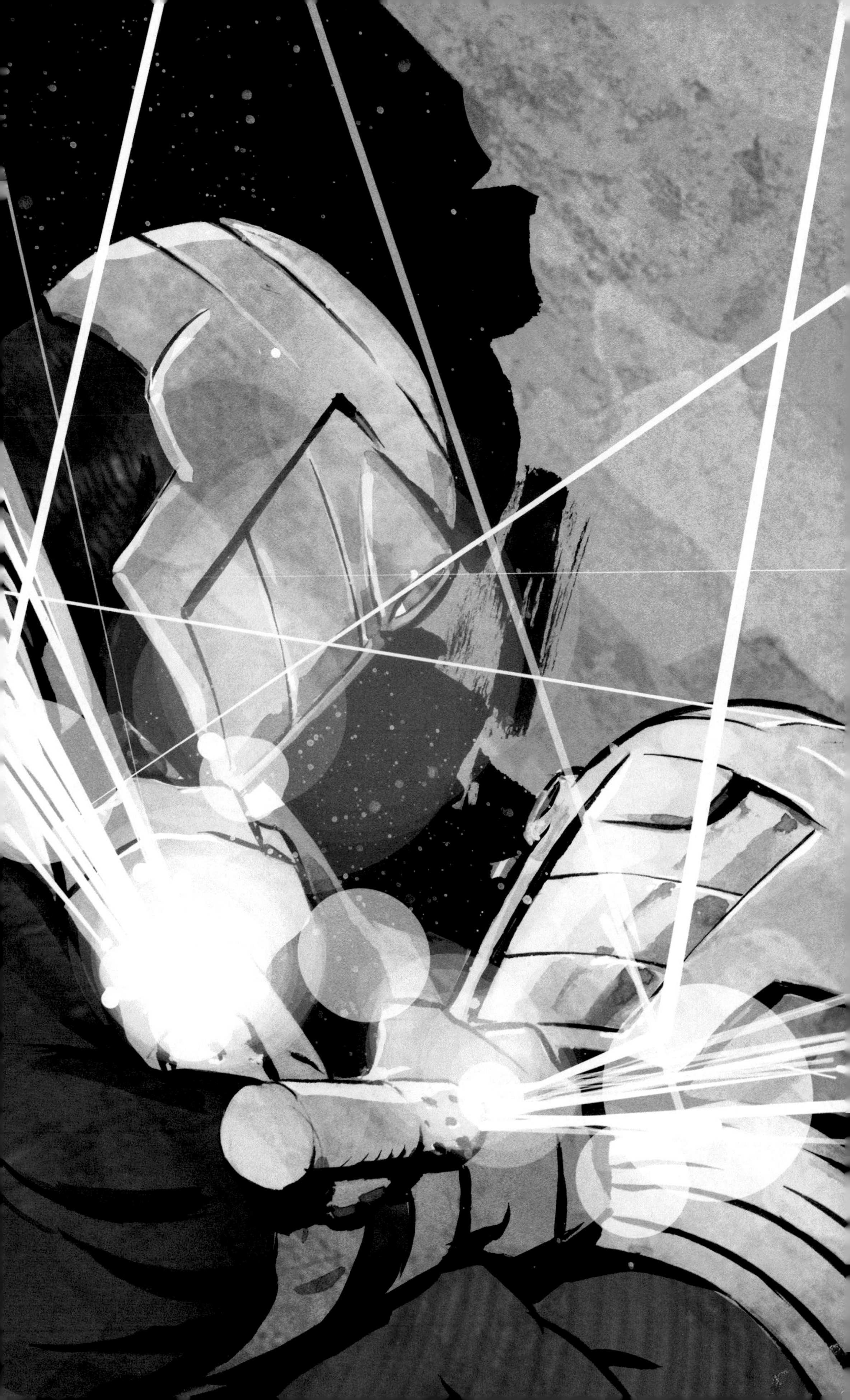

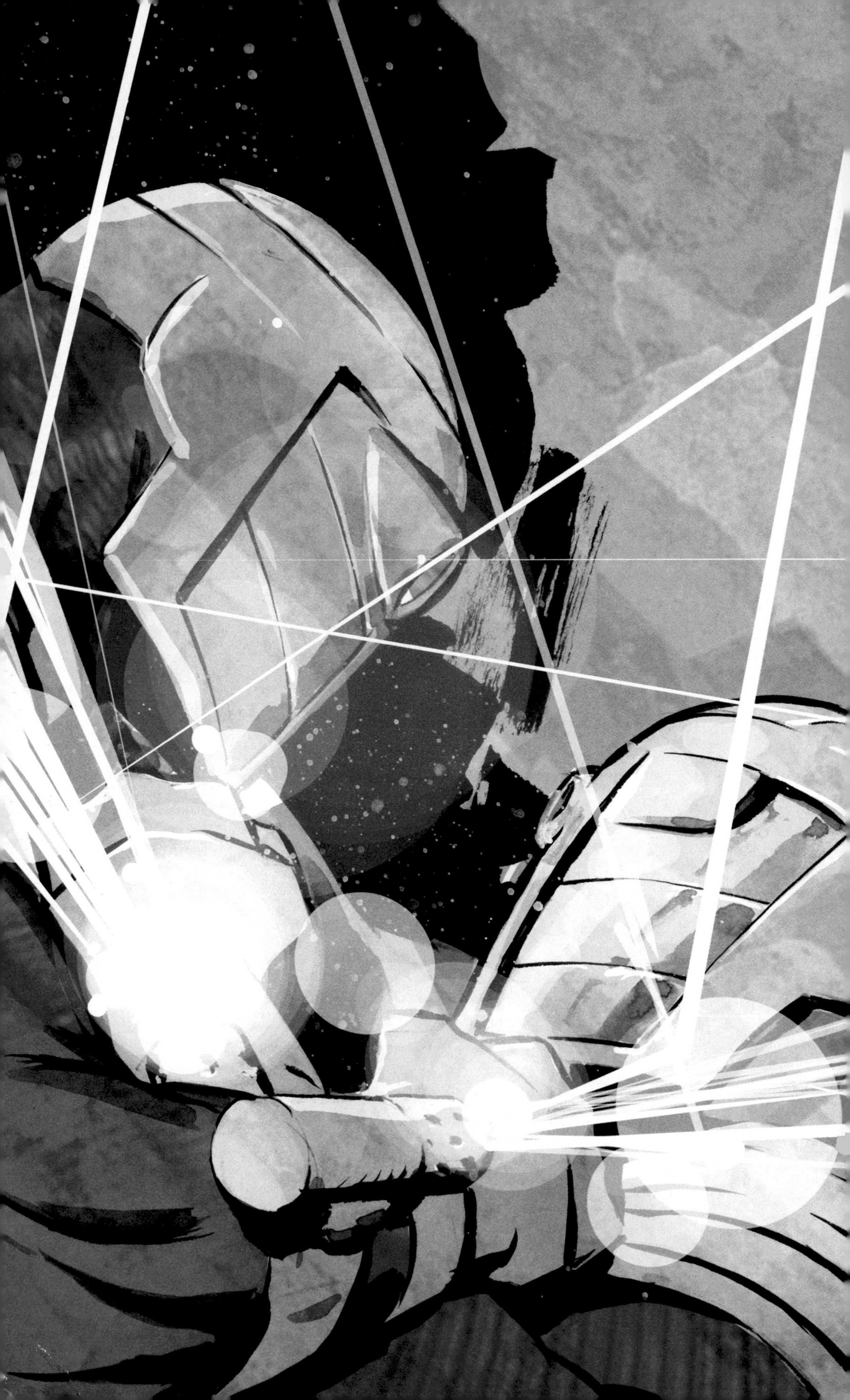

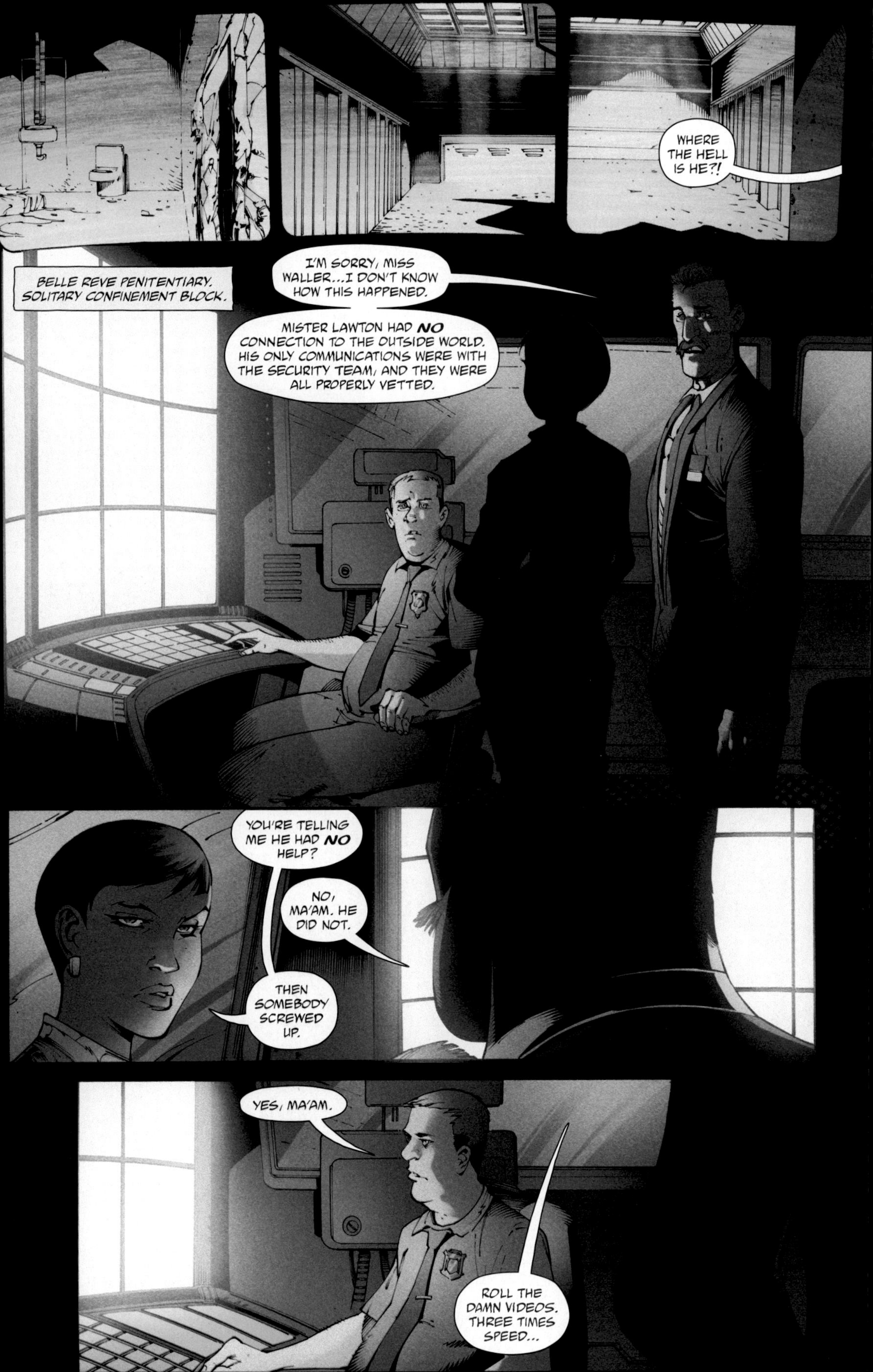
WHERE THE HELL IS HE?!
BELLE REVE PENITENTIARY. SOLITARY CONFINEMENT BLOCK.
I'M SORRY, MISS WALLER...I DON'T KNOW HOW THIS HAPPENED.
MISTER LAWTON HAD NO CONNECTION TO THE OUTSIDE WORLD. HIS ONLY COMMUNICATIONS WERE WITH THE SECURITY TEAM, AND THEY WERE ALL PROPERLY VETTED.
YOU'RE TELLING ME HE HAD NO HELP?
NO, MA'AM. HE DID NOT.
THEN SOMEBODY SCREWED UP.
YES, MA'AM.
ROLL THE DAMN VIDEOS. THREE TIMES SPEED...

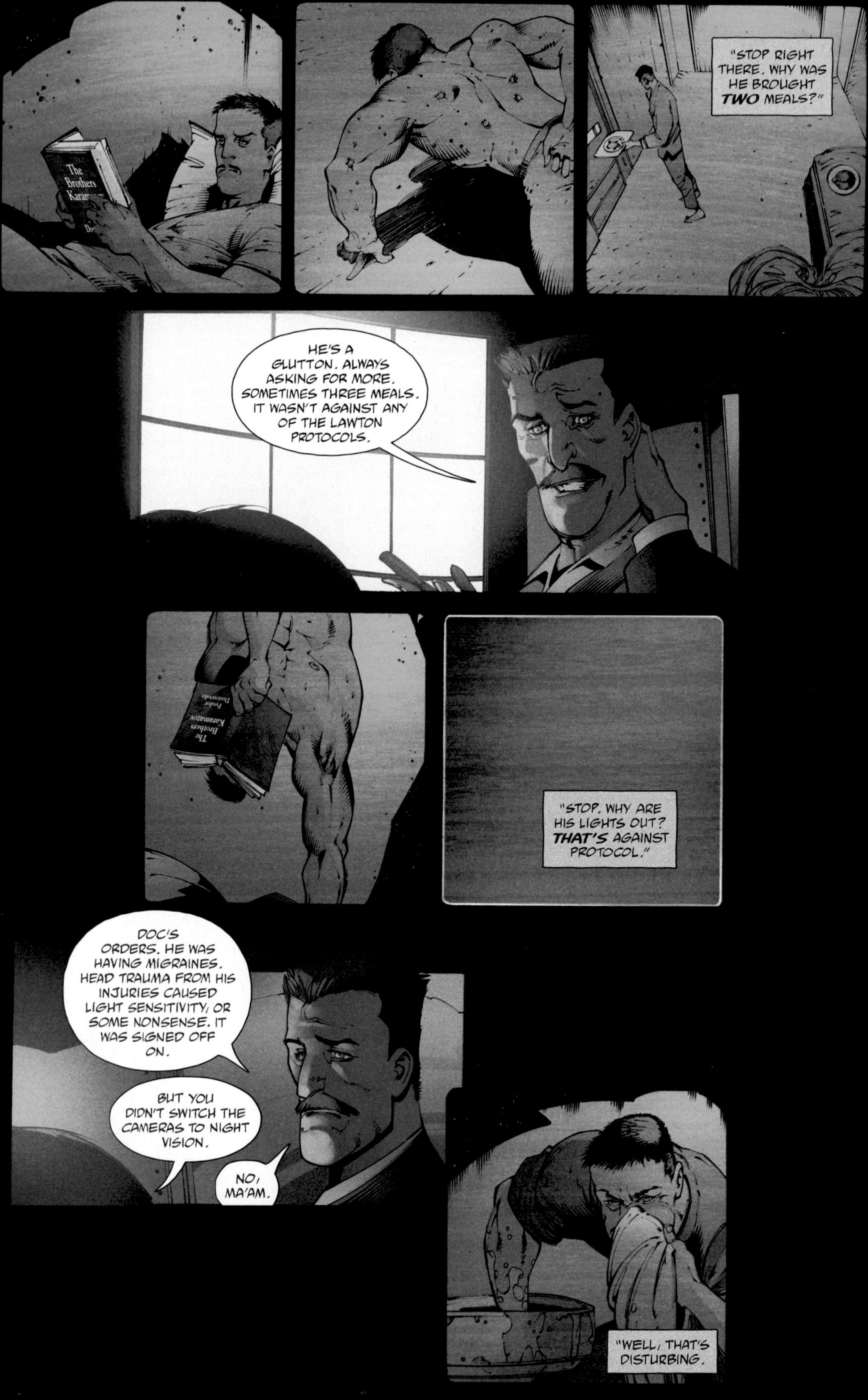
"STOP RIGHT THERE. WHY WAS HE BROUGHT TWO MEALS?"
HE'S A GLUTTON. ALWAYS ASKING FOR MORE. SOMETIMES THREE MEALS. IT WASN'T AGAINST ANY OF THE LAWTON PROTOCOLS.
"STOP. WHY ARE HIS LIGHTS OUT? THAT'S AGAINST PROTOCOL."
DOC'S ORDERS. HE WAS HAVING MIGRAINES. HEAD TRAUMA FROM HIS INJURIES CAUSED LIGHT SENSITIVITY, OR SOME NONSENSE. IT WAS SIGNED OFF ON.
BUT YOU DIDN'T SWITCH THE CAMERAS TO NIGHT VISION.
NO, MA'AM.
"WELL, THAT'S DISTURBING.

"STOP. HE'S TALKING TO SOMEONE..."

"PLAY BACK WITH AUDIO."

HEY BOSS, I'VE BEEN TELLING YOU FOR TWO DAYS. THE CRAPPER IS ALL STOPPED UP.

SUCKS FOR YOU.

CALL A PLUMBER.

SOME-THING'S GOTTA BE DONE.

SURE THING. LET ME BORROW YOUR CELL PHONE.

FOR WHAT? AIN'T NO RADIO OR CELL SIGNALS ALL THE WAY DOWN HERE--

"YOU TOLD HIM HE WAS UNDERGROUND."

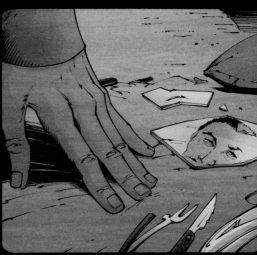

IS THAT A SCALPEL?

SURGICAL INSTRUMENTS CRAFTED FROM SILVERWARE... THAT WAS LEFT IN HIS CELL.

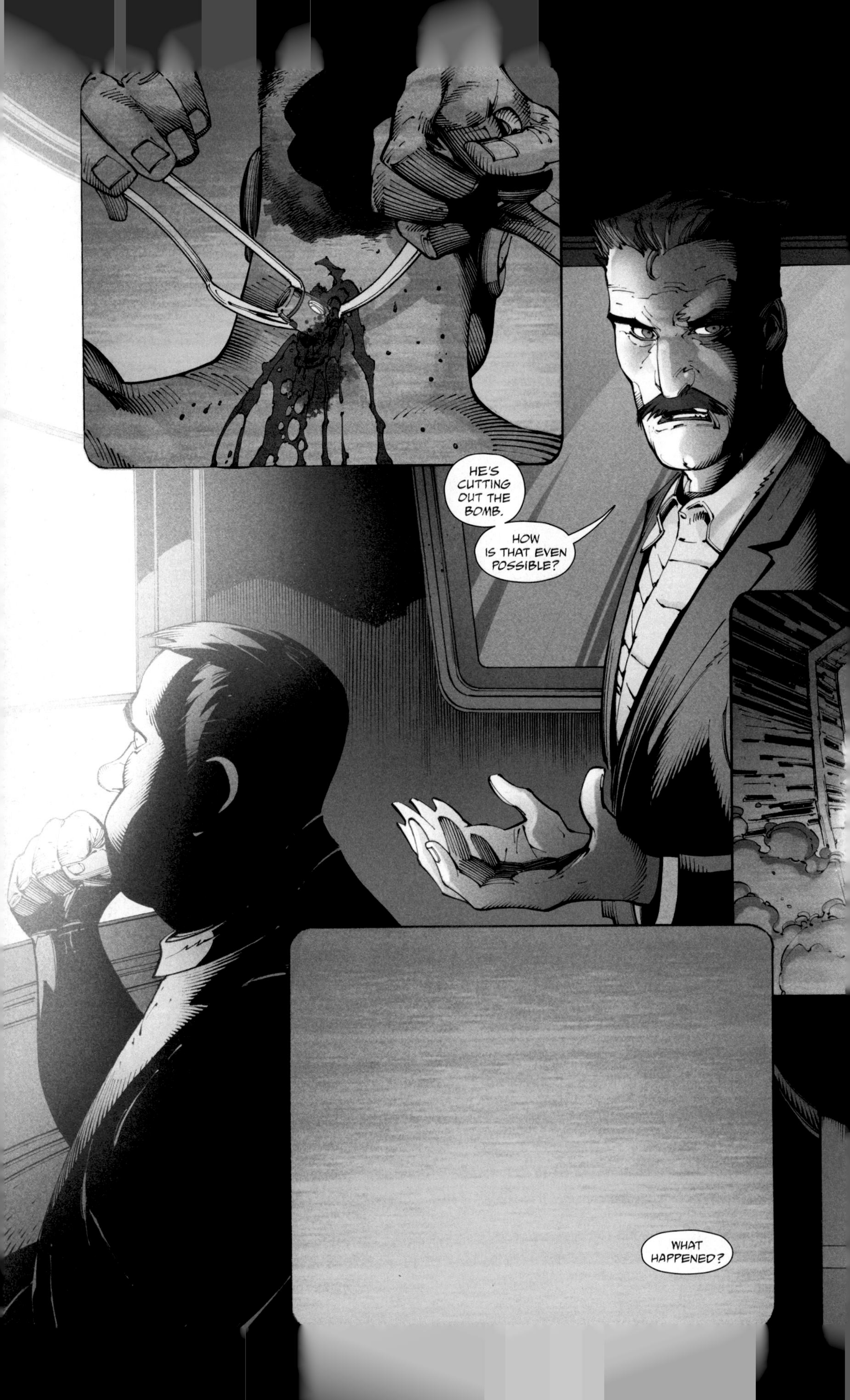
HE'S CUTTING OUT THE BOMB.
HOW IS THAT EVEN POSSIBLE?
WHAT HAPPENED?

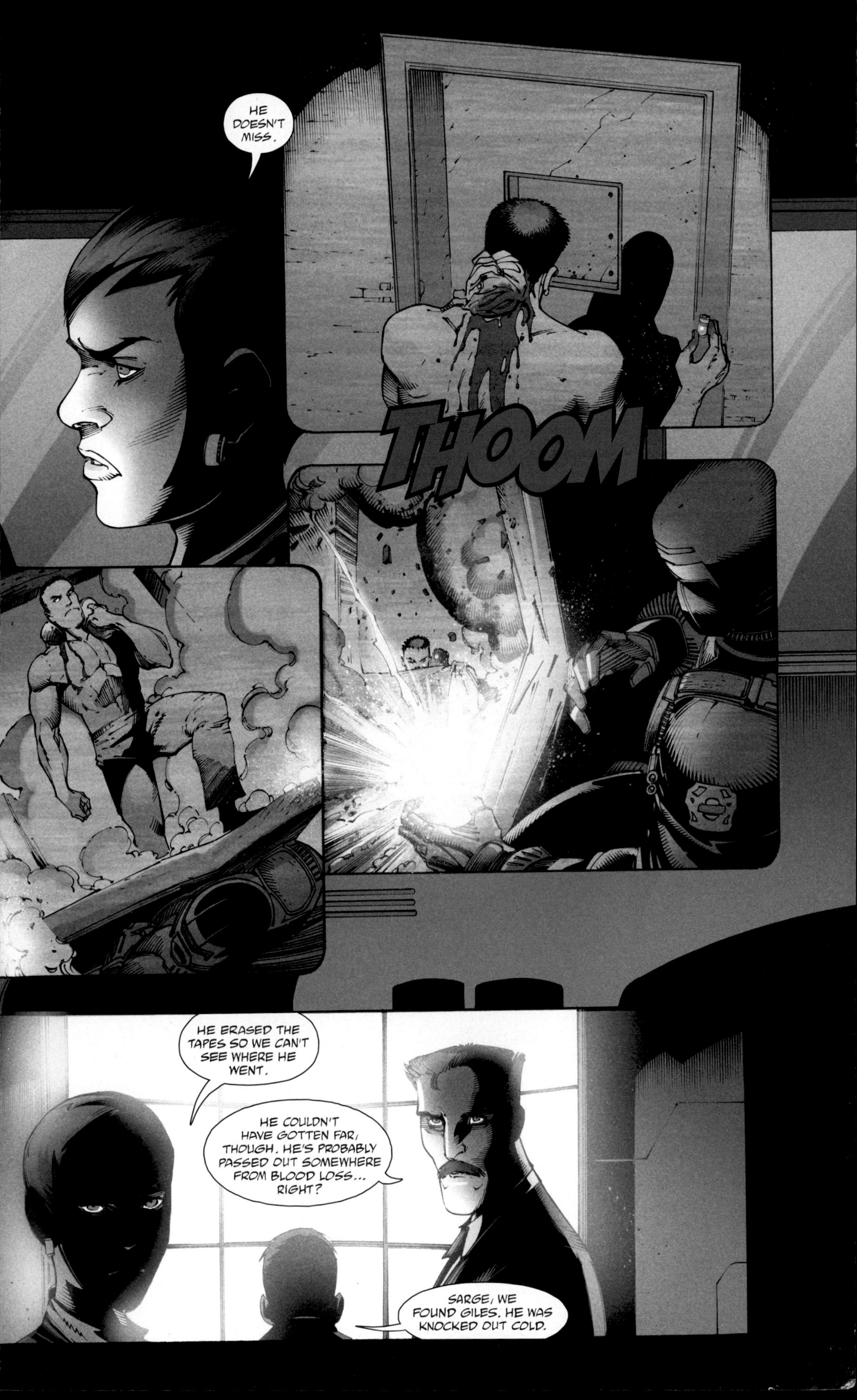
HE DOESN'T MISS.
THOOM
HE ERASED THE TAPES SO WE CAN'T SEE WHERE HE WENT.
HE COULDN'T HAVE GOTTEN FAR, THOUGH. HE'S PROBABLY PASSED OUT SOMEWHERE FROM BLOOD LOSS... RIGHT?
SARGE, WE FOUND GILES. HE WAS KNOCKED OUT COLD.

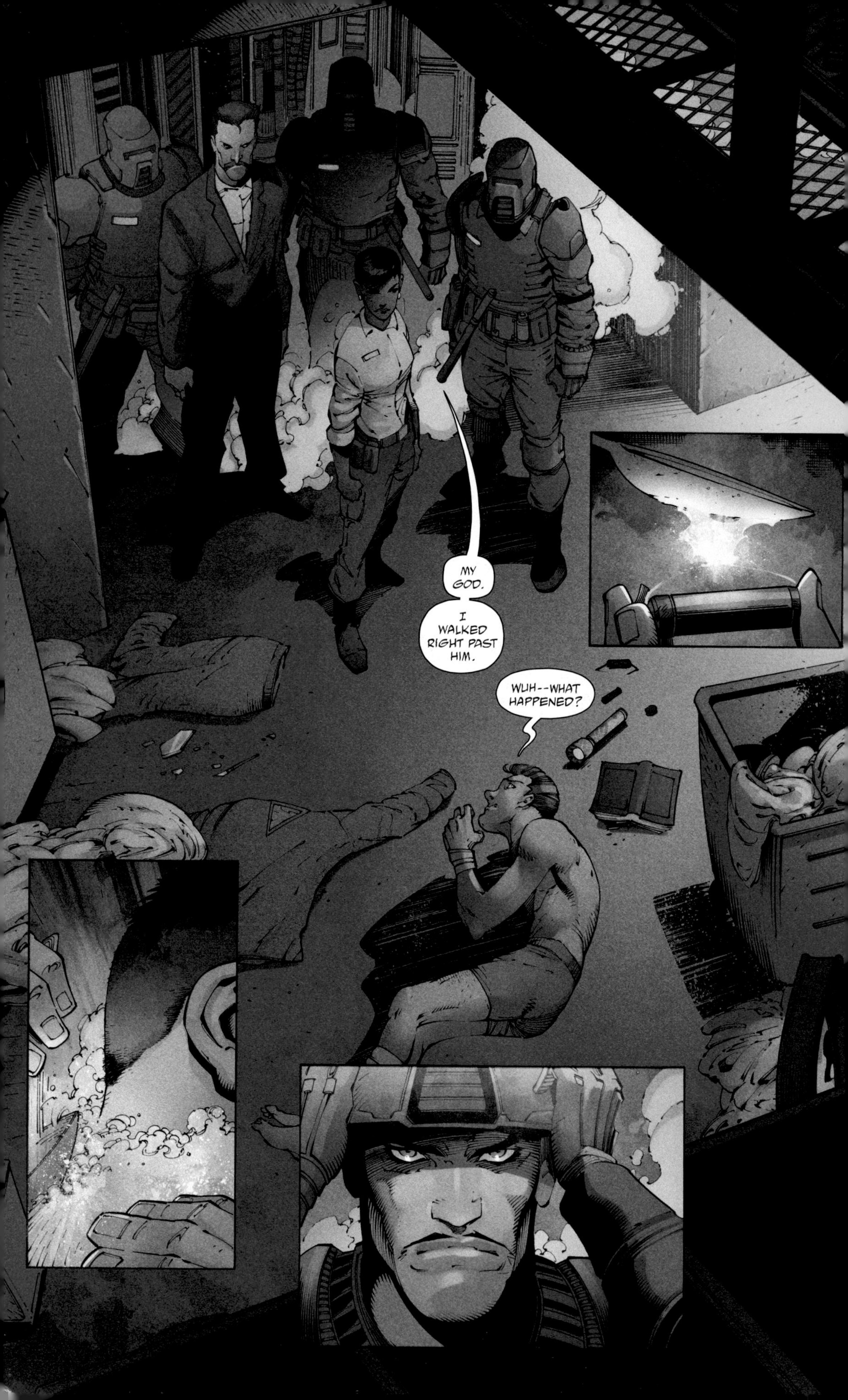
MY GOD.
I WALKED RIGHT PAST HIM.
WUH--WHAT HAPPENED?

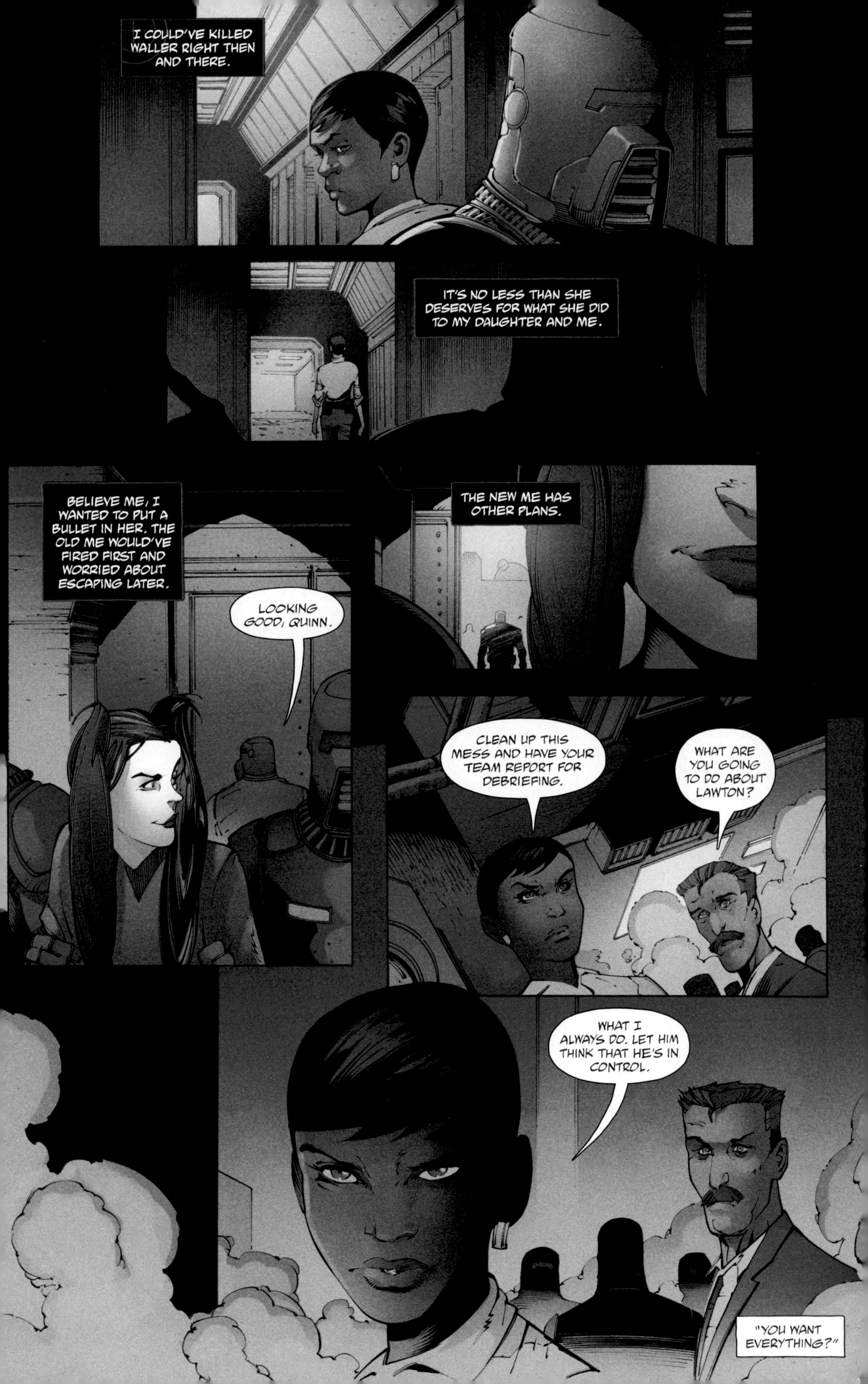

I COULD'VE KILLED WALLER RIGHT THEN AND THERE.
IT'S NO LESS THAN SHE DESERVES FOR WHAT SHE DID TO MY DAUGHTER AND ME.
BELIEVE ME, I WANTED TO PUT A BULLET IN HER. THE OLD ME WOULD'VE FIRED FIRST AND WORRIED ABOUT ESCAPING LATER.
LOOKING GOOD, QUINN.
THE NEW ME HAS OTHER PLANS.
CLEAN UP THIS MESS AND HAVE YOUR TEAM REPORT FOR DEBRIEFING.
WHAT ARE YOU GOING TO DO ABOUT LAWTON?
WHAT I ALWAYS DO. LET HIM THINK THAT HE'S IN CONTROL.
"YOU WANT EVERYTHING?"

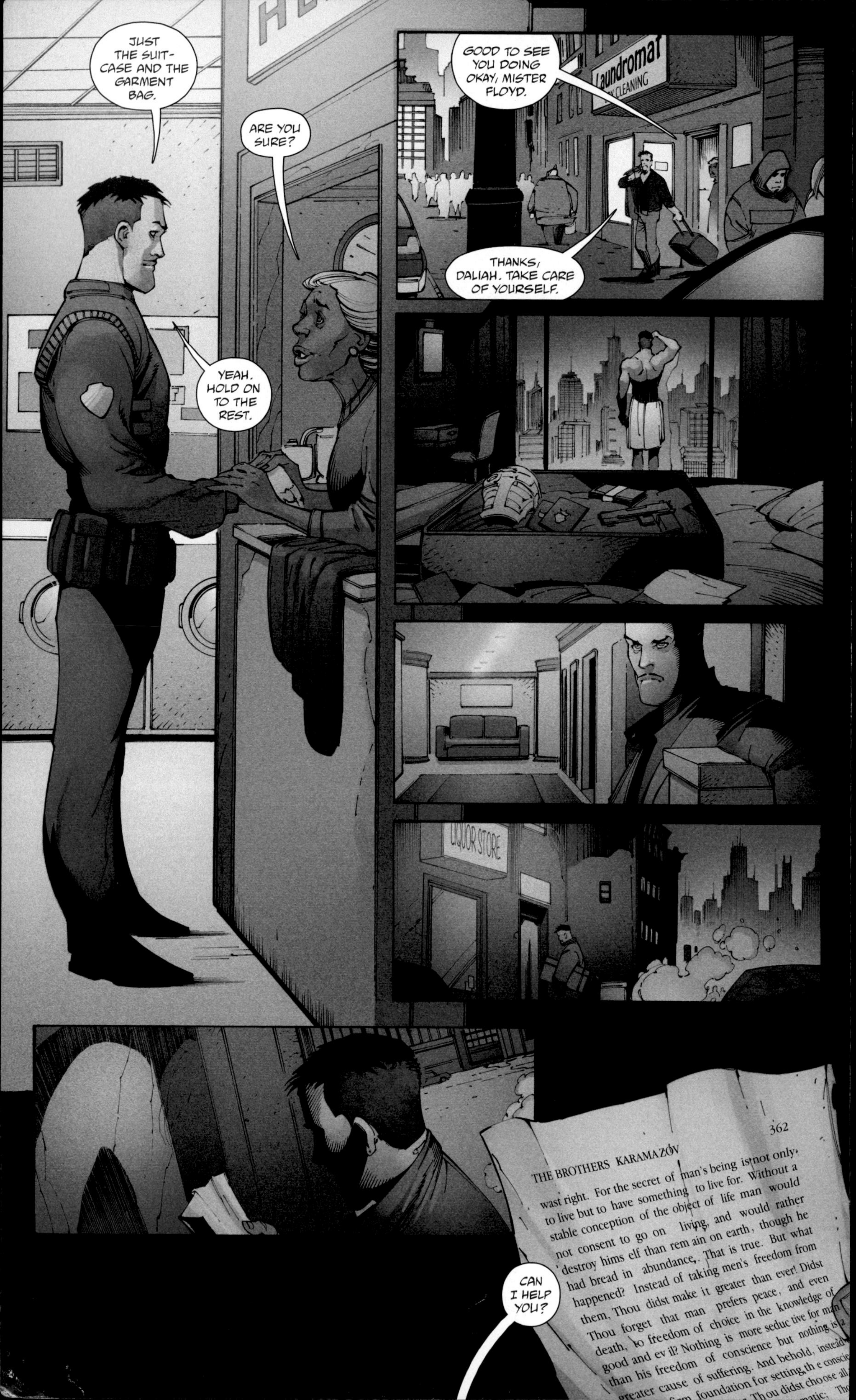
JUST THE SUIT-CASE AND THE GARMENT BAG.
ARE YOU SURE?
YEAH. HOLD ON TO THE REST.
Laundromat
DRY CLEANING
GOOD TO SEE YOU DOING OKAY, MISTER FLOYD.
THANKS, DALIAH. TAKE CARE OF YOURSELF.
LIQUOR STORE
362
THE BROTHERS KARAMAZOV
wast right. For the secret of man's being is not only
to live but to have something to live for. Without a
stable conception of the object of life man would
not consent to go on living, and would rather
destroy hims elf than rem ain on earth, though he
had bread in abundance,. That is true. But what
happened? Instead of taking men's freedom from
them, Thou didst make it greater than ever! Didst
Thou forget that man prefers peace, and even
death, to freedom of choice in the knowledge of
good and ev il? Nothing is more seduc tive for man
than his freedom of conscience but nothing is a
greater cause of suffering. And behold, instead
foundation for setting th e conscie
Thou didst choose all
CAN I HELP YOU?

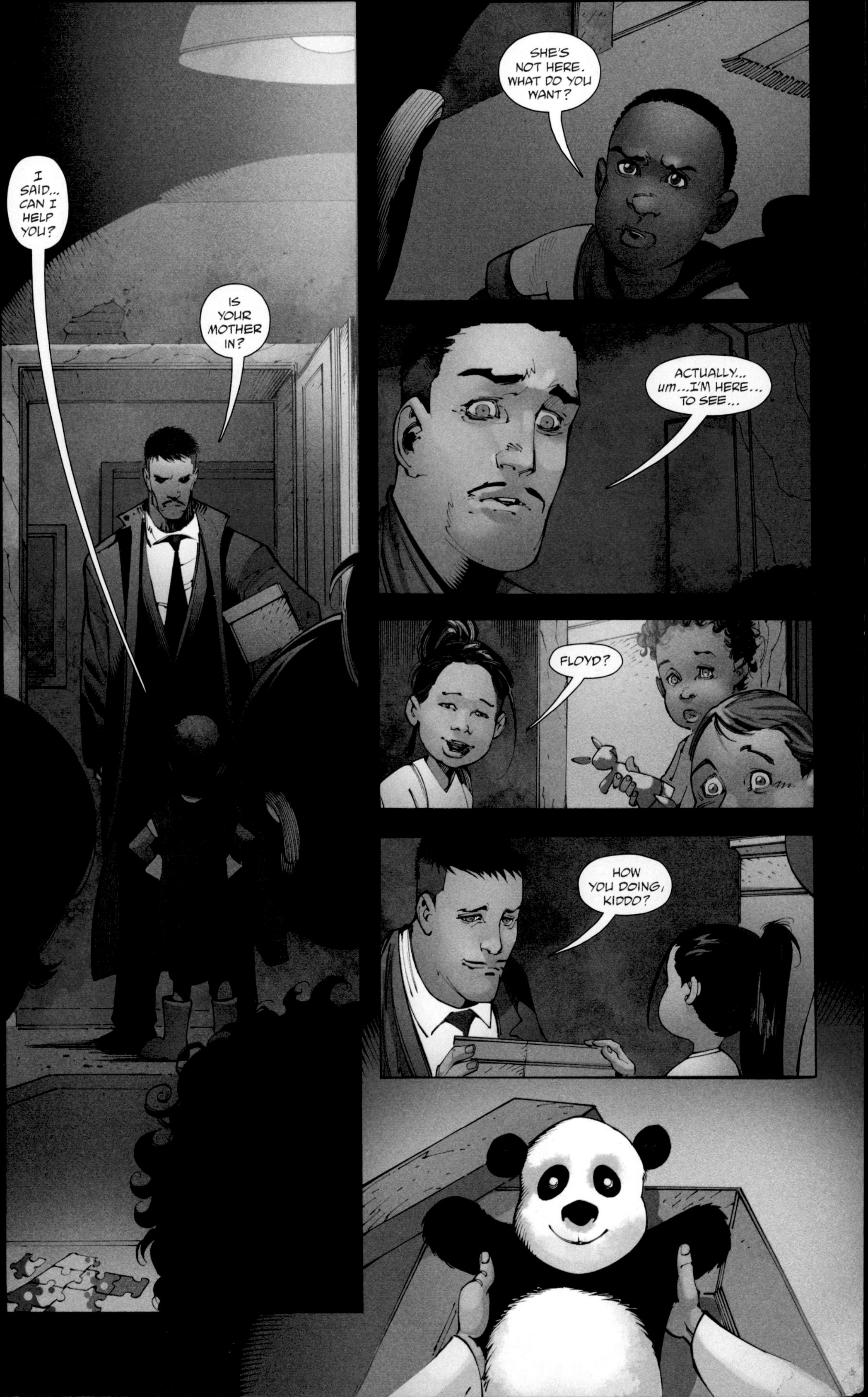
I SAID... CAN I HELP YOU?
IS YOUR MOTHER IN?
SHE'S NOT HERE. WHAT DO YOU WANT?
ACTUALLY... um...I'M HERE... TO SEE...
FLOYD?
HOW YOU DOING, KIDDO?

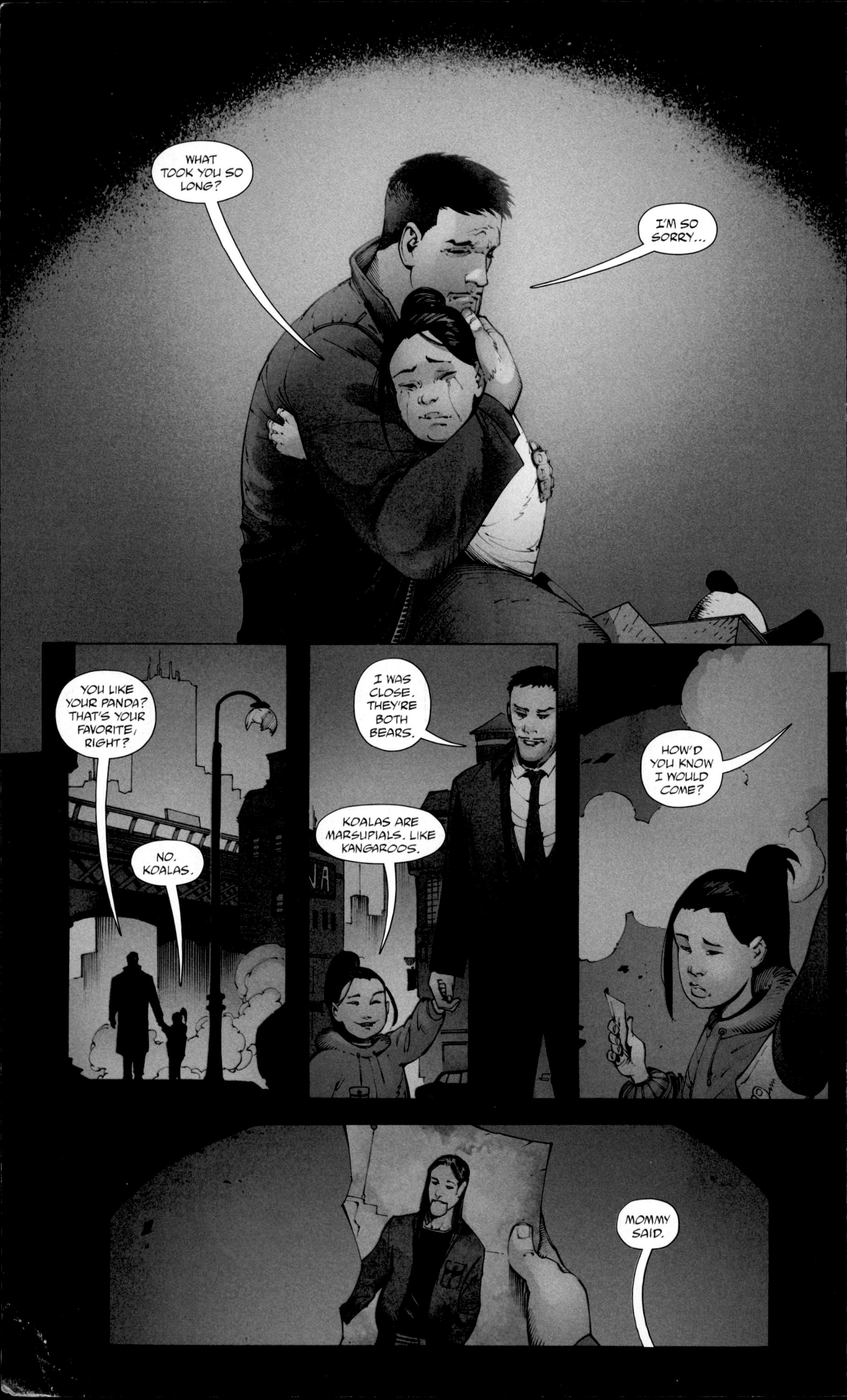
WHAT TOOK YOU SO LONG?
I'M SO SORRY...
YOU LIKE YOUR PANDA? THAT'S YOUR FAVORITE, RIGHT?
NO. KOALAS.
I WAS CLOSE. THEY'RE BOTH BEARS.
KOALAS ARE MARSUPIALS. LIKE KANGAROOS.
HOW'D YOU KNOW I WOULD COME?
MOMMY SAID.

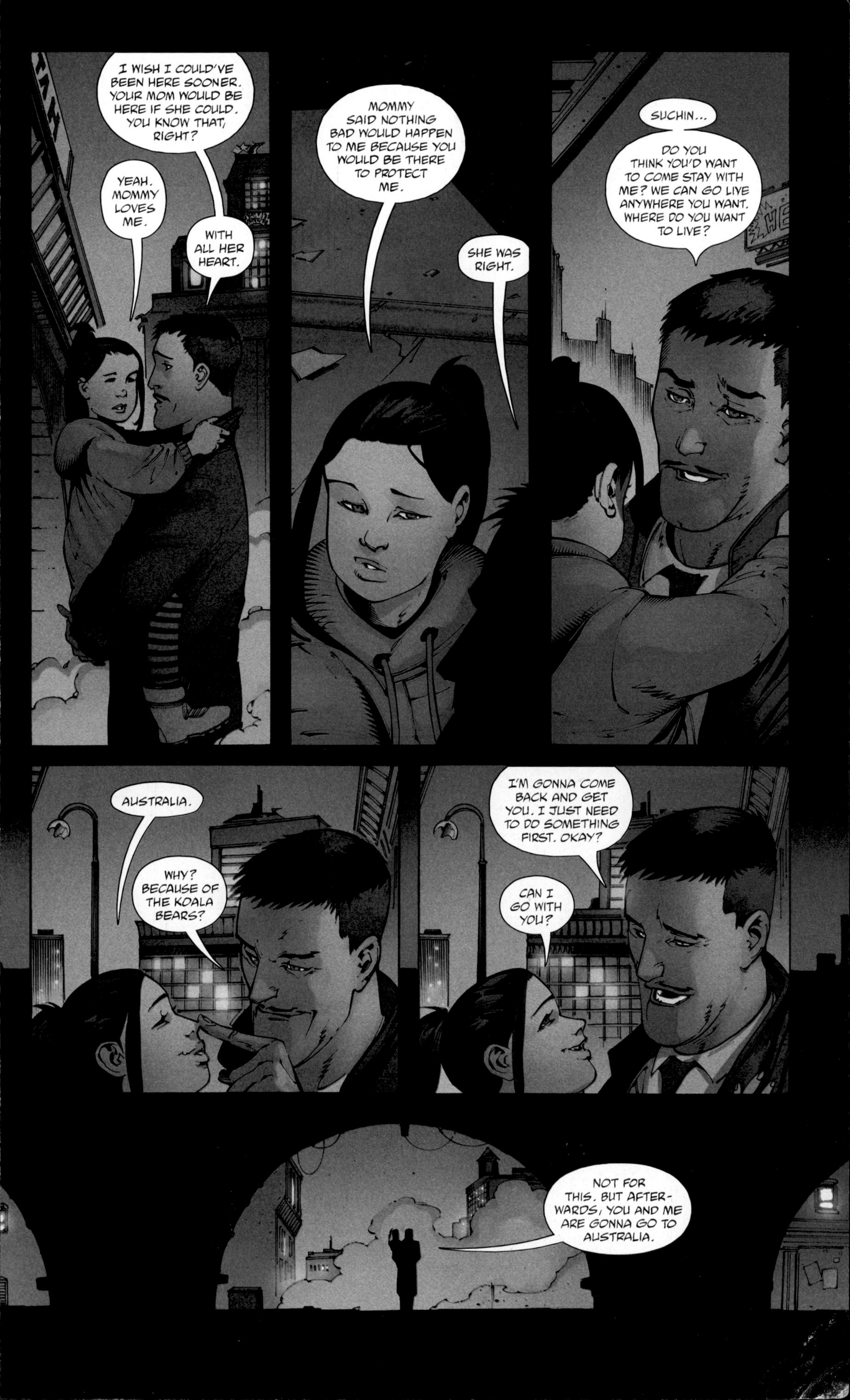

I WISH I COULD'VE BEEN HERE SOONER. YOUR MOM WOULD BE HERE IF SHE COULD. YOU KNOW THAT, RIGHT?
YEAH. MOMMY LOVES ME.
WITH ALL HER HEART.
MOMMY SAID NOTHING BAD WOULD HAPPEN TO ME BECAUSE YOU WOULD BE THERE TO PROTECT ME.
SHE WAS RIGHT.
SUCHIN...
DO YOU THINK YOU'D WANT TO COME STAY WITH ME? WE CAN GO LIVE ANYWHERE YOU WANT. WHERE DO YOU WANT TO LIVE?
AUSTRALIA.
WHY? BECAUSE OF THE KOALA BEARS?
I'M GONNA COME BACK AND GET YOU. I JUST NEED TO DO SOMETHING FIRST. OKAY?
CAN I GO WITH YOU?
NOT FOR THIS. BUT AFTER-WARDS, YOU AND ME ARE GONNA GO TO AUSTRALIA.

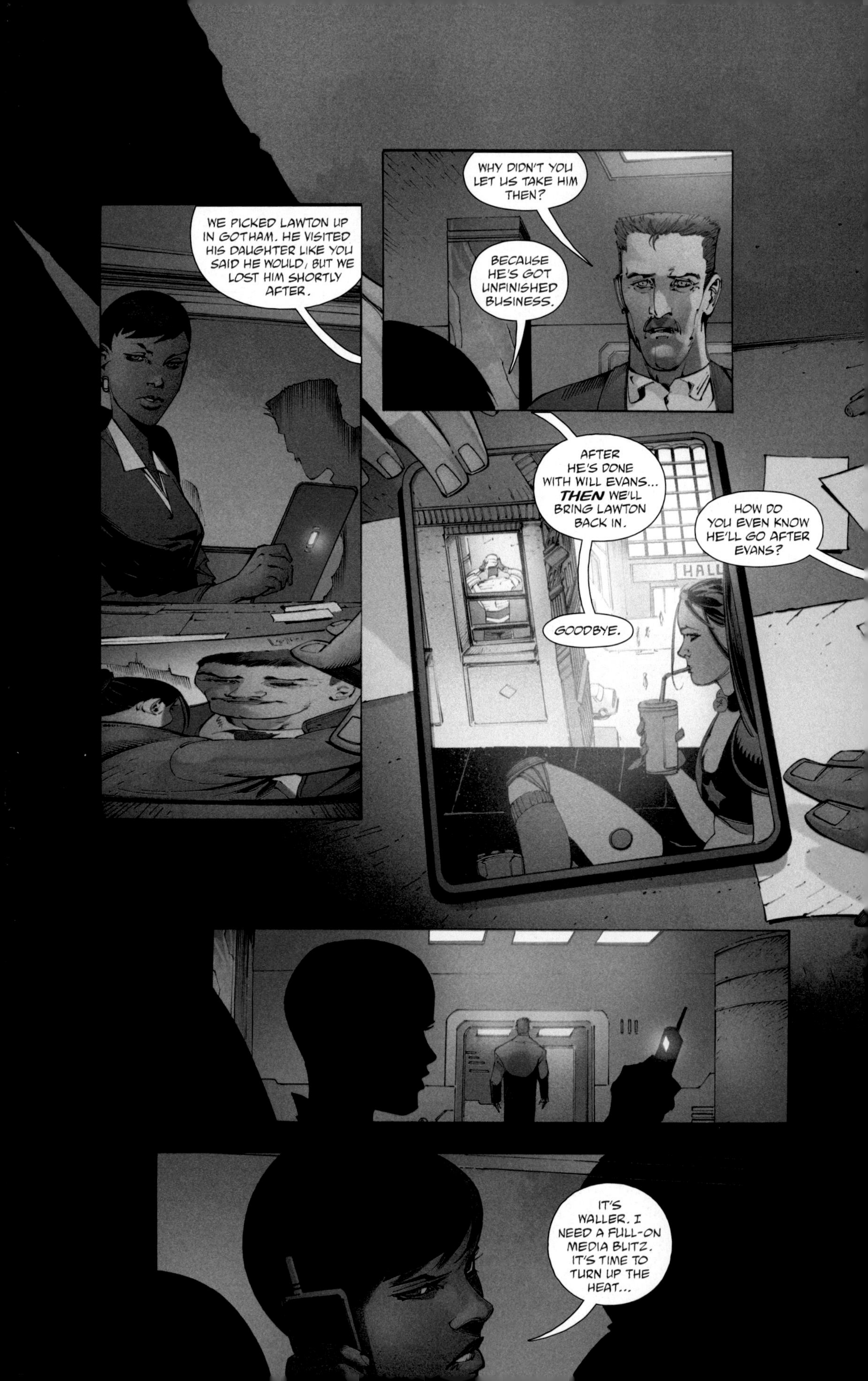
WE PICKED LAWTON UP IN GOTHAM. HE VISITED HIS DAUGHTER LIKE YOU SAID HE WOULD, BUT WE LOST HIM SHORTLY AFTER.
WHY DIDN'T YOU LET US TAKE HIM THEN?
BECAUSE HE'S GOT UNFINISHED BUSINESS.
AFTER HE'S DONE WITH WILL EVANS... THEN WE'LL BRING LAWTON BACK IN.
HOW DO YOU EVEN KNOW HE'LL GO AFTER EVANS?
GOODBYE.
HALL
IT'S WALLER. I NEED A FULL-ON MEDIA BLITZ. IT'S TIME TO TURN UP THE HEAT...

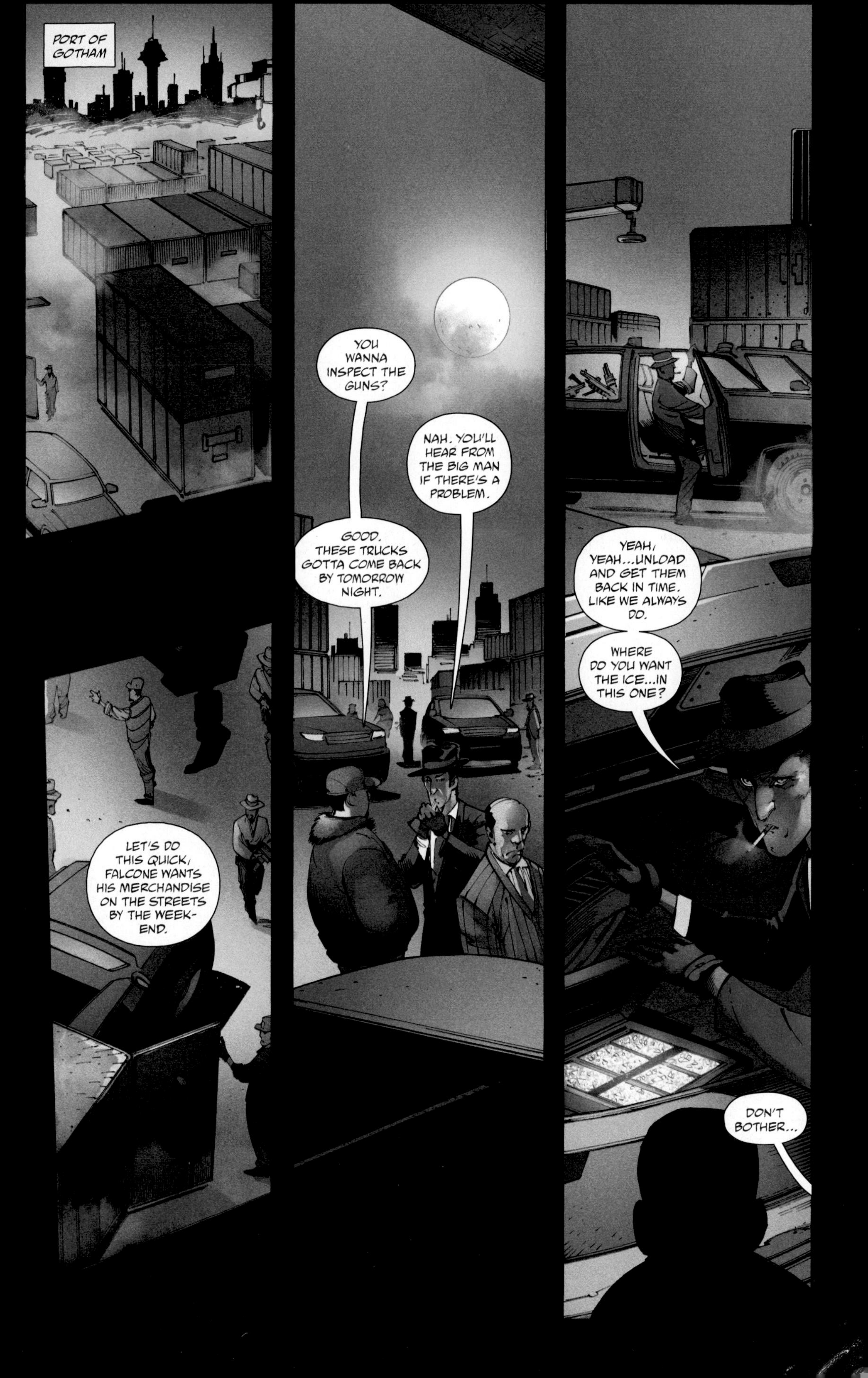
PORT OF GOTHAM
LET'S DO THIS QUICK, FALCONE WANTS HIS MERCHANDISE ON THE STREETS BY THE WEEK-END.
YOU WANNA INSPECT THE GUNS?
NAH. YOU'LL HEAR FROM THE BIG MAN IF THERE'S A PROBLEM.
GOOD. THESE TRUCKS GOTTA COME BACK BY TOMORROW NIGHT.
YEAH, YEAH...UNLOAD AND GET THEM BACK IN TIME. LIKE WE ALWAYS DO.
WHERE DO YOU WANT THE ICE...IN THIS ONE?
DON'T BOTHER...

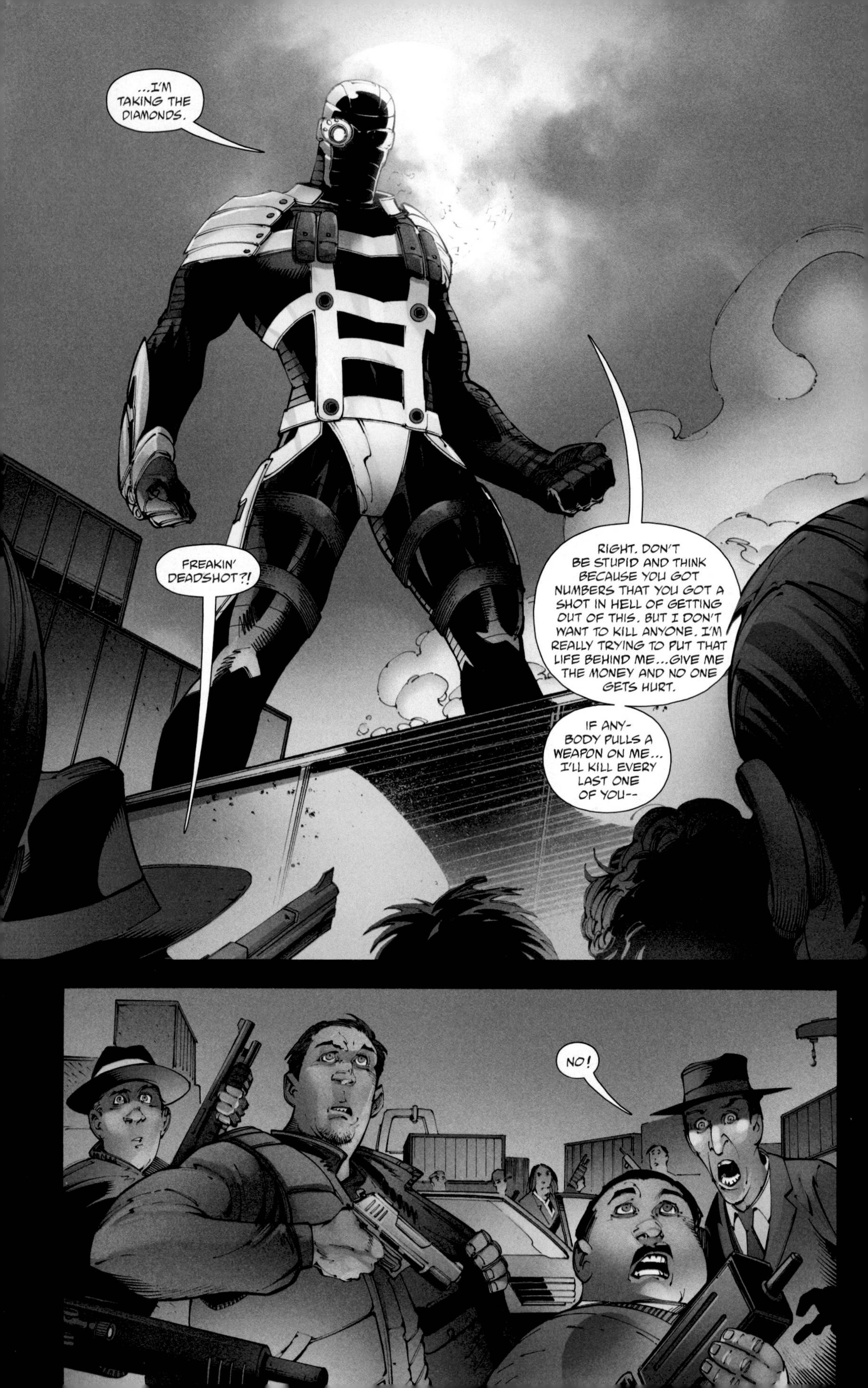
...I'M TAKING THE DIAMONDS.
FREAKIN' DEADSHOT?!
RIGHT. DON'T BE STUPID AND THINK BECAUSE YOU GOT NUMBERS THAT YOU GOT A SHOT IN HELL OF GETTING OUT OF THIS. BUT I DON'T WANT TO KILL ANYONE. I'M REALLY TRYING TO PUT THAT LIFE BEHIND ME...GIVE ME THE MONEY AND NO ONE GETS HURT.
IF ANYBODY PULLS A WEAPON ON ME... I'LL KILL EVERY LAST ONE OF YOU--
NO!

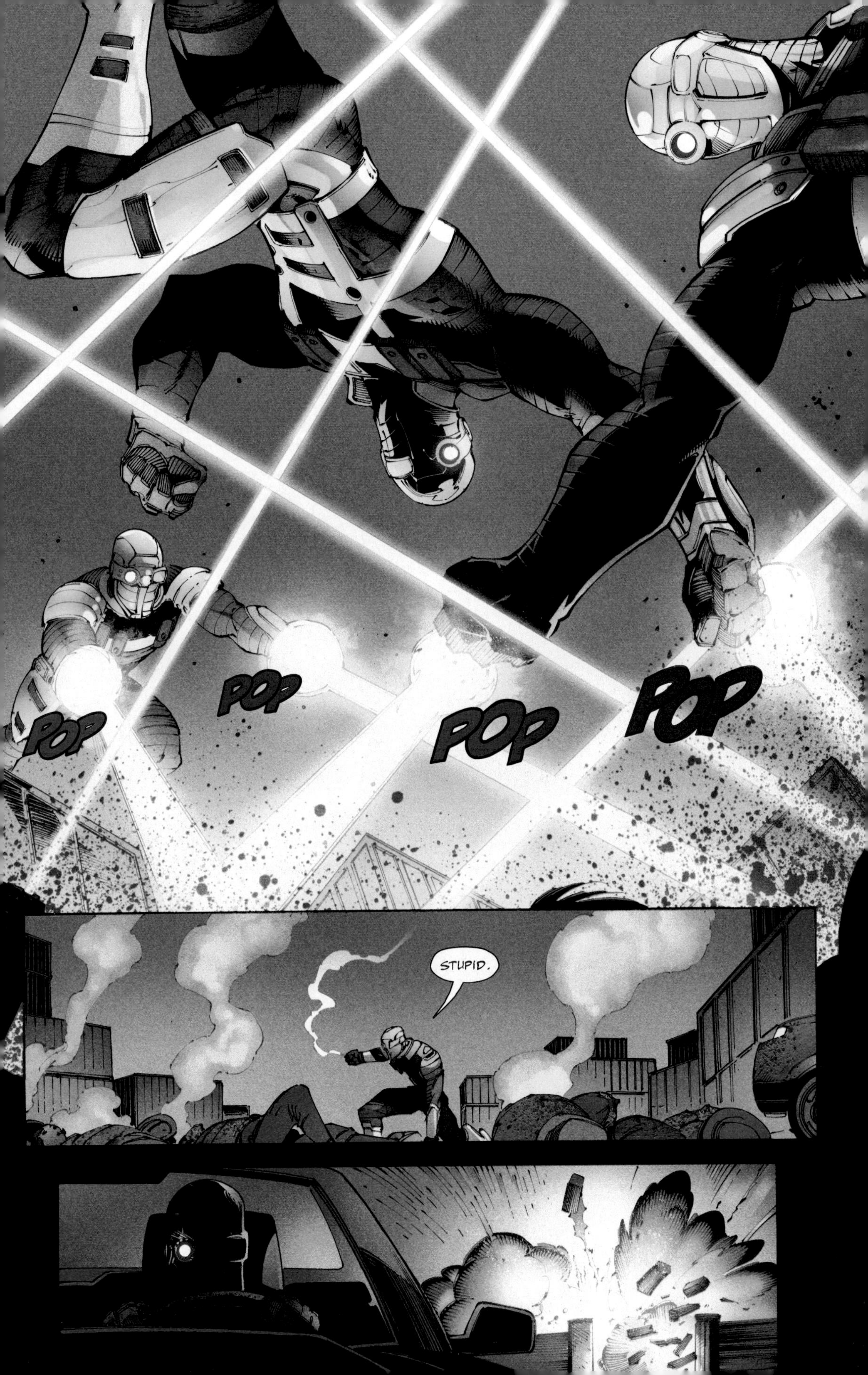
POP
POP
POP
POP
STUPID.

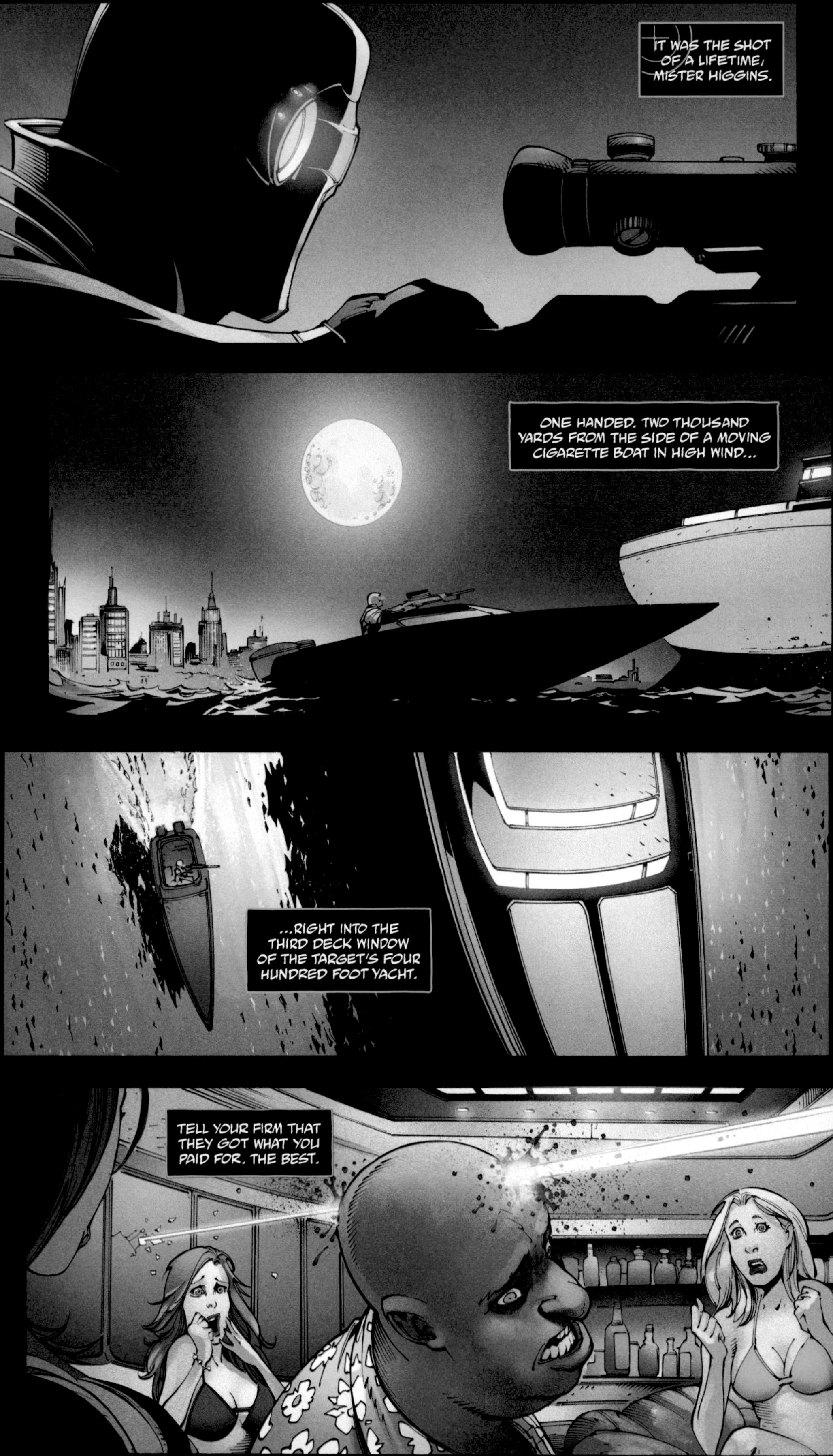
IT WAS THE SHOT OF A LIFETIME, MISTER HIGGINS.
ONE HANDED. TWO THOUSAND YARDS FROM THE SIDE OF A MOVING CIGARETTE BOAT IN HIGH WIND...
...RIGHT INTO THE THIRD DECK WINDOW OF THE TARGET'S FOUR HUNDRED FOOT YACHT.
TELL YOUR FIRM THAT THEY GOT WHAT YOU PAID FOR. THE BEST.

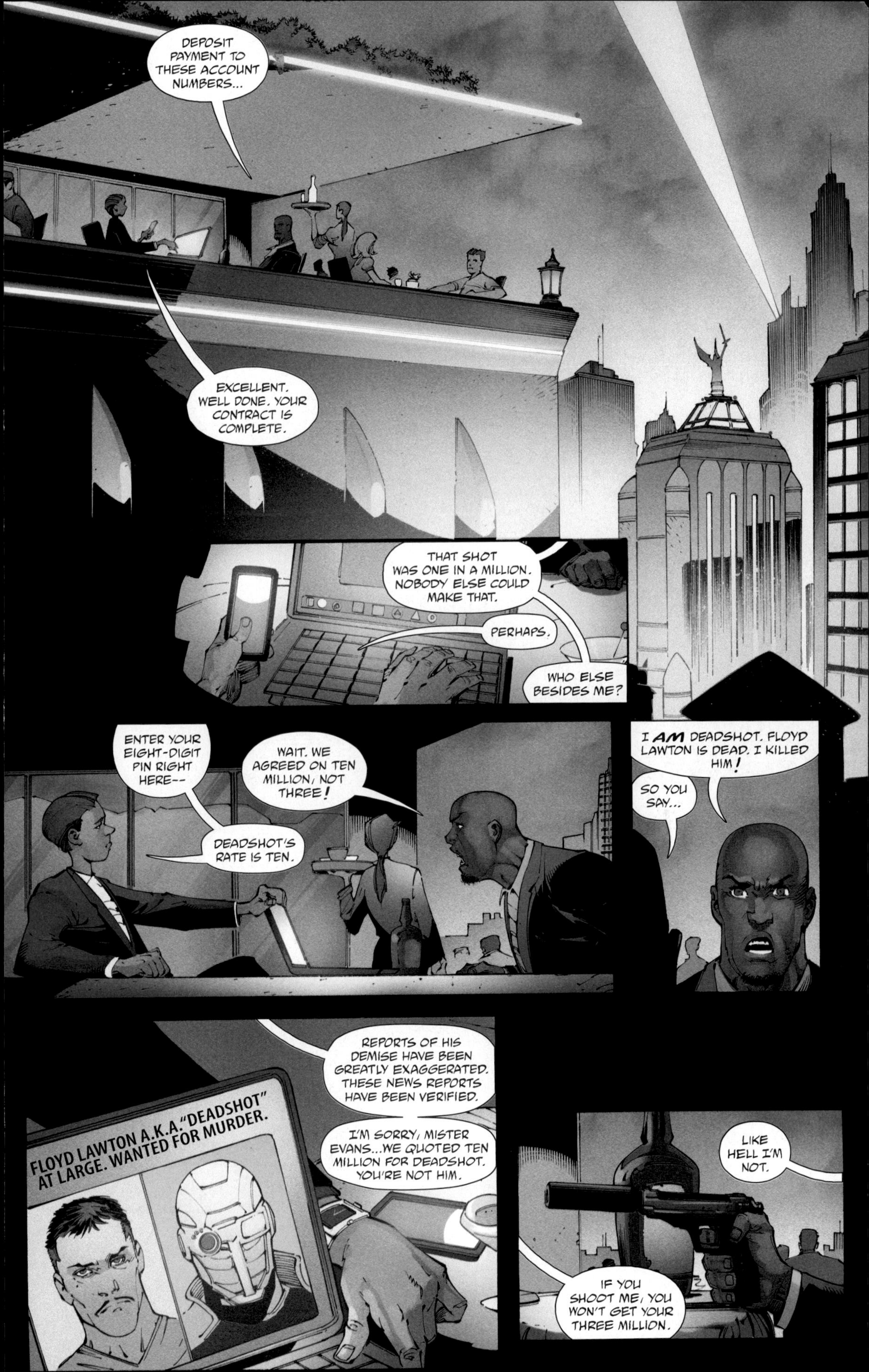
DEPOSIT PAYMENT TO THESE ACCOUNT NUMBERS...
EXCELLENT. WELL DONE. YOUR CONTRACT IS COMPLETE.
THAT SHOT WAS ONE IN A MILLION. NOBODY ELSE COULD MAKE THAT.
PERHAPS.
WHO ELSE BESIDES ME?
ENTER YOUR EIGHT-DIGIT PIN RIGHT HERE--
WAIT. WE AGREED ON TEN MILLION, NOT THREE!
DEADSHOT'S RATE IS TEN.
I AM DEADSHOT. FLOYD LAWTON IS DEAD. I KILLED HIM!
SO YOU SAY...
REPORTS OF HIS DEMISE HAVE BEEN GREATLY EXAGGERATED. THESE NEWS REPORTS HAVE BEEN VERIFIED.
FLOYD LAWTON A.K.A. "DEADSHOT" AT LARGE. WANTED FOR MURDER.
I'M SORRY, MISTER EVANS...WE QUOTED TEN MILLION FOR DEADSHOT. YOU'RE NOT HIM.
LIKE HELL I'M NOT.
IF YOU SHOOT ME, YOU WON'T GET YOUR THREE MILLION.

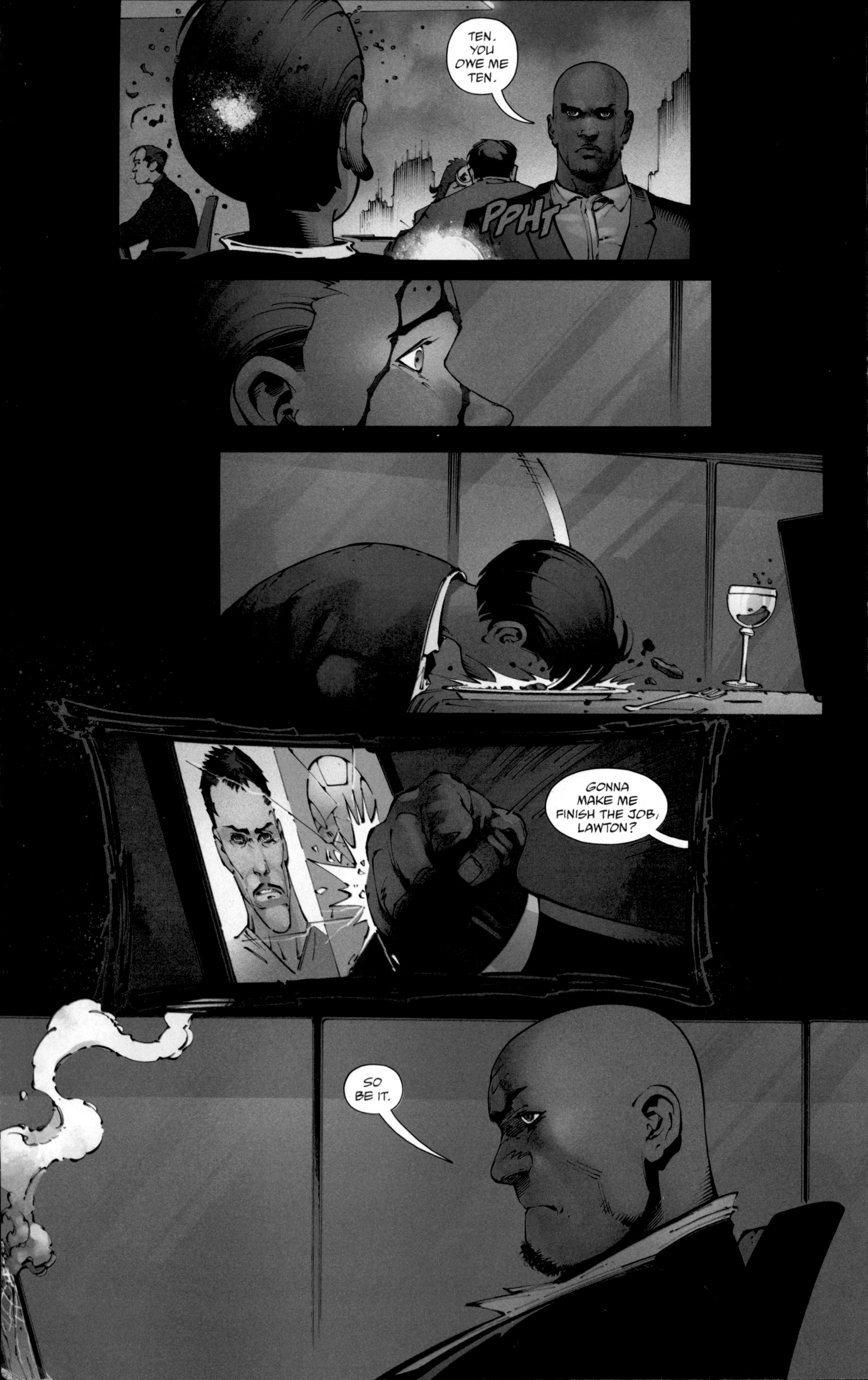
TEN. YOU OWE ME TEN.
PPHT
GONNA MAKE ME FINISH THE JOB, LAWTON?
SO BE IT.

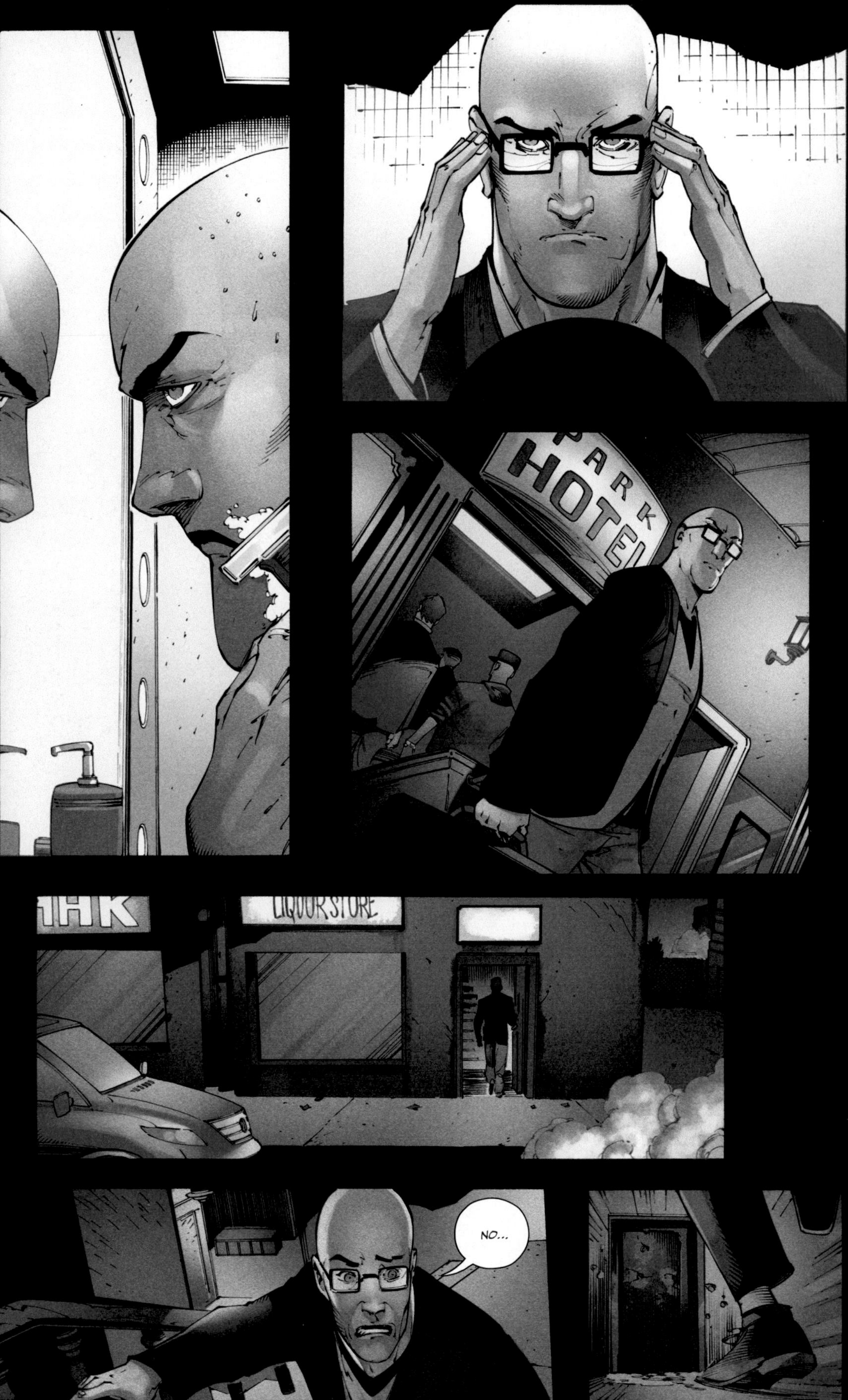

PARK HOTEL
LIQUOR STORE
NO...

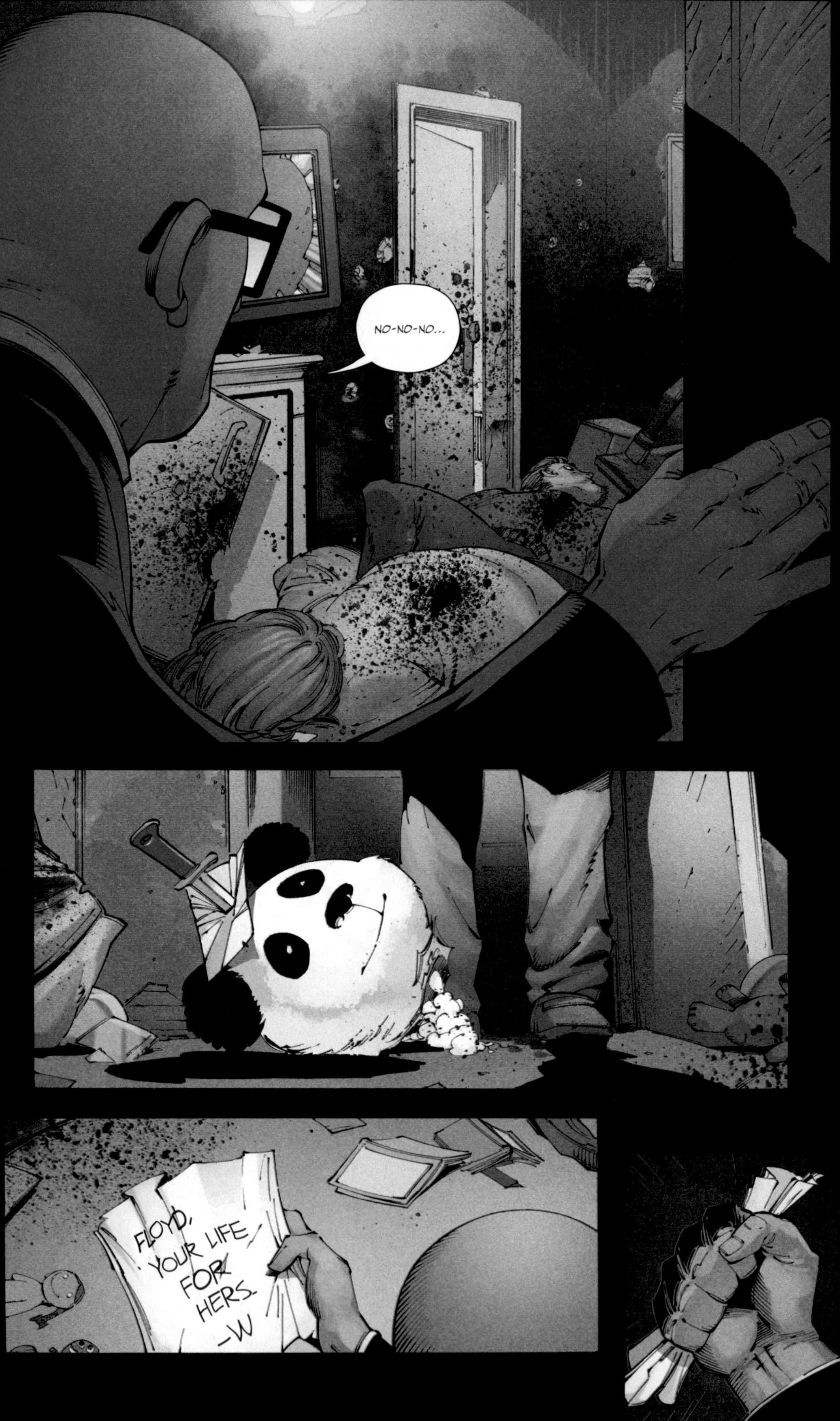
NO-NO-NO...
FLOYD, YOUR LIFE FOR HERS. -W

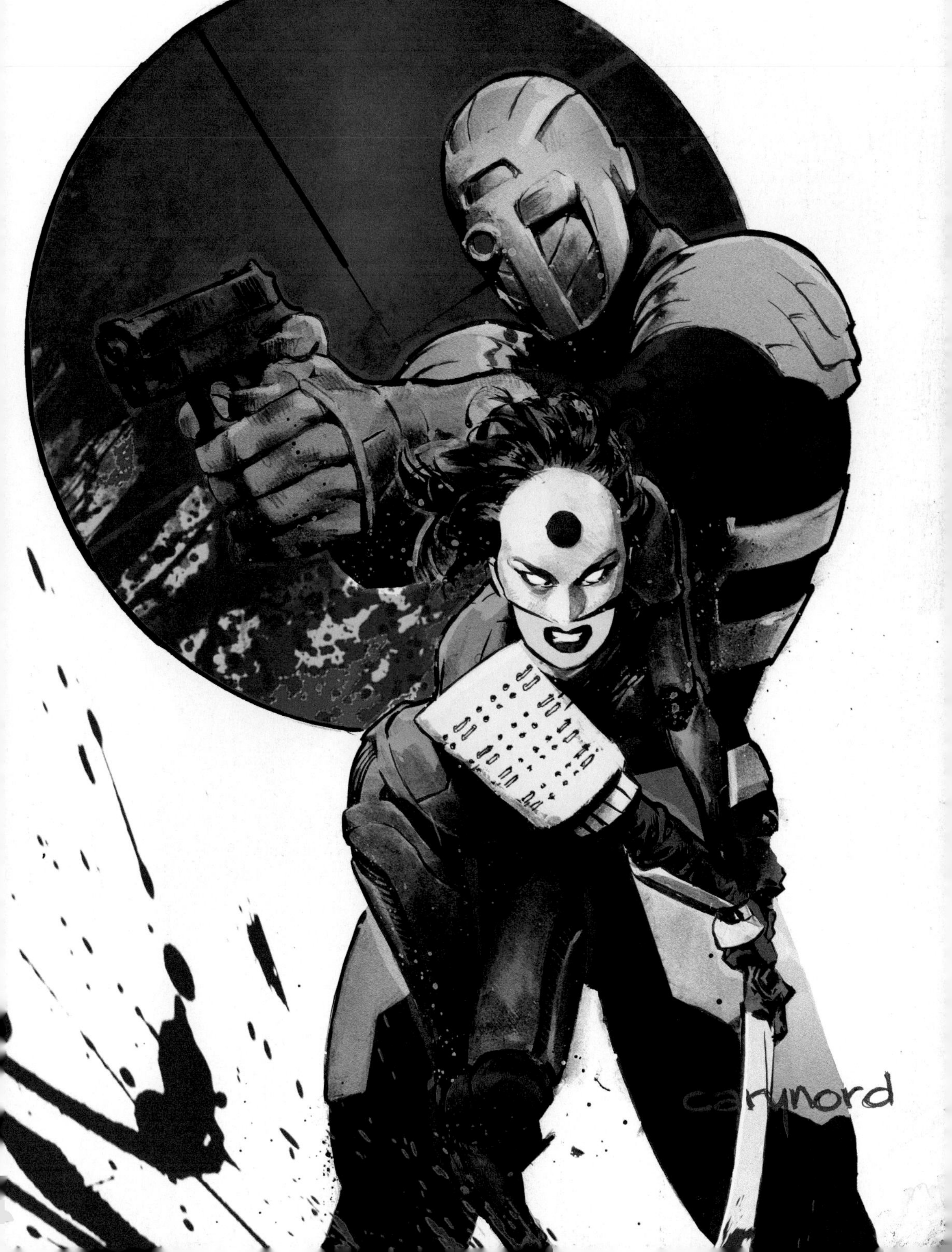
carynord

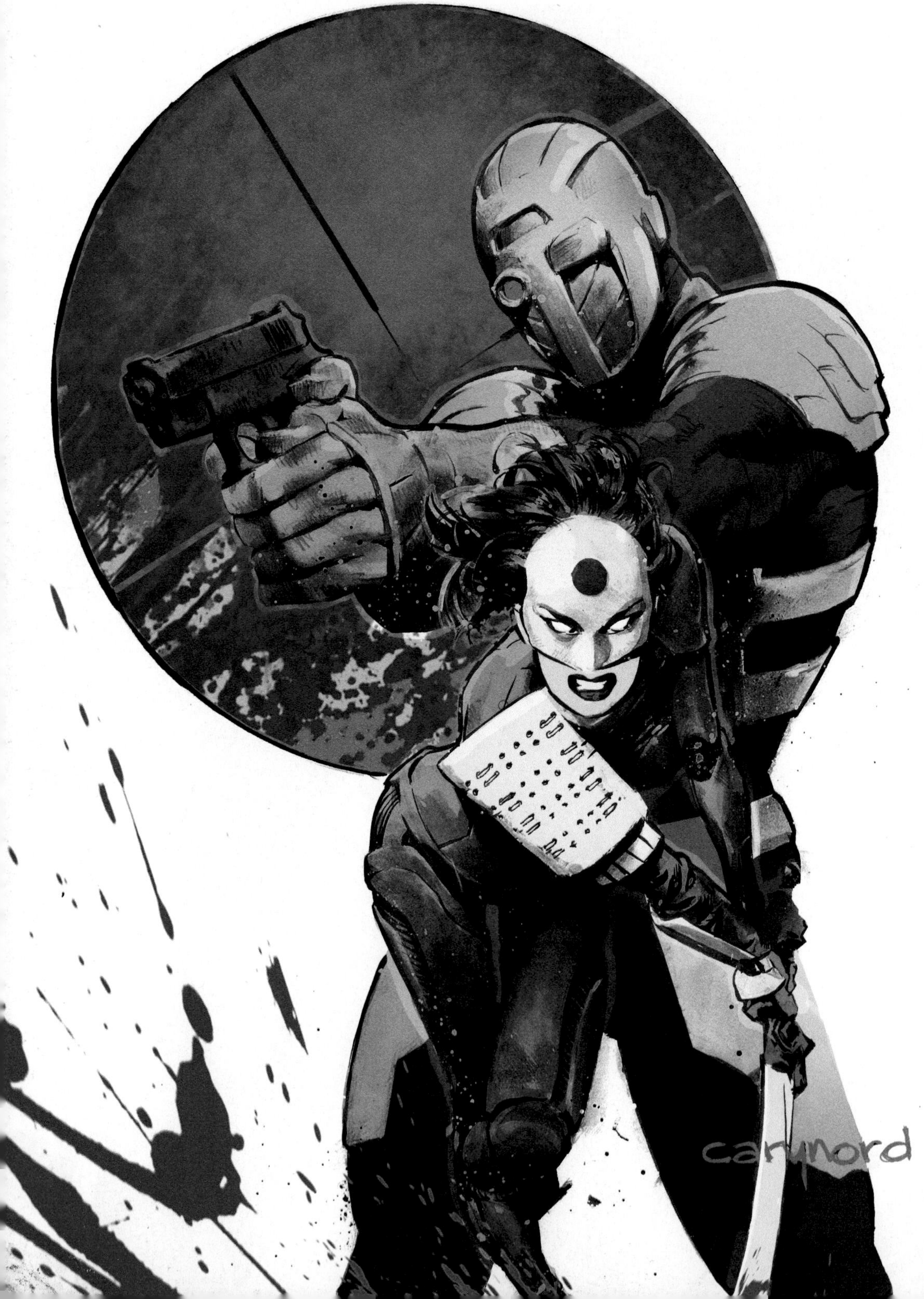
carynord

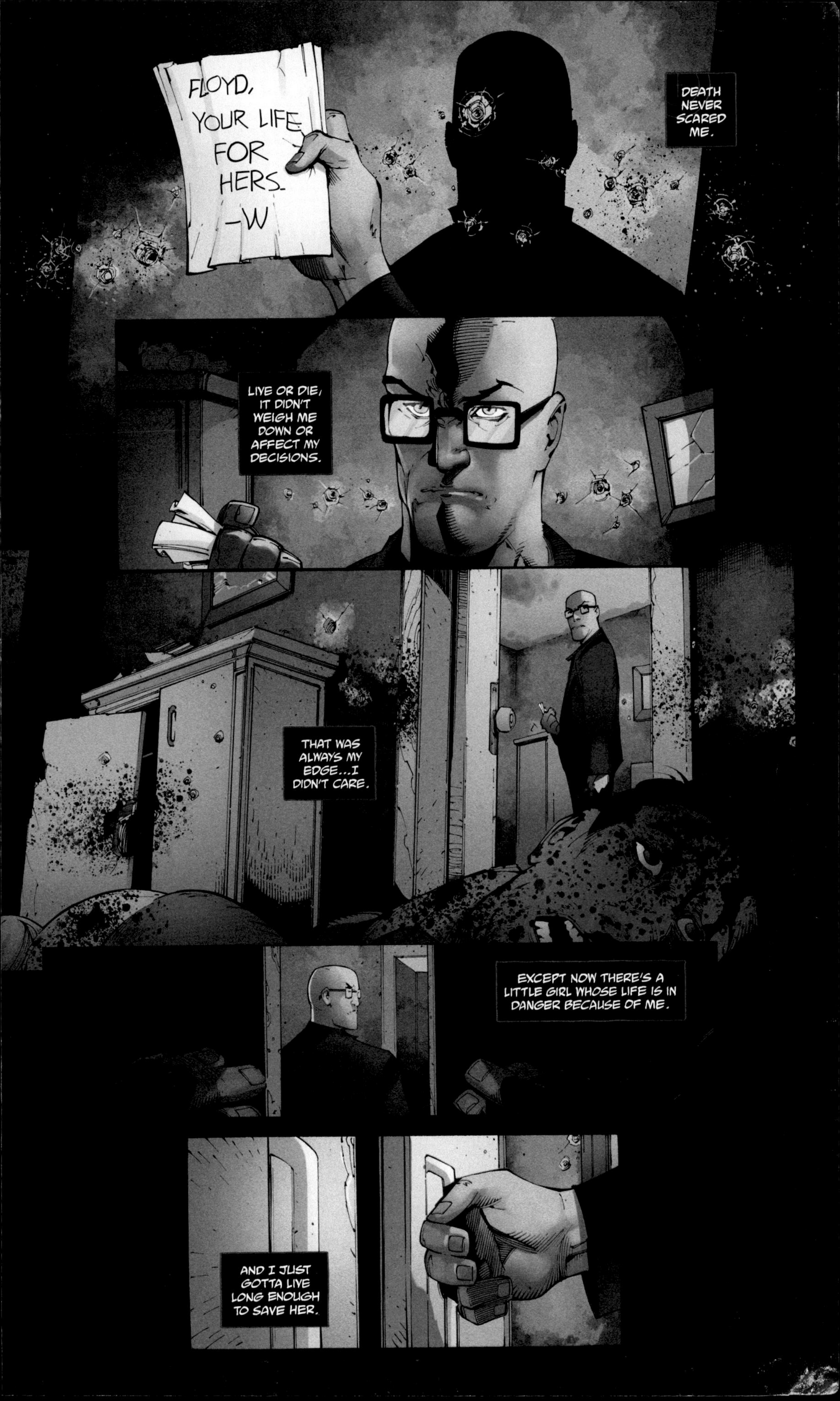
FLOYD, YOUR LIFE FOR HERS. —W
DEATH NEVER SCARED ME.
LIVE OR DIE, IT DIDN'T WEIGH ME DOWN OR AFFECT MY DECISIONS.
THAT WAS ALWAYS MY EDGE...I DIDN'T CARE.
EXCEPT NOW THERE'S A LITTLE GIRL WHOSE LIFE IS IN DANGER BECAUSE OF ME.
AND I JUST GOTTA LIVE LONG ENOUGH TO SAVE HER.

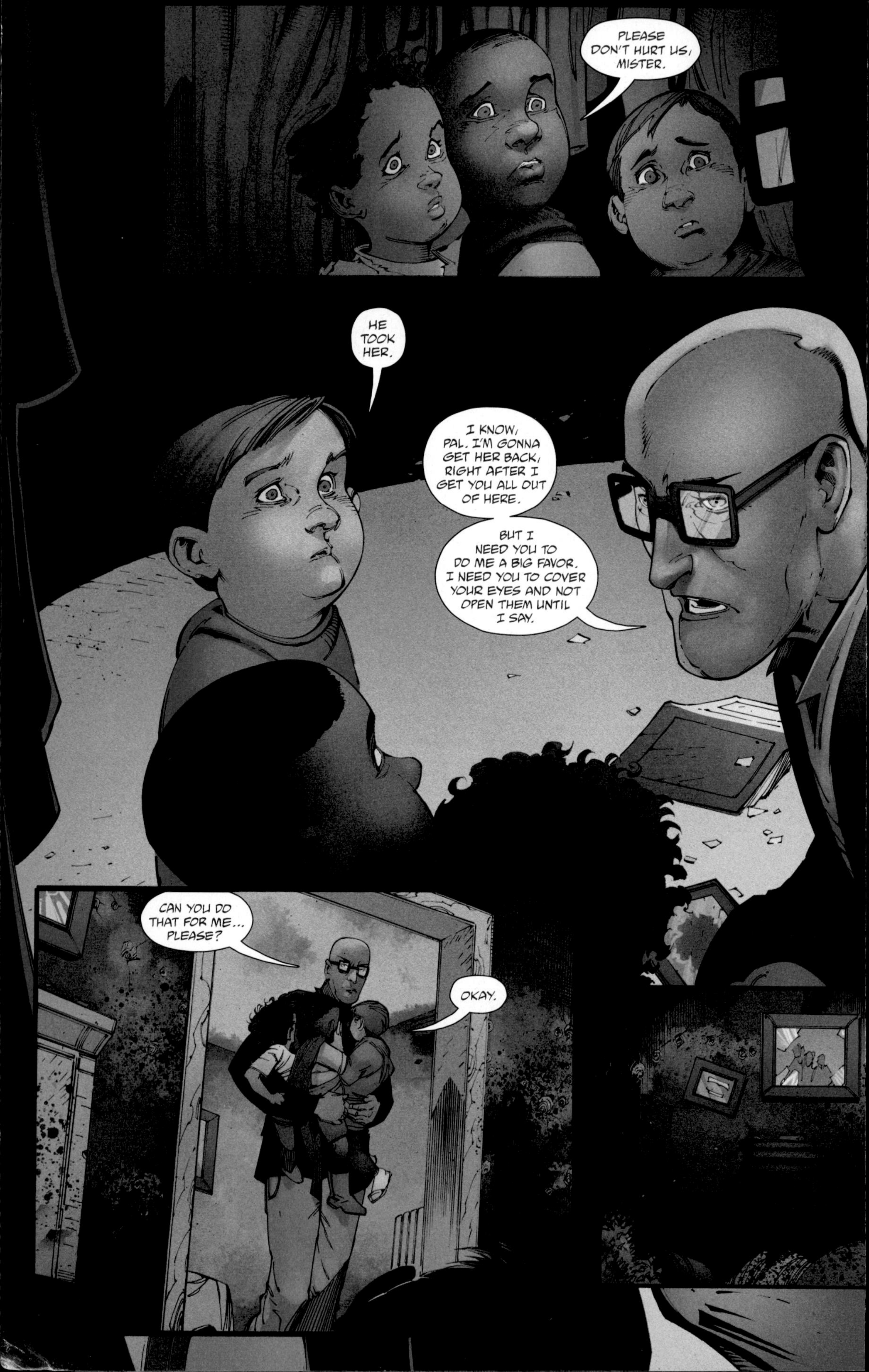
PLEASE DON'T HURT US, MISTER.
HE TOOK HER.
I KNOW, PAL. I'M GONNA GET HER BACK, RIGHT AFTER I GET YOU ALL OUT OF HERE.
BUT I NEED YOU TO DO ME A BIG FAVOR. I NEED YOU TO COVER YOUR EYES AND NOT OPEN THEM UNTIL I SAY.
CAN YOU DO THAT FOR ME... PLEASE?
OKAY.

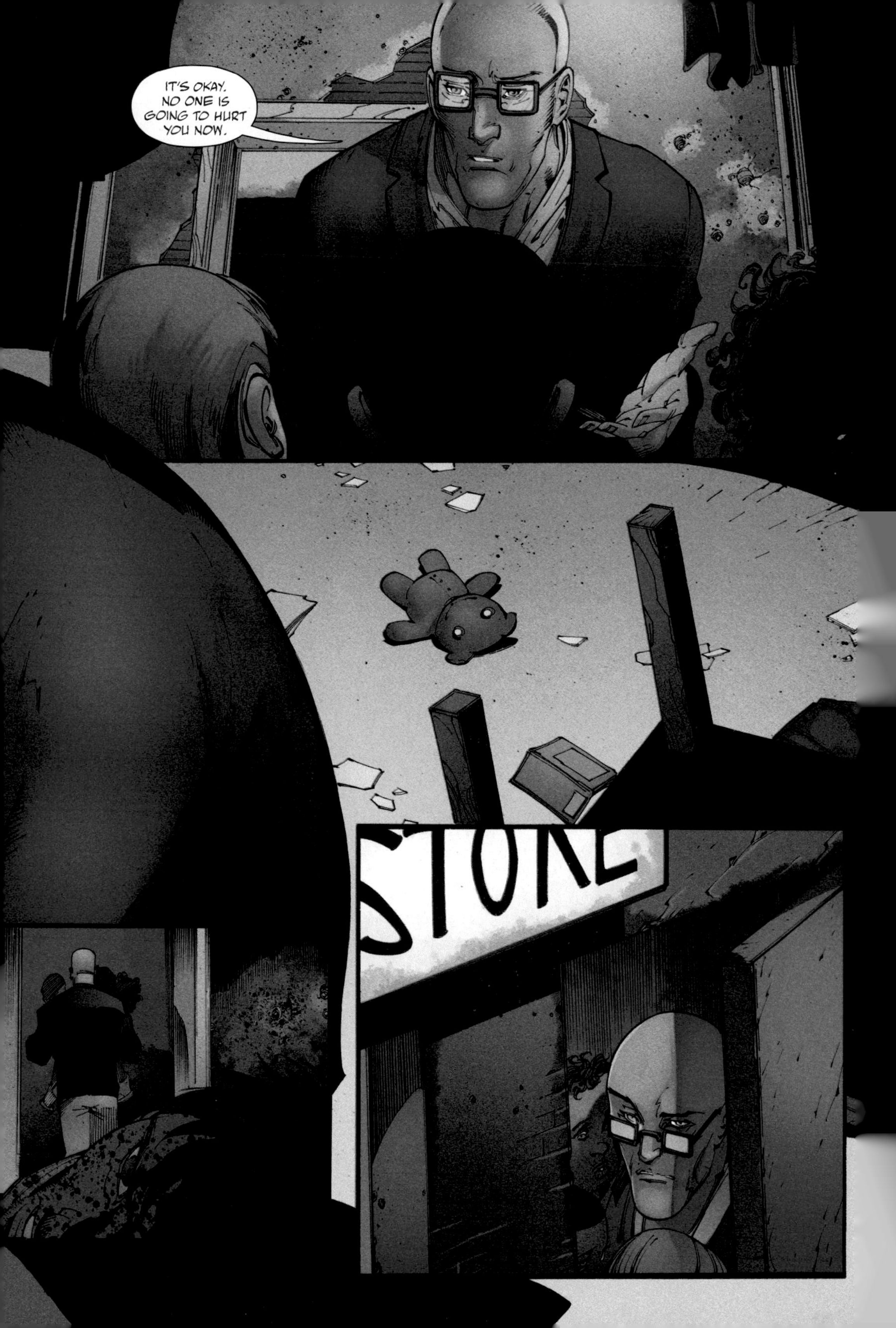
IT'S OKAY. NO ONE IS GOING TO HURT YOU NOW.
STORE

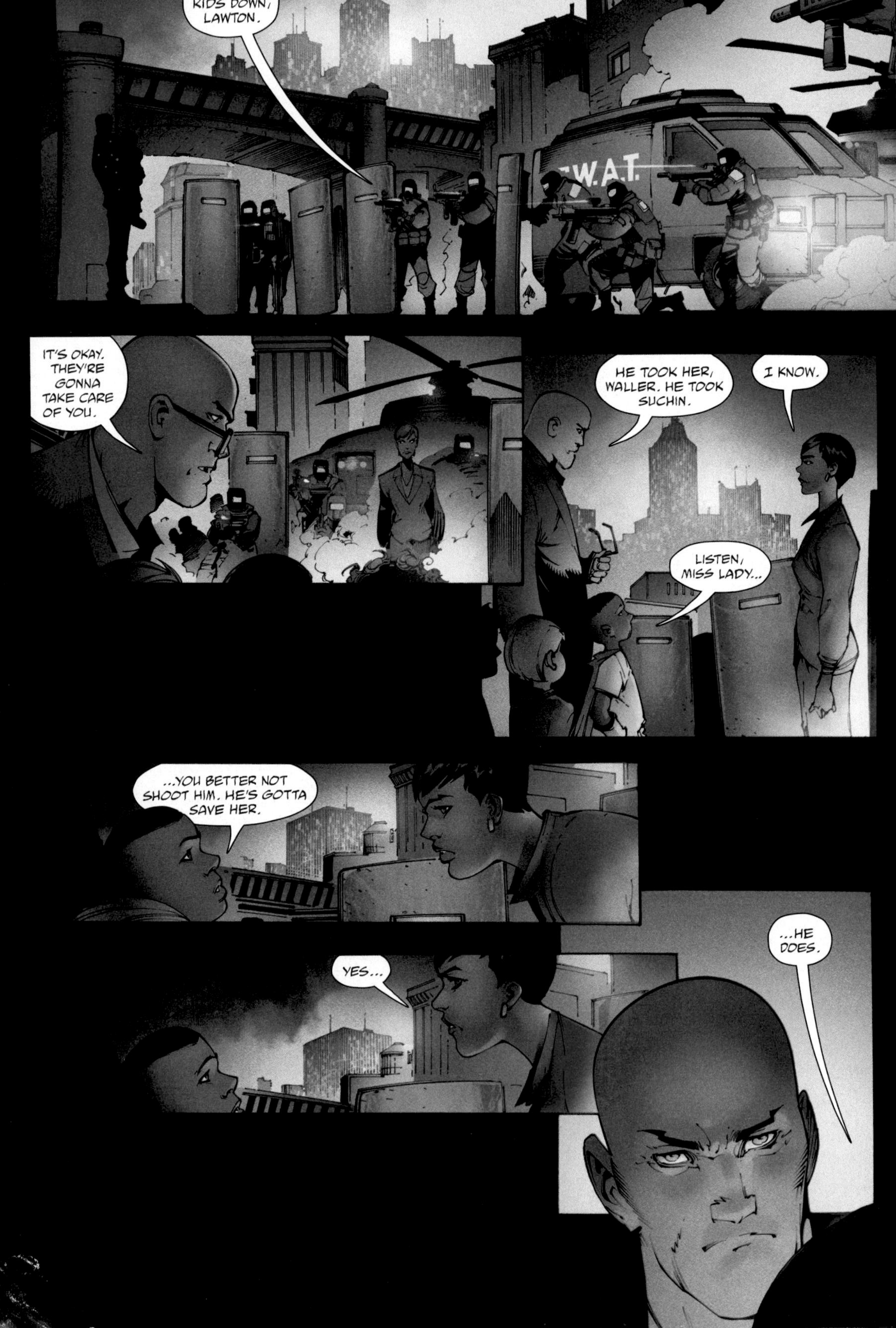
KIDS DOWN, LAWTON.
S.W.A.T.
IT'S OKAY. THEY'RE GONNA TAKE CARE OF YOU.
HE TOOK HER, WALLER. HE TOOK SUCHIN.
I KNOW.
LISTEN, MISS LADY...
...YOU BETTER NOT SHOOT HIM. HE'S GOTTA SAVE HER.
YES...
...HE DOES.

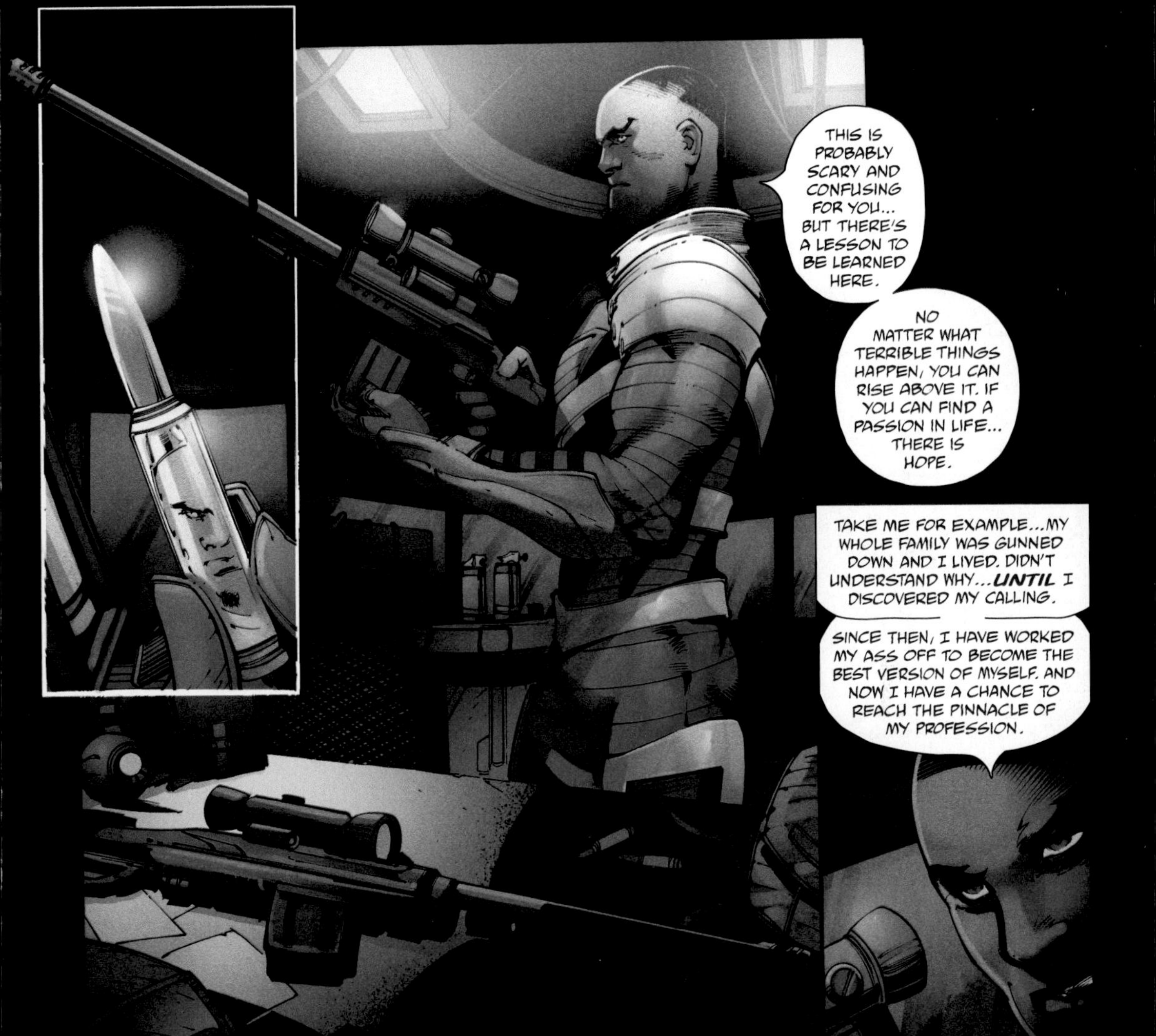
THIS IS PROBABLY SCARY AND CONFUSING FOR YOU... BUT THERE'S A LESSON TO BE LEARNED HERE.
NO MATTER WHAT TERRIBLE THINGS HAPPEN, YOU CAN RISE ABOVE IT. IF YOU CAN FIND A PASSION IN LIFE... THERE IS HOPE.
TAKE ME FOR EXAMPLE...MY WHOLE FAMILY WAS GUNNED DOWN AND I LIVED. DIDN'T UNDERSTAND WHY...***UNTIL*** I DISCOVERED MY CALLING.
SINCE THEN, I HAVE WORKED MY ASS OFF TO BECOME THE BEST VERSION OF MYSELF. AND NOW I HAVE A CHANCE TO REACH THE PINNACLE OF MY PROFESSION.

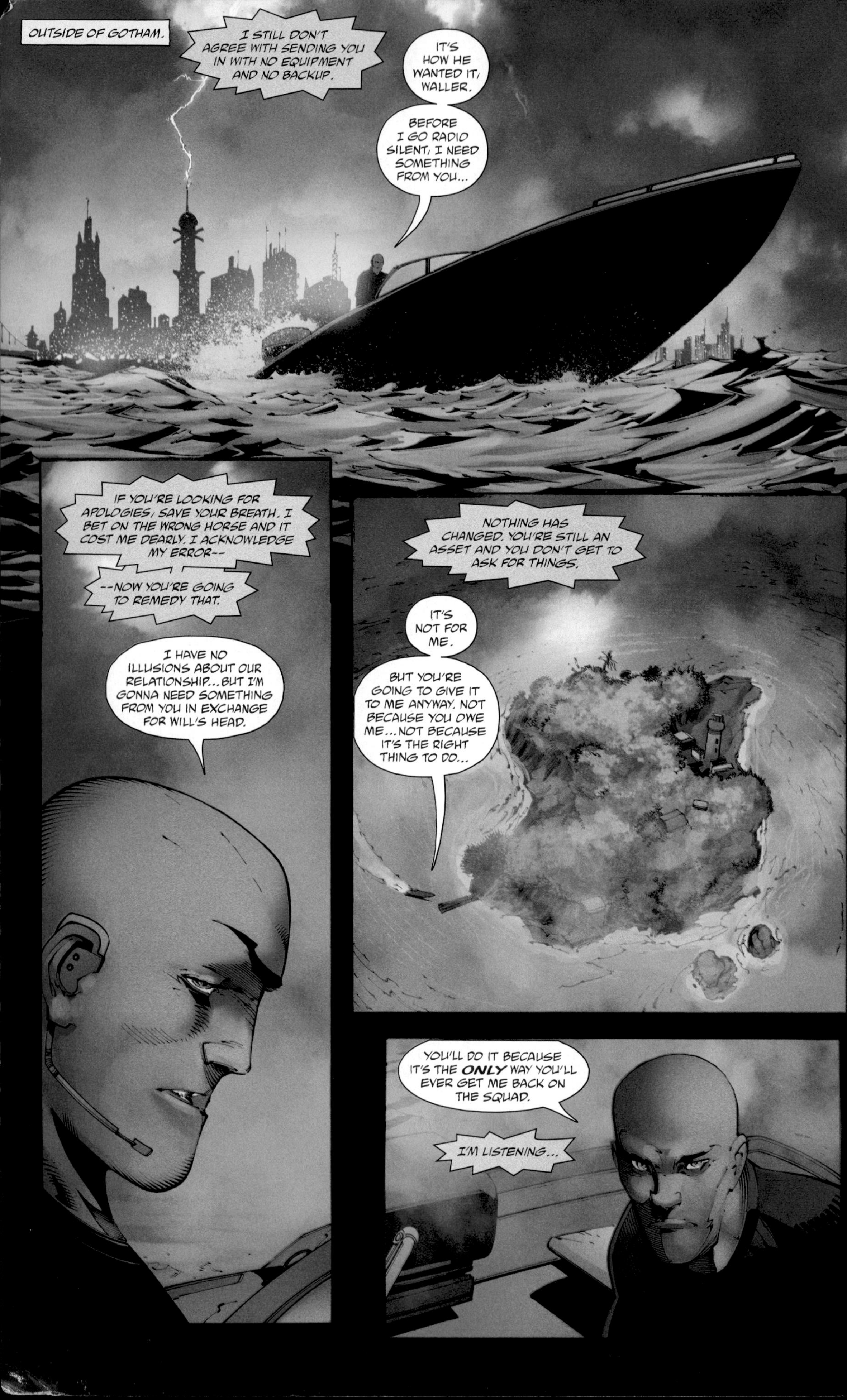
OUTSIDE OF GOTHAM.
I STILL DON'T AGREE WITH SENDING YOU IN WITH NO EQUIPMENT AND NO BACKUP.
IT'S HOW HE WANTED IT, WALLER.
BEFORE I GO RADIO SILENT, I NEED SOMETHING FROM YOU...
IF YOU'RE LOOKING FOR APOLOGIES, SAVE YOUR BREATH. I BET ON THE WRONG HORSE AND IT COST ME DEARLY. I ACKNOWLEDGE MY ERROR--
--NOW YOU'RE GOING TO REMEDY THAT.
I HAVE NO ILLUSIONS ABOUT OUR RELATIONSHIP...BUT I'M GONNA NEED SOMETHING FROM YOU IN EXCHANGE FOR WILL'S HEAD.
NOTHING HAS CHANGED. YOU'RE STILL AN ASSET AND YOU DON'T GET TO ASK FOR THINGS.
IT'S NOT FOR ME.
BUT YOU'RE GOING TO GIVE IT TO ME ANYWAY. NOT BECAUSE YOU OWE ME...NOT BECAUSE IT'S THE RIGHT THING TO DO...
YOU'LL DO IT BECAUSE IT'S THE ONLY WAY YOU'LL EVER GET ME BACK ON THE SQUAD.
I'M LISTENING...

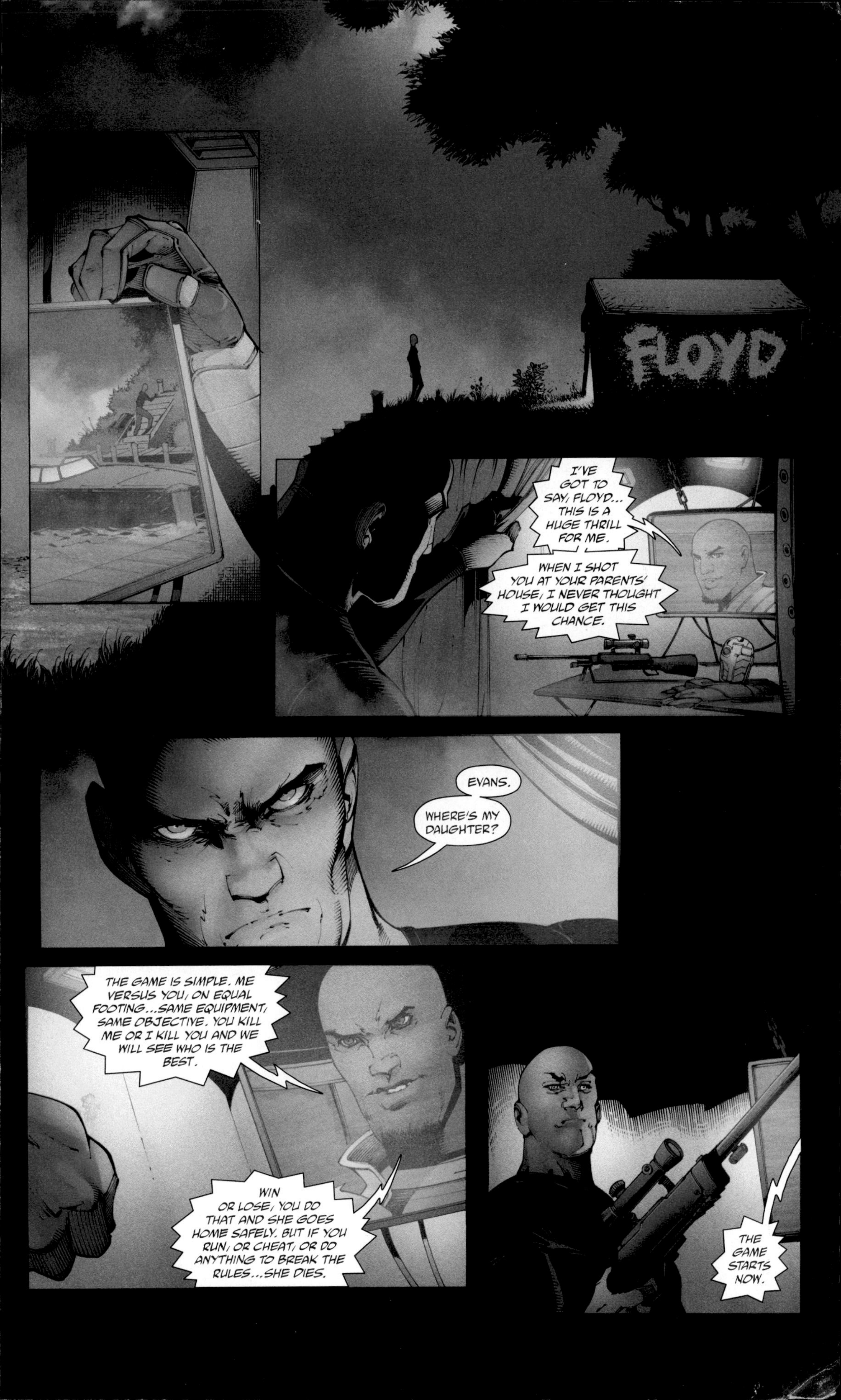

FLOYD
I'VE GOT TO SAY, FLOYD... THIS IS A HUGE THRILL FOR ME.
WHEN I SHOT YOU AT YOUR PARENTS' HOUSE, I NEVER THOUGHT I WOULD GET THIS CHANCE.
EVANS.
WHERE'S MY DAUGHTER?
THE GAME IS SIMPLE. ME VERSUS YOU, ON EQUAL FOOTING...SAME EQUIPMENT, SAME OBJECTIVE. YOU KILL ME OR I KILL YOU AND WE WILL SEE WHO IS THE BEST.
WIN OR LOSE, YOU DO THAT AND SHE GOES HOME SAFELY. BUT IF YOU RUN, OR CHEAT, OR DO ANYTHING TO BREAK THE RULES...SHE DIES.
THE GAME STARTS NOW.

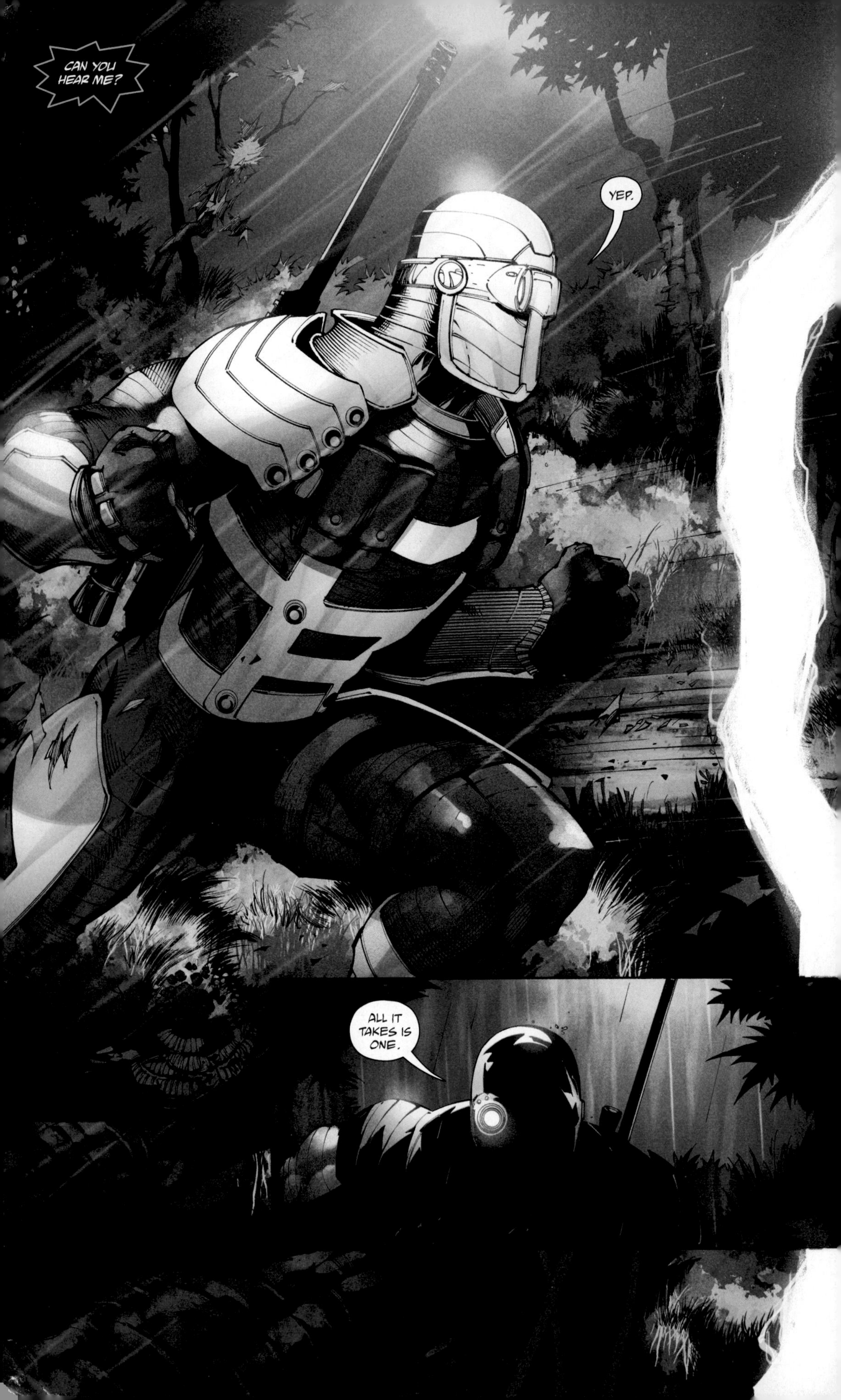
CAN YOU HEAR ME?
YEP.
ALL IT TAKES IS ONE.

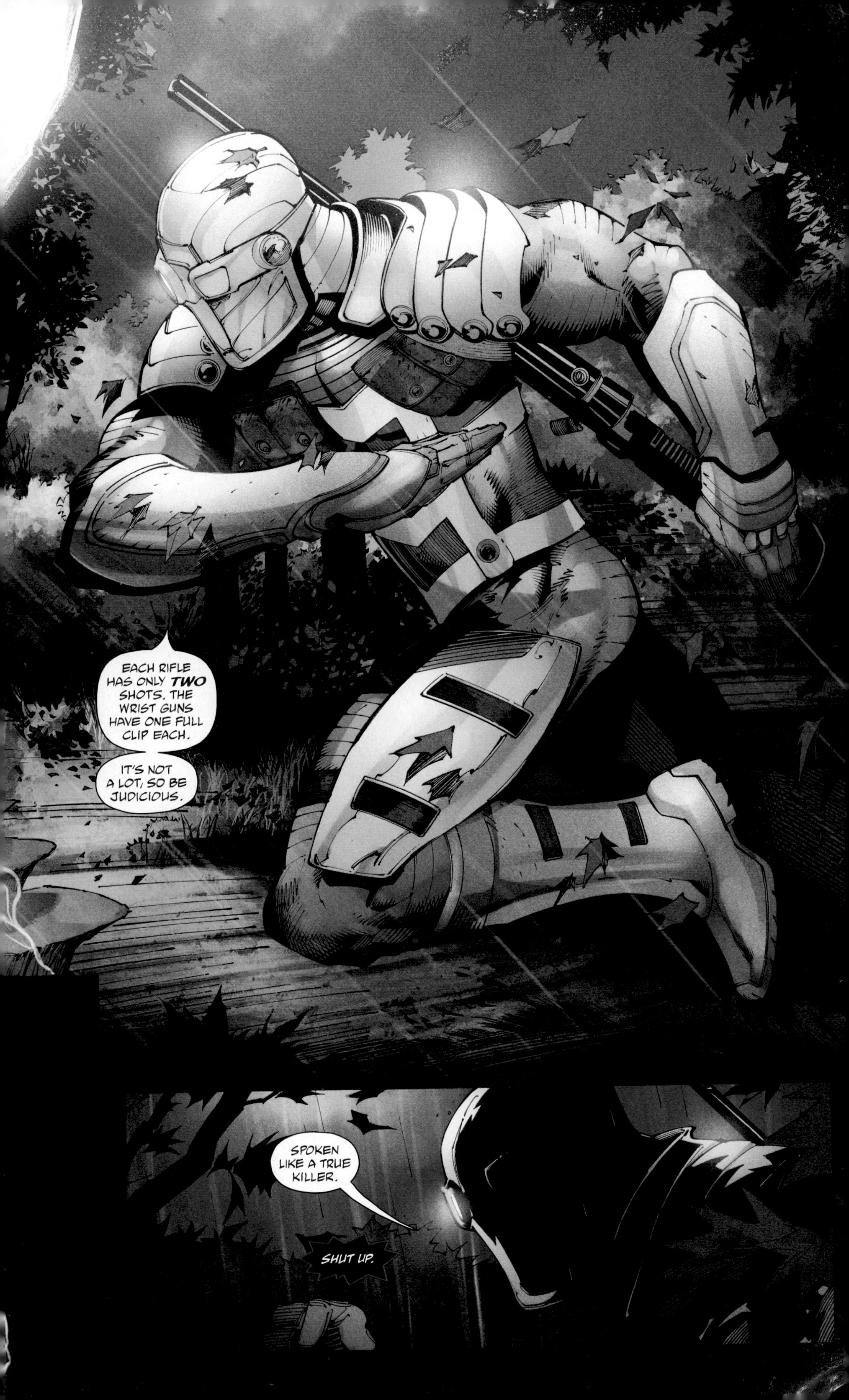
EACH RIFLE HAS ONLY TWO SHOTS. THE WRIST GUNS HAVE ONE FULL CLIP EACH.
IT'S NOT A LOT, SO BE JUDICIOUS.
SPOKEN LIKE A TRUE KILLER.
SHUT UP.

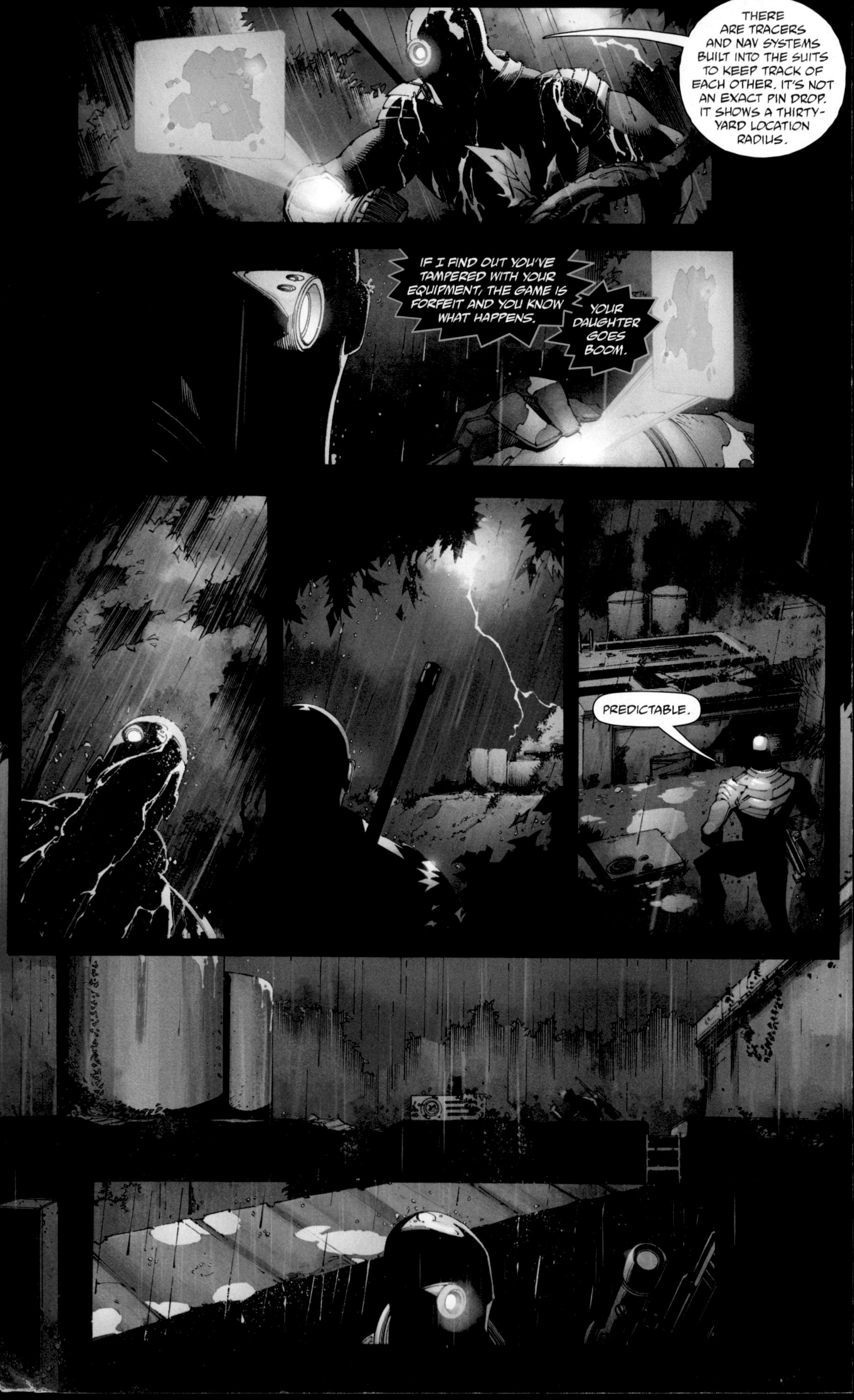
THERE ARE TRACERS AND NAV SYSTEMS BUILT INTO THE SUITS TO KEEP TRACK OF EACH OTHER. IT'S NOT AN EXACT PIN DROP. IT SHOWS A THIRTY-YARD LOCATION RADIUS.
IF I FIND OUT YOU'VE TAMPERED WITH YOUR EQUIPMENT, THE GAME IS FORFEIT AND YOU KNOW WHAT HAPPENS.
YOUR DAUGHTER GOES BOOM.
PREDICTABLE.

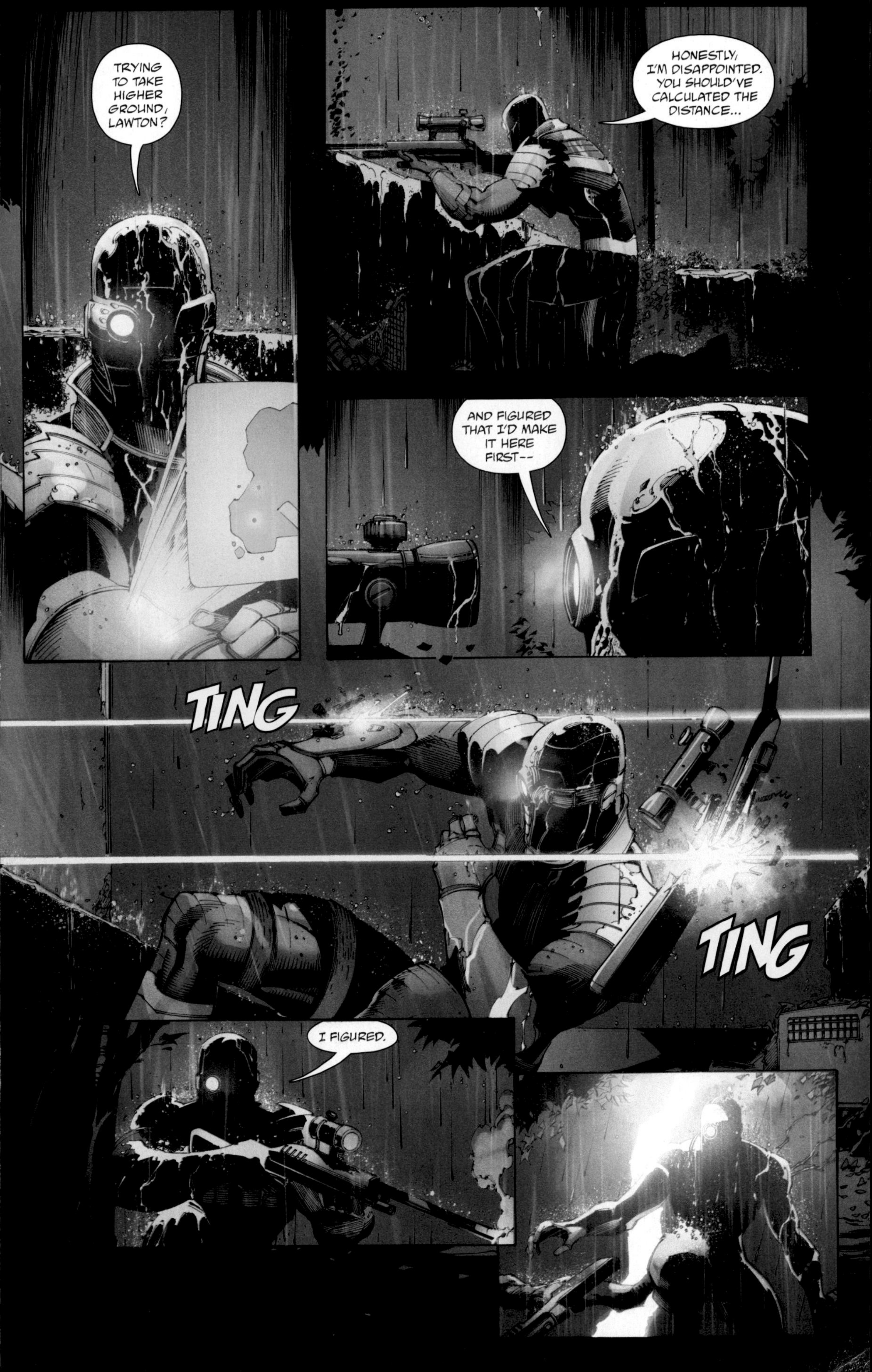
TRYING TO TAKE HIGHER GROUND, LAWTON?
HONESTLY, I'M DISAPPOINTED. YOU SHOULD'VE CALCULATED THE DISTANCE...
AND FIGURED THAT I'D MAKE IT HERE FIRST--
TING
TING
I FIGURED.

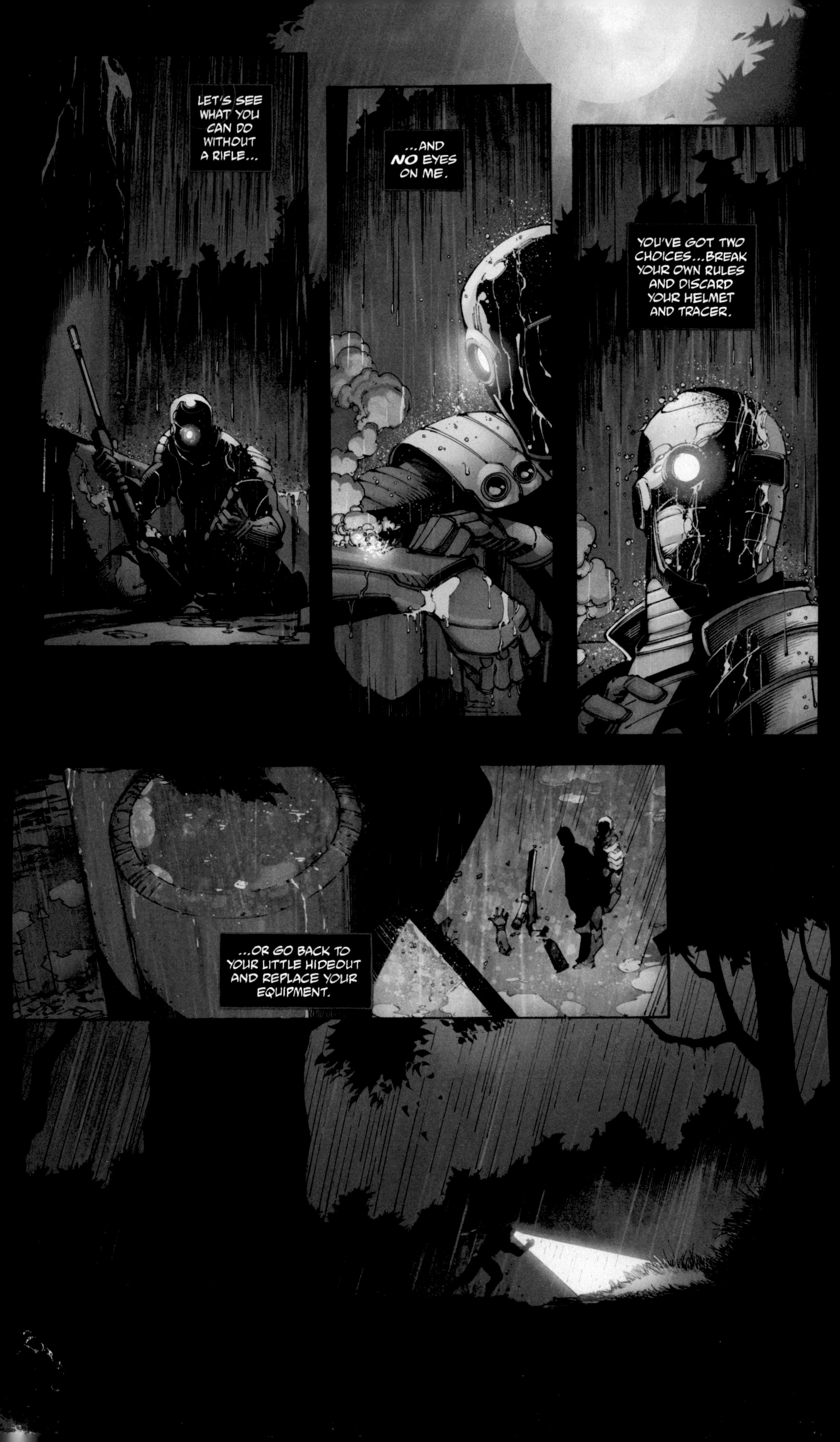
LET'S SEE WHAT YOU CAN DO WITHOUT A RIFLE...
...AND NO EYES ON ME.
YOU'VE GOT TWO CHOICES...BREAK YOUR OWN RULES AND DISCARD YOUR HELMET AND TRACER.
...OR GO BACK TO YOUR LITTLE HIDEOUT AND REPLACE YOUR EQUIPMENT.

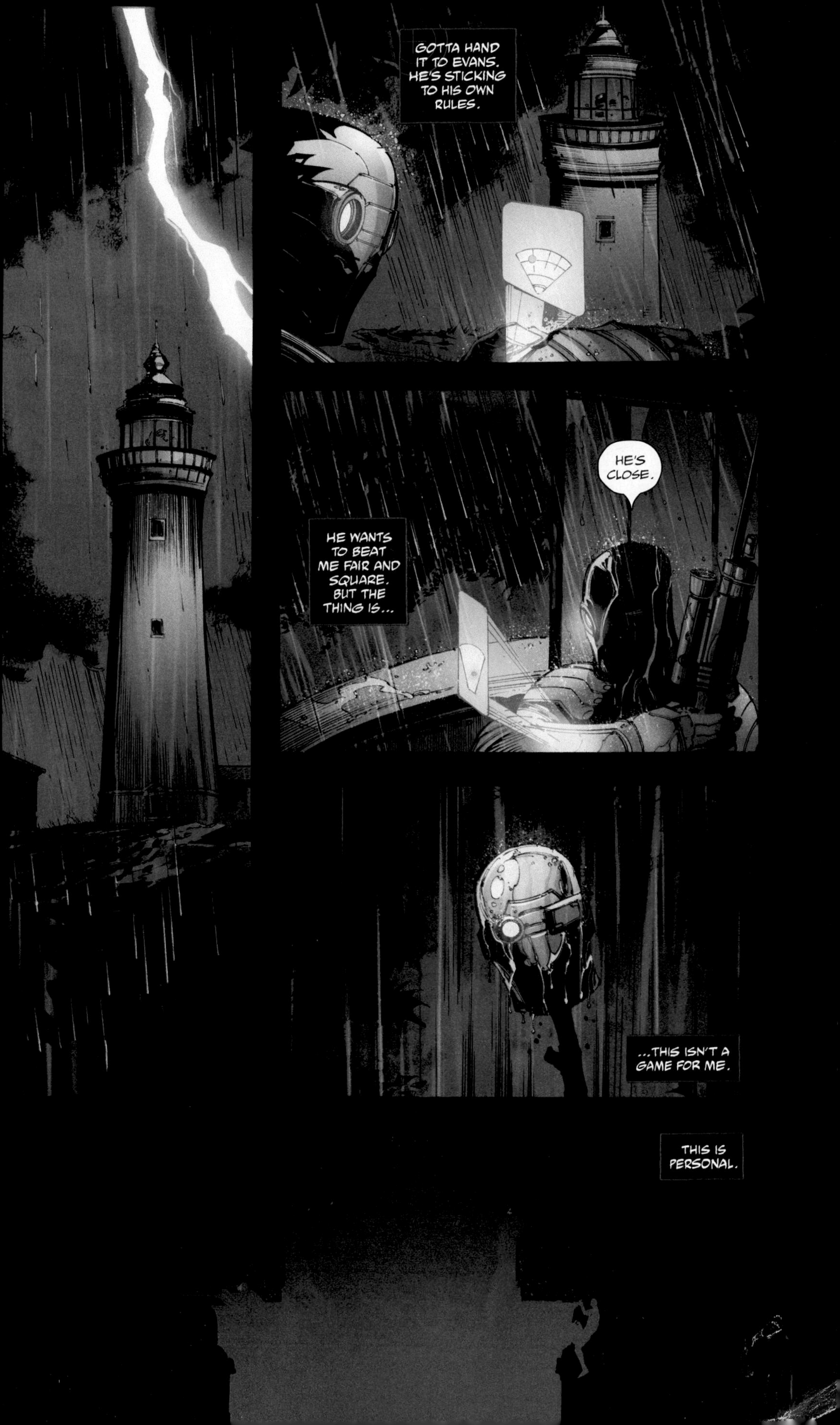
GOTTA HAND IT TO EVANS. HE'S STICKING TO HIS OWN RULES.
HE'S CLOSE.
HE WANTS TO BEAT ME FAIR AND SQUARE. BUT THE THING IS...
...THIS ISN'T A GAME FOR ME.
THIS IS PERSONAL.

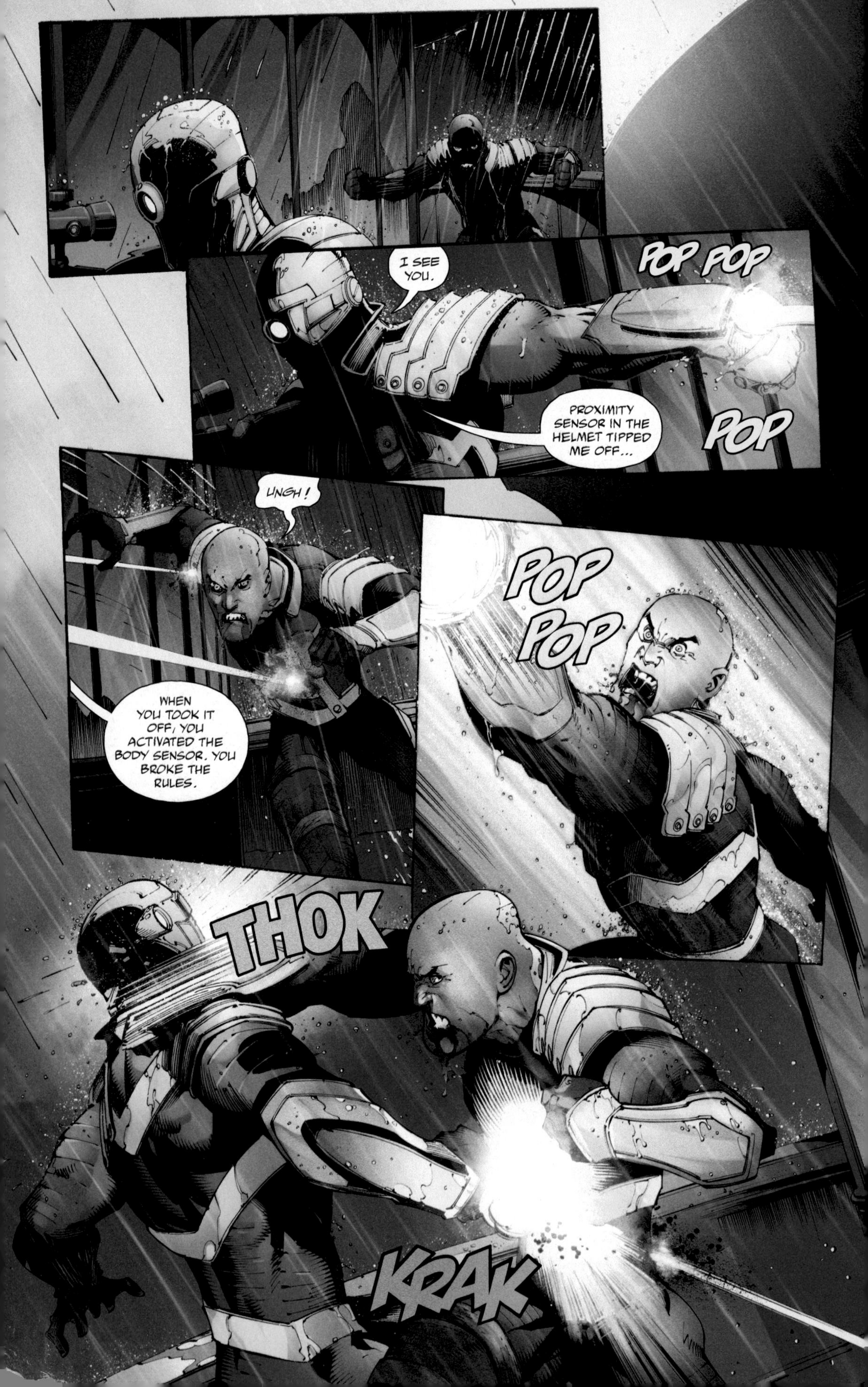
I SEE YOU.
POP POP
PROXIMITY SENSOR IN THE HELMET TIPPED ME OFF...
POP
UNGH!
WHEN YOU TOOK IT OFF, YOU ACTIVATED THE BODY SENSOR. YOU BROKE THE RULES.
POP POP
THOK
KRAK

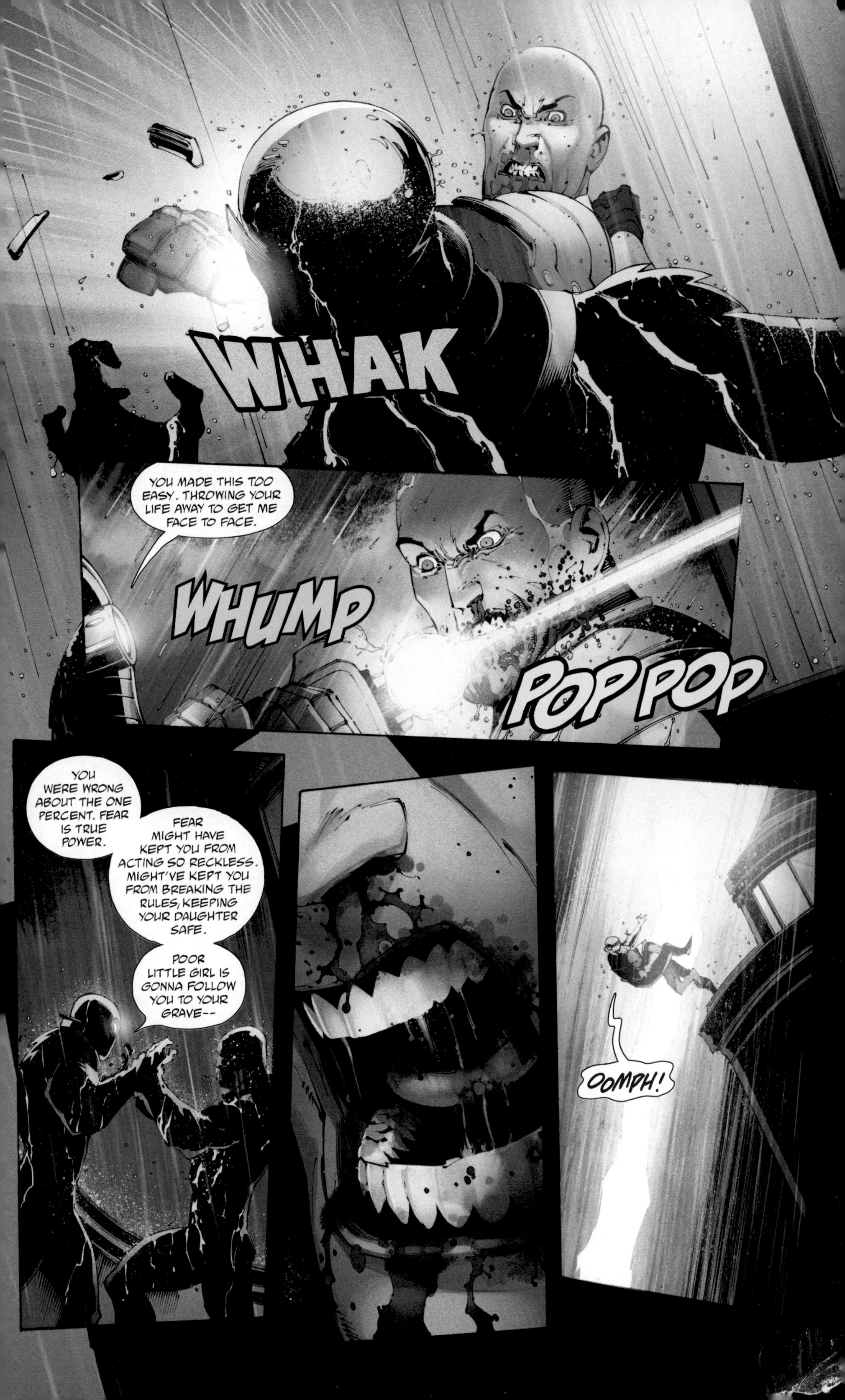
WHAK
YOU MADE THIS TOO EASY. THROWING YOUR LIFE AWAY TO GET ME FACE TO FACE.
WHUMP
POP POP
YOU WERE WRONG ABOUT THE ONE PERCENT. FEAR IS TRUE POWER.
FEAR MIGHT HAVE KEPT YOU FROM ACTING SO RECKLESS. MIGHT'VE KEPT YOU FROM BREAKING THE RULES, KEEPING YOUR DAUGHTER SAFE.
POOR LITTLE GIRL IS GONNA FOLLOW YOU TO YOUR GRAVE--
OOMPH!

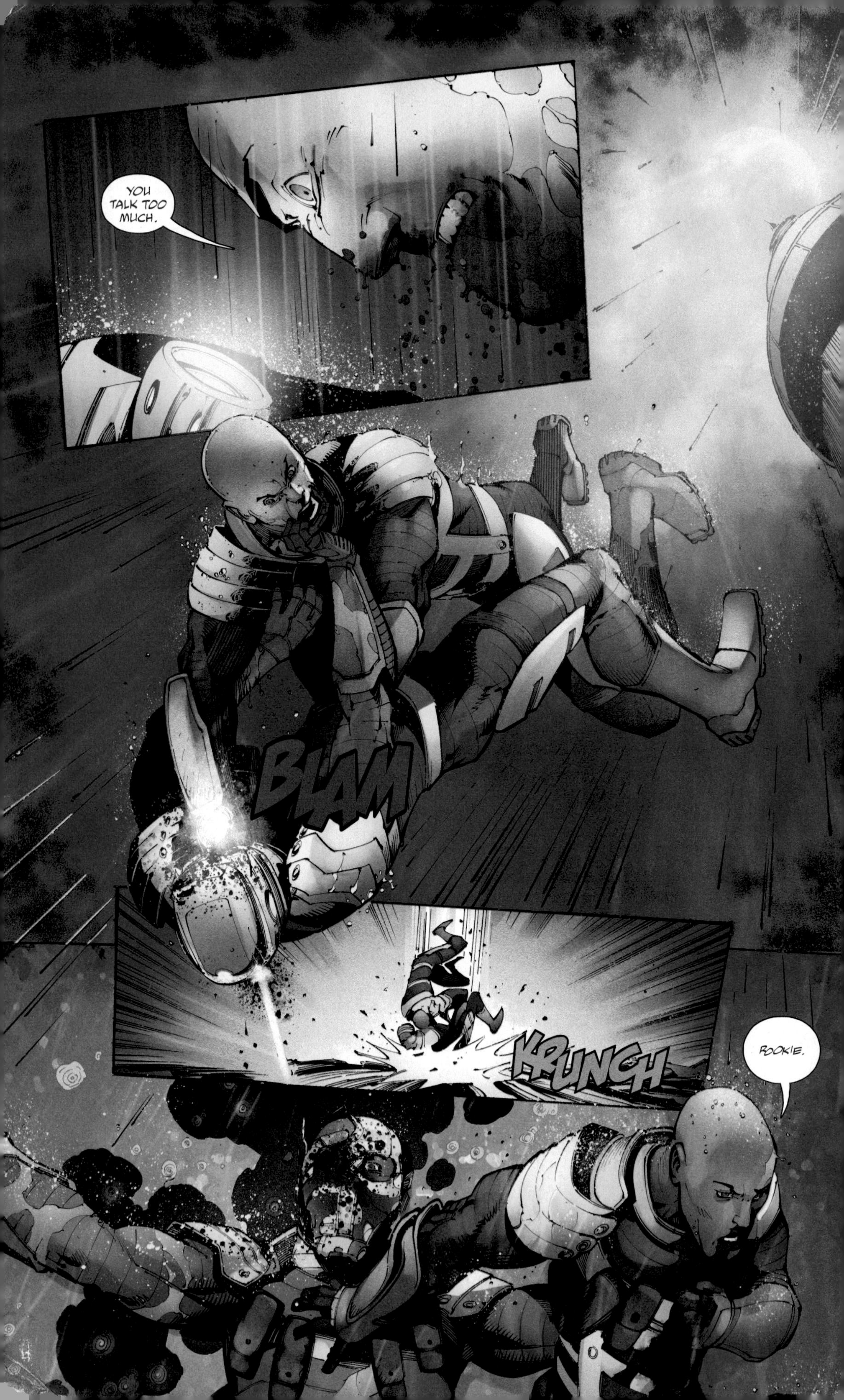
YOU TALK TOO MUCH.
BLAM
KRUNCH
ROOKIE.

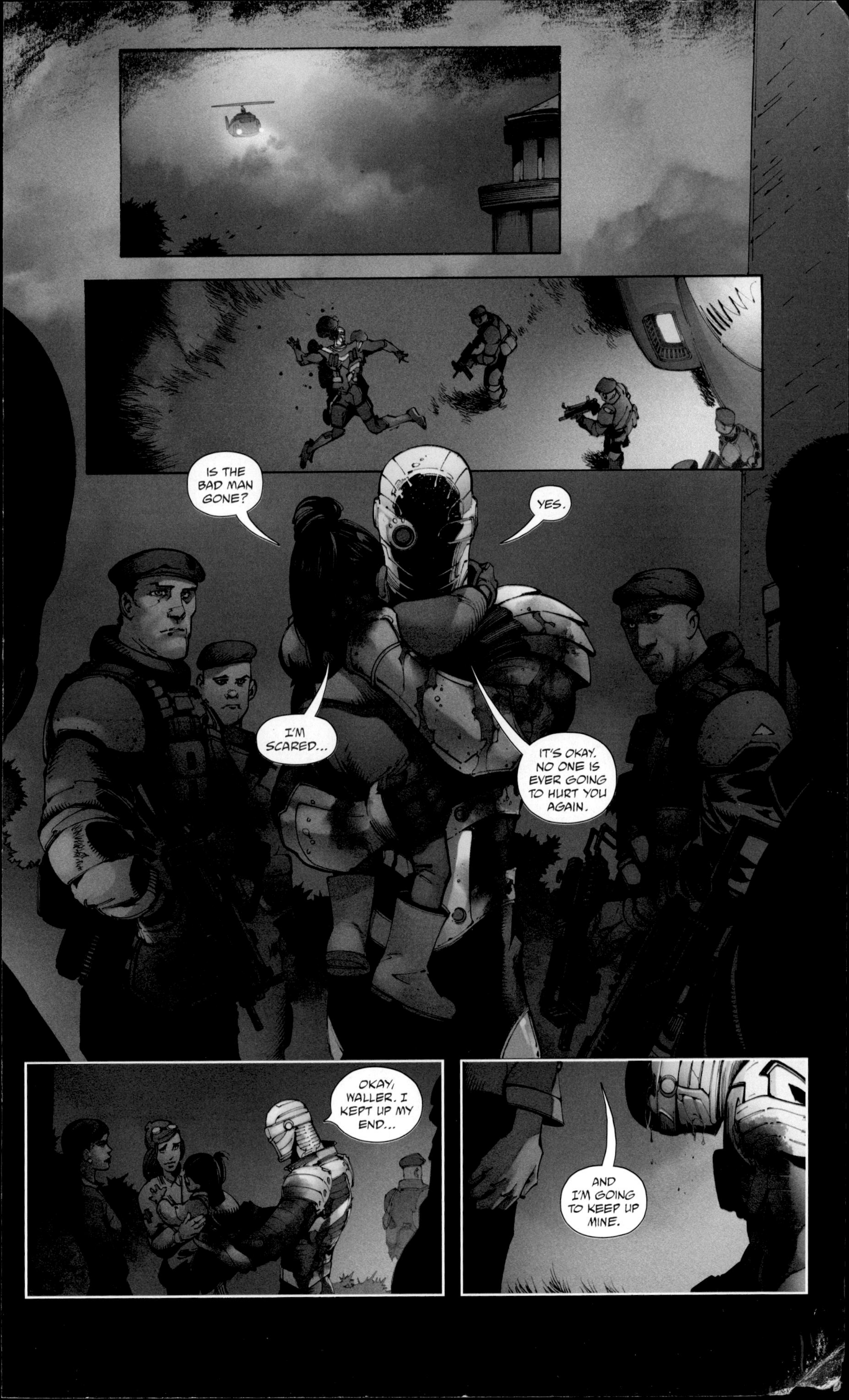
IS THE BAD MAN GONE?
YES.
I'M SCARED...
IT'S OKAY. NO ONE IS EVER GOING TO HURT YOU AGAIN.
OKAY, WALLER. I KEPT UP MY END...
AND I'M GOING TO KEEP UP MINE.

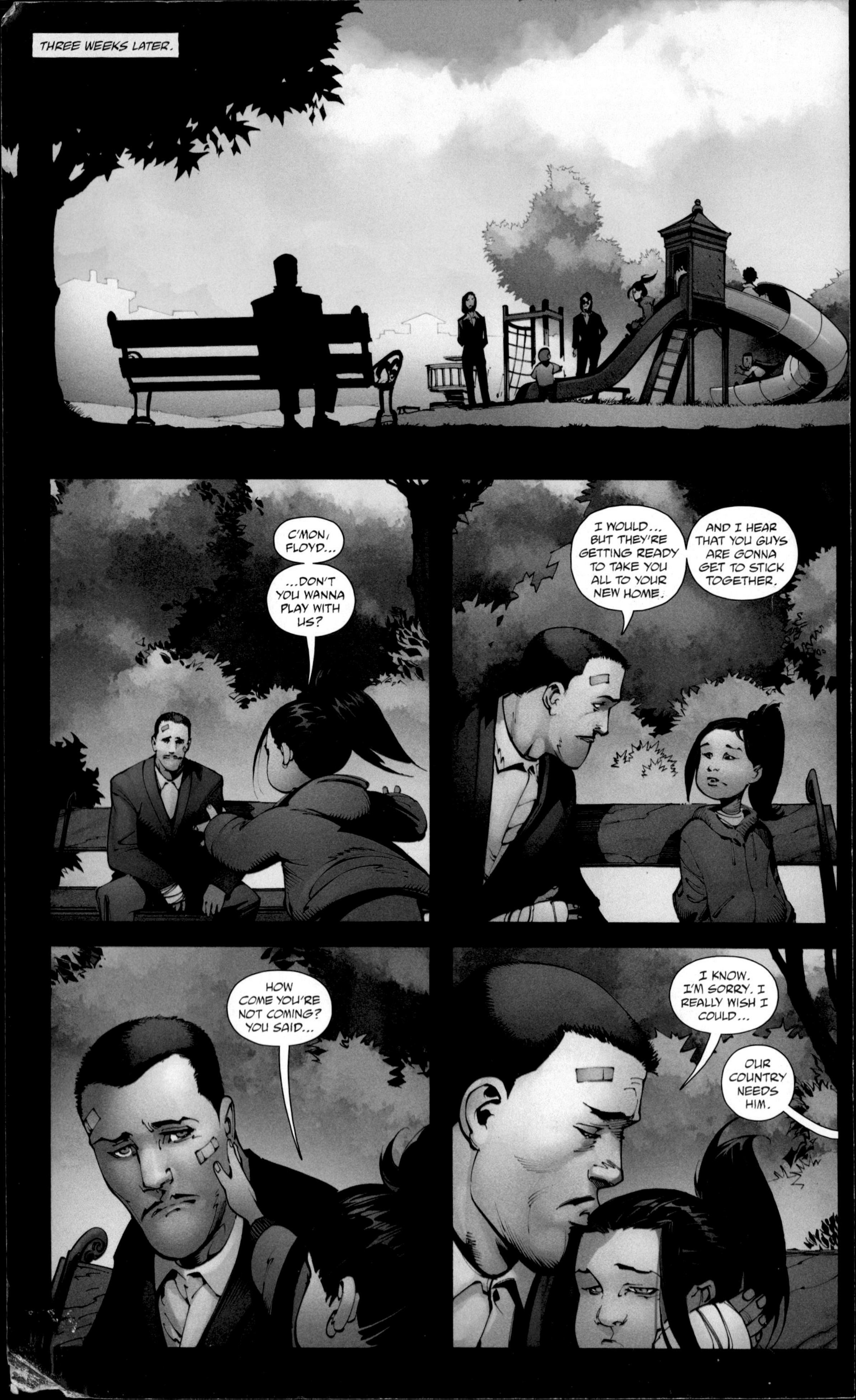
THREE WEEKS LATER.
C'MON, FLOYD...
...DON'T YOU WANNA PLAY WITH US?
I WOULD... BUT THEY'RE GETTING READY TO TAKE YOU ALL TO YOUR NEW HOME.
AND I HEAR THAT YOU GUYS ARE GONNA GET TO STICK TOGETHER.
HOW COME YOU'RE NOT COMING? YOU SAID...
I KNOW. I'M SORRY. I REALLY WISH I COULD...
OUR COUNTRY NEEDS HIM.

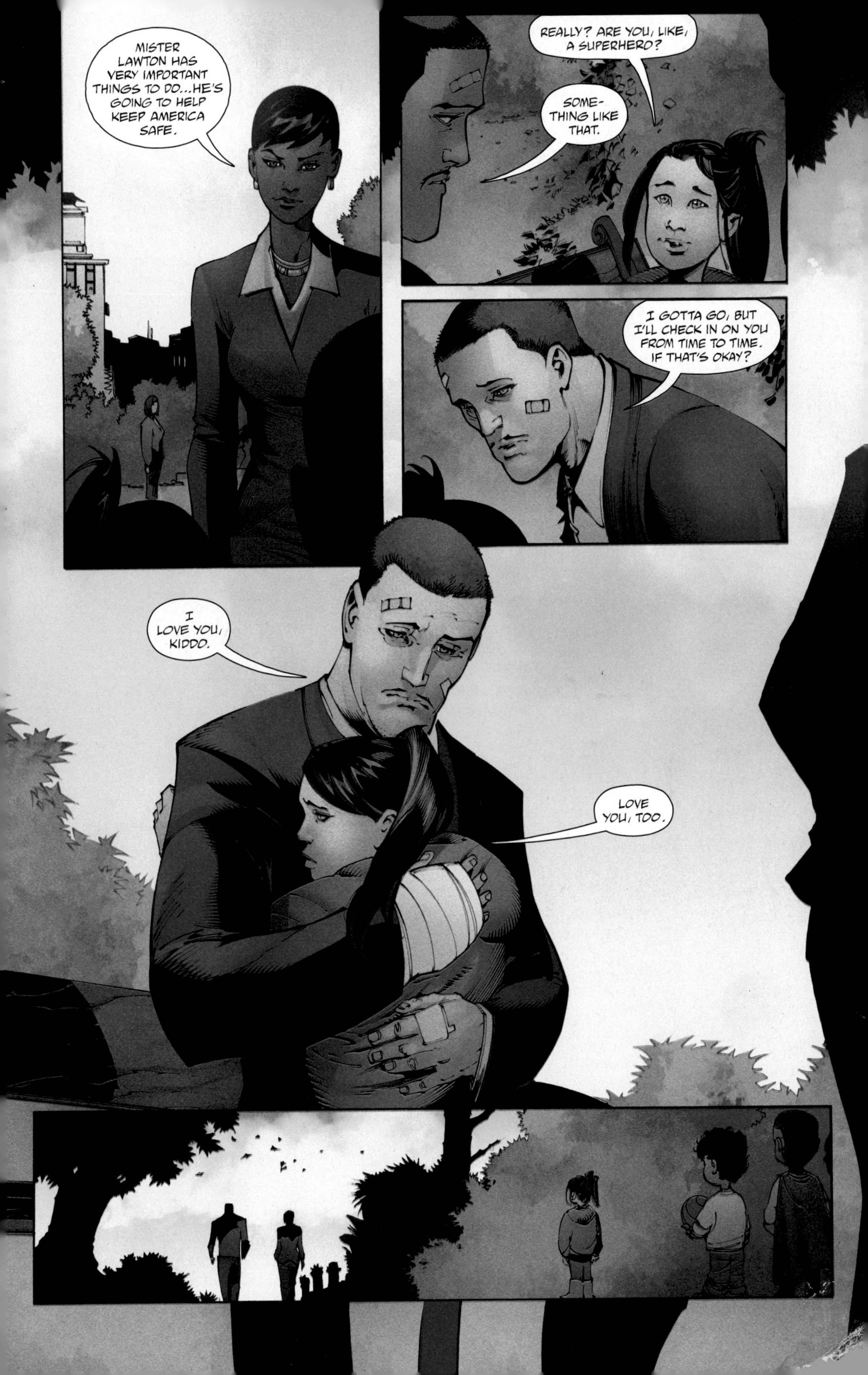
MISTER LAWTON HAS VERY IMPORTANT THINGS TO DO...HE'S GOING TO HELP KEEP AMERICA SAFE.
REALLY? ARE YOU, LIKE, A SUPERHERO?
SOME-THING LIKE THAT.
I GOTTA GO, BUT I'LL CHECK IN ON YOU FROM TIME TO TIME. IF THAT'S OKAY?
I LOVE YOU, KIDDO.
LOVE YOU, TOO.

BELLE REVE PRISON.

HEY! THE 'STACHE IS BACK!

DIDN'T FEEL RIGHT WITHOUT IT.

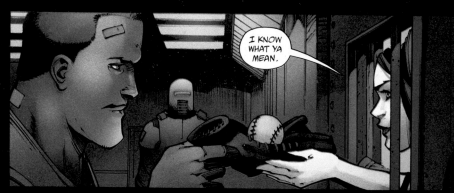

I KNOW WHAT YA MEAN.

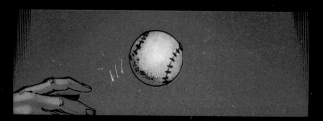

END.